Singing Softly to the Light

The Biography of Mary Louise Coulouris

Singing Softly to the Light

The Biography of Mary Louise Coulouris

Gordon Wallace

Published by Unicorn Press Ltd 2015

66 Charlotte Street
London W1T 4QE
www.unicornpress.org

5 4 3 2 1

ISBN: 978-1-910065-884

Designed by Tora Kelly
Cover Picture: 'Mandraki Bend' by Mary Louise Coulouris.
Photo: Nikolaos Kiafis.
Private Collection: James Browning.
Printed and bound in the UK

To our daughter Saro and son Duncan, in memory of my wife

CONTENTS

CHAPTER 1

Shortly before midnight on a hot July evening in 1939, a doctor looking a bit older than his years left the Le Roy Sanitarium in mid-town Manhattan and began making his way home. He was Ned Shnayerson and his gaunt features hadn't been improved any by the lateness of the day and the hours he'd spent in the hospital's maternity unit. All had gone well though, and his turn of duty had ended with the safe delivery of a baby girl, immediately named Mary Louise. She was the second child of a couple who were close friends of the doctor as well as his patients, and before leaving the hospital Shnayerson had telephoned the baby's father assuring him that mother and baby were both comfortable and looking good.

On the drive home, however, Shnayerson might well have reflected a little more on the birth of Mary Louise, considering it somewhat of a miracle that the baby had been conceived at all. A few years earlier he had been instrumental in saving her father's life when peritonitis threatened. At the time, the use of antibiotics was still something being debated in medical journals: so a ruptured appendix, spilling its poison into the abdomen, often ended in painful and predictable death. Shnayerson's speedy appendectomy had been a testament not only to his nerve, but also to his meticulous surgical skills and had endeared him to the family thereafter.

Shortly after recovering his health however, Mary Louise's father had further cause to cement his bond with the good doctor when he was injured after being bowled over by a taxi on Times Square. The taxi driver could not have been expected to recognise the tall, broad-shouldered figure that had stepped inattentively from the pavement, his face stuck in the book he was reading. Nor would he have appreciated the fierce looks he got from the deep, hooded eyes of the man as he got shakily to his feet. In time, however, the cab driver like many others would come to recognise him courtesy of the cinema screen, for he was George Coulouris – an English actor who was later to appear in almost a hundred movies alongside some of the biggest names in Hollywood. The vivid bruises caused by his collision with the taxi would soon give way to a colourful career spanning the next half-century.

Before that career got seriously underway however, there was a new baby to consider. A few days after she was born, Mary Louise and her mother left hospital and were taken to their home in Spuyten Duyvil, an area of New York lying north of the Harlem River. The Coulouris family was now complete, consisting of parents George and Louise and Mary Louise's older brother, George junior. They all travelled home from the hospital in the family car which was soon to be replaced by a cherry-red, fully-automatic Oldsmobile convertible which the children loved and were to remember with great affection long after it had been forced into scrap-yard retirement. This car, like the family, soon became a familiar sight on the streets of Spuyten Duyvil.

Long before Mary Louise's birth, Spuyten Duyvil had become one of New York's most desirable places to live. With its leafy thoroughfares and breezy open spaces it had an almost-rural atmosphere about it, something underlined in several parts by unmade roads and stores whose interiors had changed little in over a hundred years. It was much like London's Hampstead district which exerted a magnet-like effect on those working in the arts and a variety of other media-related occupations. And although it was located in the Bronx, it had never been associated with the sort of images that came to mind when people mentioned that particular area of New York. In all respects, the place was removed from the poverty, violence and crime that sullied the streets of the Borough further to the east. Indeed, the spread of weeds like ragwort, hackweed and wild bamboo, were about the only manifestations of unruliness ever likely to trouble the residents of Spuyten Duyvil.

The Coulouris's lived in a comfortable, detached property at

775 Kappock Street, Mary Louise's parents having moved there from the cramped downtown rooms they'd rented in Lower Manhattan soon after being married. And it was here that George Coulouris, in a short interview for the New York Times, explained his reasons for leaving England to pursue his acting career in the United States. It was due, he said, to the stranglehold a small number of people had on the theatre in England, especially in Shakespearian drama – Coulouris's main passion as an actor.

'Everything's done on the old boy network' he'd said. *'It's not ability but who you know that counts in England.'*

It was a theme Coulouris returned to frequently in his career, endowing it with more heat and intensity the older he got. Unabashed, however, the Times correspondent proceeded to describe the couple (photographed taking afternoon tea on a chintzy sofa), as *'quintessentially English.'* What Louise Franklin Coulouris made of this, she being a proud Philadelphian, no one thought to ask.

By the time Mary Louise appeared on the scene, her father was already busy establishing himself as an actor on the Broadway stage, playing roles opposite the likes of Katherine Cornell and Helen Hayes, both leading ladies of their time. And living close to the Coulouris's in Spuyten Duyvil were others who were also becoming favourites with the public. One of these was Valerie Cossart whose looks, together with her talents as an actress got her roles in some of the first television shows ever to be broadcast in America. Valerie was also an accomplished musician and would arrive at the Coulouris home to play piano in the conservatory attached to the house. And it was a musical connection that led the family to encounter someone else who was arguably Spuyten Duyvil's most famous resident – the celebrated Italian conductor, Arturo Toscanini.

Toscanini – a refugee from fascism in his native country – was in New York working with the NBC Symphony Orchestra. In between rehearsals, he was often to be seen taking his daily constitutional around the Hudson Memorial Park adjacent to where the Coulouris's lived. *'Look...'* people would say, nudging their companion in the ribs *'here's Toscanini coming along.'* But if people seldom failed to recognise Toscannini, it was pretty certain Toscannini never saw much of them. Notoriously short-sighted, personal vanity persuaded the great man to eschew any idea of wearing spectacles.

To parents like George and Louise Coulouris, Spuyten Duyvil must have seemed like a dream location for raising children. It was safe and brimming with creative personalities: and if the ceaseless cacophony of noise coming from the more-distant streets of Manhattan might still be heard from across the Harlem River, it only served to underscore the relative peace enjoyed by those living in the city's northern-most suburbs. So why would anyone choose to give it all up and move, something Mary Louise's parents decided to do?

The answer is probably familiar to anyone with an itch to make progress - to find better paid work, to rise to new and different challenges, and to provide more security for a family whose breadwinner, in this case, was subject to the fluctuating fortunes of a professional actor. Add to that the perennial restlessness of George Coulouris, something that was never assuaged for long no matter how much success he achieved on the Broadway stage. So, when Hollywood beckoned he didn't hesitate for long before accepting the offer of taking part in the movies. He'd said the opportunities America offered actors didn't exist for him in the country of his birth. Now, when they presented themselves he was about to grab them.

The call from Hollywood came via a controversial and astonishingly-young individual who was by turn writer, broadcaster, actor and director – roles he frequently wrapped-up into a single package. Revered by as many as came to revile him, he was accustomed to being hailed at one moment as brilliant and innovative, at the next vain and manipulative. One thing no one could ignore, however, was that Orson Welles was in Hollywood to make his first big motion picture, and he wanted George

Coulouris to be a part of it. The movie, which today continues to be lauded as a masterpiece, was called *Citizen Kane*.

Exactly four months from the day of her birth, Mary Louise was embarking on the first of several trips she would make with her family across America. Swathed in enough clothing to keep the chill of approaching winter at bay, she left New York for California – a journey that began with an overnight sleeper to Chicago, then onward by Union Pacific to Los Angeles. The journey took all of three days to complete, although it wasn't entirely farewell to New York and Spuyten Dyvil. The house on Kappock Street would stay in the family's possession for a while yet.

Over the next few years, return journeys between Los Angeles and New York were to be a regular feature of Mary Louise's life as she grew from babyhood to infancy, leaving her with enduring images that would in time find an outlet in her own chosen profession as an artist. The grandeur of New York's Grand Central Station was one of these: the crackling humour of the porters, the cigar-smoking passengers packing the observation car and the sleek locomotives that carried her and her family on its way, were just a few of the others. Eventually, however, the long journeys between cities reduced in frequency as her father established himself as a movie actor, although for Mary Louise this simply ushered in a fresh era of fascination and excitement. Within a few months of arriving in L.A. her parents bought a house in Beverly Hills, and their daughter was adjusting to life amongst the Hollywood stars.

CHAPTER 2

After clambering on to the man's knee, the chubby four year-old gazed up at him as earnestly as her soft-brown eyes would allow.

'When I'm all grown up,' she said. 'I want you to marry me.'

The man threw back his head and boomed with laughter. As a Hollywood screen idol, Jose Ferrer wasn't unused to receiving romantic overtures from females. But never had they been made as simply and directly as this!

'I'll keep that in mind,' he promised graciously 'but if you ever feel differently about it, be sure to let me know.'

Mary Louise nodded and slid to the floor. Outside her home in Beverly Hills humming birds had invaded the garden, and through a hole in the hedge the unruffled surface of a neighbour's swimming pool was signalling its own alluring propensities. For the moment Ferrer would have to wait, although Jose being Jose, wasn't the sort to hang around. Long before Mary Louise had reached the marrying age, Ferrer would be enjoying connubial bliss with a string of Hollywood's leading actresses. One of them, Rosemary Clooney – aunt of current movie star George Clooney – he would marry twice...........

After arriving in Los Angeles the Coulouris family had lived in rented accommodation before buying 608 North Roxbury Drive – a street in Beverly Hills that ran diagonal-fashion between the boulevards of Wilshire and Sunset and then further towards the mountains. They moved in shortly before their daughter's fifth-birthday. The street was no stranger to celebrities at the time, or since for that matter. Further along lived Jack Benny and Lionel Barrymore: further along still stood the homes of Lucille Ball and the songwriter-brothers, George and Ira Gershwin. More recently actors such as Peter Falk and Mia Farrow have chosen to live on North Roxbury Drive.

The Coulouris home with its steeply-sloping roofs, sharply-angled bay windows and unfenced lawns had been purchased from another actor, the extremely youthful Farley Granger, who was just beginning his movie career at the time. Granger had been somewhat hasty in buying the property, realising only after the deal had been done that a street mostly given over to families (albeit of the showbiz sort) wasn't quite the place someone in their late-teens wanted to be. So, when the opportunity to sell came along he was only too pleased to take it. To Mary Louise, Granger's role as a property vendor was to be the best part the young actor was ever to play.

Inside the house a long corridor separated the room shared by Mary Louise and her brother from the apartments used by their parents and the little room off the kitchen which housed the family's latest addition – their Japanese maid, Taz. This corridor often became a stage for ad-hoc performances of opera, Carmen mostly, in particular the Smugglers March, which was belted out on a radiogram while the children, led by father George, paraded up and down the parquet flooring. It was also the place where Mary Louise recalled bursting into tears when she heard the music of Haydn and Beethoven for the first time. Music, and the people who made it, was to become a source of great inspiration for her, and just as in New York when Valerie Cossart came to play piano, she'd become excited and animated by it. Later, when she became an accomplished artist an entire series of pictures would be devoted to music.

Growing in the garden of 608 North Roxbury Drive was a variety of fruit trees, including an avocado which produced more fruit than the family could ever consume. When the season for picking arrived it presented an opportunity for the Coulouris children to practise what today would be called 'retail enterprise.' Taking the avocados to the pavement's edge, they set up a stall using some salvaged building blocks and began offering passers-by the chance to buy at greatly-reduced prices. Among the first to take an interest were two bulky officers from the L.A. Police Department, scratching their heads over where things stood in respect of unlicensed street-trading. Soon however, they were driving away tunic-pockets bulging with avocados. At ten cents a piece, who was *gonna get heavy with a cupala kids?*

Lemons from the garden attracted similar entrepreneurial interest. The children squeezed lemon juice into a pitcher, topped-up with tap water, and set off round the neighbourhood selling their homemade lemonade. At one grand residence they were ushered into the presence of someone who had been known in Hollywood as the *'Prima Diva of the Silent Screen.'* She was Gloria Swanson, who at the time was making the first of two major comebacks following the introduction of talking pictures. Whether she ever consumed the 'lemonade' bought from Mary Louise and her brother cannot be vouched for, and Swanson's biographers failed dismally to say if the concoction had anything to do with her soaring success. But her performance in the 1951 production of 'Sunset Boulevard' restored her reputation and she became a household name again at the age of 52.

By now Mary Louise's father had completed his role in *Citizen Kane* and the film had been released. Coulouris played Walter Parks Thatcher in the movie – a glacially unsympathetic banker and trustee of the young Kane's inherited fortune. Coulouris gave a hallmark performance in the role, revealing many of his approaches to acting which were to become familiar to cinema-goers over the next four decades. But as far as 'Kane' went he wasn't at all impressed with the film. One of his fellow-actors in the movie recalls meeting him in the street the day after 'Kane' had its first public preview in Los Angeles. Coulouris was railing against the film in a way only Mary Louise's father could.

'*Do you see what that fool Welles has done now?*' he blustered. '*Thinks he's made a classic, but it'll be the biggest flop of all time, I can tell you!*'

Hardly a prescient view you might think, considering the status of the movie today. Yet Coulouris was right in a couple of ways. *Citizen Kane* attracted lots of attention immediately after its release, but it was never big box-office. After a year of dwindling

George Coulouris as
Walter Parks Thatcher
in Orson Welles' classic
film 'Citizen Kane'

audiences and frantic attempts to re-package publicity for the film, it was finally withdrawn from circulation. It had lost around $150,000. But it also failed in another way which Coulouris was quick to identify.

Before arriving in Hollywood he'd understood the main business of the movie industry in America was providing cinema audiences with what it was told they wanted. Despite making some first-rate movies which drew their inspiration from the Great Depression and the Second World War, Hollywood never ventured far from its roots in escapist drama. It wasn't much different from what Hollywood does today where the stock elements of romance, family values, the virtues of individual success and most of all the triumph of good over nastiness, point the way to meeting the expectations of audiences and box office both. *Citizen Kane* in its depiction of the collapse and ultimate destruction of its central character didn't qualify on any of those counts.

Only years after its release did the picture come to be viewed as a masterpiece, though the ones saying so were usually other film directors and movie buffs, who hailed Orson Welles as a brilliant innovator which he undoubtedly was. Even before his film was previewed however, Welles departed Hollywood and had an uneasy relationship with it thereafter. George Coulouris on the other hand stayed, although his association with Welles, which had begun in the mid-Thirties in theatre and radio, was broken for ever.

While waiting for problems affecting the shooting of *Kane* to be resolved, Coulouris had acted in two other movies, one starring Bette Davis and Charles Boyer, the other Rita Hayworth and Glenn Ford: and he'd continued with his stage career by appearing in theatres back on New York's Broadway. After the release of *Citizen Kane* he embarked on a hectic schedule of acting commitments, appearing in 4 films and 3 stage-plays in a short, two-year period. With her father absent for long periods, the physical and emotional support for Mary Louise and her older brother was left for their mother to provide.

The house in Beverly Hills where Mary Louise spent her childhood days.

Louise Franklin Coulouris was a charming, self-effacing, yet quietly determined woman who had been born and raised in Overbrook, Philadelphia. Her mother had died shortly after giving birth to Louise and her twin sister, and the girls had been brought up by a governess, Miss Shoemaker. Her father, a Philadelphian dentist, encouraged his daughter to attend the city's Academy of Fine Art, which she did before a prolonged spell of ill-health forced her to quit. Eventually, she re-joined the art-world but this time as a stage-designer – an occupation that took her at one point to the Cambridge Festival Theatre in

England. There she met George Coulouris, and two years later they married. The couple waited more than seven years before having their first child, followed eighteen months later by their second, Mary Louise.

An interesting fact about Louise Franklin Coulouris was that she could trace her descent back to a family that had given America one of its greatest geniuses, Benjamin Franklin. Ben Franklin was a model example of how to fuse intellectual power with endless energy and practicality. Starting at around the mid-point of the 18th century he developed from being a journalist and newspaper proprietor to becoming a scientist and inventor and then a diplomat, statesman and civic leader. Frequently he performed all of these functions simultaneously. He provided America with its first fire service, its first police force, its first pair of spectacles, and its first seat of learning – now the University of Pennsylvania. In between times he invented the lightning conductor, water wings, and an energy-saving stove (the Franklin stove) still around today in various guises.

What isn't so well known is that Franklin also possessed a great sense of humour. Arguably, his biggest contribution to the development of the United States was his part in writing the Declaration of Independence: but Thomas Jefferson, recognised as the founding father of modern America, is said to have commented that the only reason Benjamin hadn't been allowed to draft the entire document was because he would have included too many jokes! Perhaps this sense of fun passed down through the genes of the Franklin family to Mary Louise's mother. With two demanding children to manage, the ability to see the lighter side of things was a parenting tool never far from her grasp. She is remembered amongst many other things for her soft chuckle and her insistence on not being gloomy for long.

Most weeks, after school, she took her children swimming in the ocean off Santa Monica, just a thirty-minute car journey away. Then there were trips to see the ice age fossils at the La Brea tarpits, summer picnics on the beach, and for Mary Louise ice skating lessons with Olympic gold-medallist, Sonja Henie at the Los Angeles Figure Skating Club. This established a life-long enthusiasm for ice skating in Mary Louise, and on winter trips back to New York she would take to the frozen lake in Hudson Memorial Park. For many years ice skates would become a permanent part of her luggage wherever she went.

On Sunday mornings the entire family would descend on the Brown Derby restaurant situated on a corner of Wilshire Boulevard. The Brown Derby – so called because its entire structure was shaped to look like a giant, derby hat – was always a big hit with the Coulouris children. Here, in varnished booths enclosed by polished glass and chrome, Mary Louise and her brother would set about demolishing plates of crackly bacon, hash browns and pancakes inundated with maple syrup.

The Brown Derby was also a favourite meeting place for Hollywood actors and film directors: so on those occasions when George Coulouris was in L.A. he would avail himself of the opportunity to network and hear about the latest film projects in the pipeline. He would also update himself on the latest gossip and scandal which easily outstripped the supply of strawberry shortcake and sugared-doughnuts on offer in the restaurant. At the Brown Derby on Sunday mornings, your mouth wasn't just for eating with.

Following lunch, visits to the Hollywood film studios became an additional treat for Mary Louise and her brother George. Mary Louise would wander the factory-like complexes which made up MGM, Warner Brothers and other studios making the popular films of the day. She was mesmerised by the film sets and costume design on show. But even more-intriguing was the activity of the studio crews – the sound, lighting and camera operators who suddenly sprang into action when a scene was ready for shooting. The hush called for at such moments helped reinforce the idea that something important was about to take place, something to which the skilled, technical work of the crew was indispensable. This, and the frantic activity of the screenwriters, working and reworking scripts in the glass-walled booths lining the studio walls, was Mary Louise's first exposure to people working in what was virtually an industrial environment. Years later, images of people at work were to become a focus for her art, forming the basis of several series of paintings and prints which she exhibited in galleries in various parts of the world. Many of these entered the private collections of labour and trade union leaders, including John Smith who before his untimely death was leader of the British Labour Party.

When the summer heat began pounding the pavements of Los Angeles the Coulouris's headed for the hills, renting a log cabin in Idlewild close to Huntingdon Lake. Melons were submerged in a nearby stream to keep them fresh, forest trails were explored and camping trips became a frequent undertaking. The experience provided Mary Louise with an enduring delight in woodland and the scent of pine and wild herbs. The landscape fascinated her too, as did the fleeting, fragile beauty of the wildflowers which carpeted the lower slopes of the surrounding hills. Both were to become central to her artwork in years to come.

Back in Hollywood, if all other distractions failed, there was always cricket to fall back on. Such was the number of British actors living around L.A. at the time it was possible to form up to four, full-strength cricket teams. It was not unusual for an arriving ex-pat (Laurence Olivier being a good example) to find a note waiting for him at his hotel, saying '*...there will be cricket practice tomorrow at 4 p.m. I trust you'll be there.*' And usually they were. One of the first things George Coulouris did after moving into 608 North Roxbury Drive was to lay out a strip of coconut matting on the driveway, and after chalking a set of wickets on the garage door invite his friends around for some cricket practice. His son, George Jnr. remembers taking part in these 'nets' and also umpiring in actual matches which were played in Griffin Park, Los Angeles, and at Pasedena.

The motivating force behind what eventually became the Hollywood Cricket Club was an English actor, C. Aubrey Smith.

He it was who imported five cartloads of English grass seed to make the pitch, and raise $30, 000 to build the pavilion in Griffin Park. By 1936 the club was well established and could list the likes of Ronald Coleman and David Niven as members. Not that Americans were excluded, however: a wonderful picture exists showing Boris Karloff – star of many Hollywood horror films – keeping wicket, as the great man himself, Aubrey Smith, takes guard.

Mary Louise and her mother would often be part of these events, Louise keeping score while her daughter made sure the metal numbers on the scoreboard kept pace with the runs being made on the field. On days when the run-rate wasn't exactly flowing, the shadowy interior of the structure supporting the scoreboard would intrigue her more than what was taking place in the game. With its peephole-views of the outside world, the structure would in some ways provide her with an introduction to the laws of perspective and the need of every artist to filter out and focus, free of surrounding distractions. In the long run her view from the scoreboard would amount to more than just helping to manage a simple game of cricket.

CHAPTER 3

When cricket didn't appear at the top of the weekend's priorities, Mary Louise's home on North Roxbury Drive became an alternative gathering place for many Hollywood actors, some of them already establishing themselves as household names. They would arrive around lunchtime to talk, debate, swap gossip, and by all accounts swallow prodigious amounts of alcohol. Bette Davis was one such visitor, as was John Garfield – the original rebel-hero of the cinema screen and prototype for later legends like James Dean and Marlon Brando.

The story is Garfield had become an actor to escape a delinquent's life on the Lower East Side of New York. If this was true then he made good use of his upbringing in several Hollywood productions. His first movie performance in 'Four Daughters' saw him nominated for an Academy Award, and his second won him best actor in 'Body and Soul.' But his meteoric-rise to stardom ended abruptly when he died in the apartment of his Los Angeles lover, aged just 39. Falsely accused of being a communist by his country's House Committee on Un-American Activities (HUAC), the intense pressure he endured as a result finally caused him to suffer a fatal heart attack.

Other guests at North Roxbury who were to feel the wrath of HUAC and have their careers disrupted and destroyed included screenwriter Lester Cole, and Larry Adler - a talented composer remembered best during his exile in Britain for his harmonica playing when guesting on radio and television shows. Adler played tennis with Mary Louise's father on a regular basis in Hollywood and London and their friendship   - cemented this time by the union of ball and racquet - continued for many years afterwards. I asked Adler on a couple of occasions what he felt about being blacklisted and exiled from his country, but he wouldn't say. Like a soldier returned from the horrors of the battlefields he was reluctant to talk about it. On the second occasion he pulled a couple of small harmonicas from his pocket and gave one to each of my children, whereupon they blew so noisily on them that further conversation became impossible.

Despite being at an end the experience of surviving the ravaging effects of America's 'Great Depression' remained embedded in people's minds. The fate of friends and family members during the decade-long economic catastrophe was too recent to be banished entirely from their thoughts: and this applied as much to the Franklin side of Mary Louise's family as anyone else.

A great uncle of her mother's, having watched his investment in an Illinois rose-farm disappear like so much water down a drain, took his own life. He wasn't the only one who had resorted to such drastic measures rather than suffer the ignominy of financial ruin and the loss of social status. A vein of grisly humour related to this soon surfaced on Wall Street suggesting that every share bought in the banking conglomerate of Goldman Sachs came with a complimentary revolver: and the story was told of the hotel receptionist who asked clients booking a room, 'Is it for sleeping, or jumping?' At the time when Mary Louise's parents were being married, as many as one-half of America's workforce was unemployed, millions were undernourished, and an uncountable number hovered on the edge of starvation. As a result, efforts were made by government to investigate child-care issues with an emphasis on the nutritional needs of infants and young people. It was a similar process to that which led to Churchill's endorsement of a strategy to provide fresh milk, cod liver oil and orange juice for schoolchildren in Britain.

As a modern mother Louise Franklin Coulouris would not have been unaware of the outcomes to this research which gave rise eventually to the commercial production of an infant cereal called pabulum which she was later to feed to her children. Pabulum was a yeasty mix of wheat, oats, and corn, fortified with several types of vitamins. Boiled in water it provided a bland, uninviting meal that looked like porridge and was swallowed by Mary Louise and her brother only on the promise of a recuperative visit soon to somewhere like the Brown Derby. What pabulum consisted of however, when you deducted its vitamins and minerals from the equation, was starch: and starch could lead to a child putting on weight. At birth Mary Louise had proved to be a 'big' baby weighing in at almost nine pounds, two pounds heavier than the average: 18 months later she was five-and-a-half pounds heavier than the average. Little of this was due to pabulum, of course, which Mary Louise didn't begin taking in serious quantities until later in her infancy: but it didn't help. The result was a healthy and attractive child, but a chubby one nonetheless. In terms of leaving a lasting legacy, healthy eating, nutrition and weight-control were to become important factors in how she felt about herself thereafter.

Something else during the Depression years that was to have a lasting influence on the Coulouris's, especially father George, was a government-led economic recovery plan called the 'New Deal'. The 'New Deal' used public funds to create jobs by investing in a wide range of new initiatives including road and harbour construction and large housing developments. Listed as one of these initiatives, was the Federal Theatre Project (the FTP).

The FTP was designed to provide unemployed actors with work, and unemployed citizens with cheap access to the theatre. During its four years of existence, the FTP delivered over a thousand theatre productions giving more than 12 million people the chance to watch plays and other stage-based cultural events in schools and community centres across the land. In New York alone the project employed five-and-a-half thousand people in a single year, among them Orson Welles who staged an all-black Macbeth in Harlem, and a controversial play called 'The Cradle Will Rock'. Such was the hostility to this latter production's leftist-content by conservatives, that the day before its public preview the theatre doors were padlocked, obliging the cast and their audience to walk over 20 blocks north in Manhattan where another theatre had been found to stage the show.

It was in this period that Mary Louise's father first met and worked with Orson Welles, appearing with him on both radio and the stage then shortly afterwards as part of the Mercury Players – a group Welles got together when FTP funding looked like it was beginning to dwindle. But their friendship got off to a less than auspicious start. In a Broadway play called Ten Million Ghosts – an anti-war story in which Coulouris played a munitions tycoon and Welles the young hero – there were accusations that Welles had fallen asleep at points in the performance. The two rowed and the play ran for no more than a week before being pulled. Its failure didn't help create the symbiosis between Coulouris and Welles which the latter seemed to elicit from the other senior actors around him.

Going to sleep, on the other hand, was seen as no more than a necessary inconvenience for Mary Louise as she focused on cramming as much fun as possible into each day. Her brother George was to say of that time, 'We were typical California kids, always doing something outside or playing in the garden.' One afternoon they were startled by the noise of an aircraft flying low over the rooftops. Seconds after it disappeared there was an almighty bang followed by a plume of smoke. With Mother trailing in their wake the children raced along an alley at the rear of their house in time to see a familiar figure stumble from the wreckage where the plane had hit the ground. The figure was that of billionaire Howard Hughes, a man whose life was to become the subject of much intrigue and sensationalist media attention.

Hughes emerged relatively unscathed from his wrecked aircraft although the same couldn't be said for his reputation thereafter. Drug abuse, paranoia and an obsession with diets and infections deranged his mind and led to him becoming a total recluse who refused to cut his fingernails and trim his hair. In recent times it has emerged that he was a central figure in funding plots to invade Fidel Castro's Cuba, and claims have been made that his right-wing political views encouraged his involvement in the assassinations of John F. Kennedy and his brother, Bobby. He died in 1976 leaving a fortune worth two billion dollars.

Away from the environs of North Roxbury Drive, the sandy beaches of Southern California provided the now school-age Mary Louise with a further range of fun things to do. Swimming was just one option: another was barbecues especially when the amazing grunion made their appearance.

Grunion are small, silvery fish which come out of the ocean to lay their eggs on the beach. They do this almost like a surfer, allowing themselves to be carried ashore by one wave then having deposited their eggs quickly in the sand, catching the next wave back to the ocean. They carry out this ritual only on certain nights of the year, and only on certain beaches – Santa Monica being one of them.

Catching grunion with a view to barbecuing them meant people had to be as quick off the mark as the slippery little creatures themselves. But such was the regularity of their arrival, that plans to catch them could be made a year in advance resulting in the sight of thousands of people lining the Californian beaches in anticipation of a 'grunion run.' The fish were caught at night (legally, only when they were on the beach and you used bare hands to catch them), then stored on ice ready for the big barbecue parties the following day. The smell of barbecued grunion, coated in corn flour and olive oil, was often strong enough to overpower other odours generated by increased traffic volumes around Santa Monica at the time.

One of Mary Louise's friends who was a regular at these grunion picnics and at North Roxbury, was a girl called Judy Chaplin. Judy was later to marry the theatrical producer, Hal Prince, who produced and directed dozens of hugely successful musicals including West Side Story and Fiddler On The Roof. He also collaborated with Andrew Lloyd-Webber to stage Phantom Of The opera in 1986. When Judy visited 608 North Roxbury Drive, she and Mary Louise would bring out their dolls and avail themselves of the wooden play house built at the rear of the property. Later they'd help the Coulouris's maid, Taz, prepare lunch and practice ballet in the front room to music which Mother arranged on the record player. Dying swans now replaced grunion on the menu of available distractions.

It was Judy's father Saul Chaplin, however, who was to have a hand in deciding the next step into the future of his daughter's friend Mary Louise. Saul Chaplin was a talented composer and songwriter working in films, whose successes were to include 'An American In Paris' starring Gene Kelly, and 'High Society' featuring Frank Sinatra, Bing Crosby and Bob Hope. It was through her father's work in Hollywood that Judy Chaplin first met, and then married, Hal Prince. And it was Saul Chaplin who advanced the idea of staging a musical that held a great deal of interest for Mary Louise's father.

From his earliest days George Coulouris had practised singing alongside his main passion to develop as an actor. His motivation in this respect stemmed from his admiration of the Russian bass, Fydor Chaliapin, many of whose recordings were made in an era known as 'pre-electric.' George Coulouris had a library of Chaliapin's work which had been transposed on to 78-discs, and listening to them enabled him to see how great moments in singing were like the great moments in acting – moments that caused an audience to hold its breath and experience an intensity of feeling that bordered on the magical. So, when Saul Chaplin proposed staging a new musical and invited George Coulouris to be part of it, Mary Louise's father – despite what he was to say several years later - didn't take long to make up his mind.

The musical was Bonanza Bound based on a book by Adolph Green and Betty Comden, and it was scheduled for rehearsal in New York before it transferred down the coast to open in Philadelphia. Unlike previous theatre appearances in New York which had seen Coulouris become the absent father to his children, this time he decided to take his family with him. On the surface it seemed a reasonable thing to do, especially if Bonanza Bound was to receive favourable reviews and enjoy a longish-run before transferring to the New York stage. Added to this was the awareness that Hollywood wasn't providing him with the acting roles he most wanted to play. He was still imbued with the ambition of using his talent performing Shakespeare and plays in the classical repertoire. Film roles as a villain which he inevitably played, and the way movies were shot was by comparison at odds with how he wanted his acting career to develop.

Within a few weeks of George Coulouris taking the decision to play in Bonanza Bound his family were once again packing their suitcases and preparing to move house. But if there was any sadness felt at leaving Beverly Hills, it was soon assuaged by the excitement of facing life in a new and different part of the country. For Mary Louise it meant opening a fresh chapter to what was already shaping to be a varied and interesting start to life. It was destined to go on being so, even if along the way the unexpected was waiting in the wings, preparing to make its own entrance.

CHAPTER 4

Bidding farewell to Beverly Hills the Coulouris's travelled the long diagonal which marks the route between Los Angeles and the north-eastern state of New York. They took the train while their maid Taz followed in the family car driven by a student hired to do the job. Awaiting them on the outskirts of Port Chester – a town known for making sweets and producing chat show host Ed Sullivan - was a property that had the proportions of a mansion.

Sitting on eleven acres of land close to the border with Connecticut, 'Hill House' was a timber-clad property consisting of twenty-three rooms and surrounded by pine forests and lakes. Although a sandy beach running up to some spectacular cliffs was close at hand, it was the two winters spent here that Mary Louise remembers best. Blizzards, somewhat reminiscent of those depicted in the opening scenes of *Citizen Kane*, left behind them several feet of snow and frozen lakes. Mary Louise and her brother ice skated, built igloos and developed their skills at skiing on the steep driveway leading from the road up to the house. Thanks to Doctor Ned Shnayerson who'd taught them how to ski back in Hudson Park, both children were equal to anything flung at them during that first winter in their new home.

At times though there seemed to be almost as much space for adventure and exploration inside 'Hill House' as outside of it, although such were the distances between rooms – especially between the huge living room and the kitchen – that a system of bells had been installed by the original owner for summoning his servants. What Taz and Mary Louise's mother made of this only their aching feet could be relied on to say.

The house was owned by the widow of a wealthy New York businessman, and Mary Louise's parents rented the property at a rate that must have been considerable even if its location was conveniently close to New York where George Coulouris was due to rehearse 'Bonanza Bound.' What persuaded him to take on the onerous financial burden of renting 'Hill House' isn't clear. Certainly its accommodation vastly exceeded what his family required. Compared to 608 North Roxbury Drive where Mary Louise and her brother had shared a room and Taz had taken up what was left of the available space, 'Hill House' must have seemed like stepping into somebody else's world – a veritable Xanadu in fact, like that occupied in the movie by Charles Foster Kane. Such was its size that one of the Coulouris's best friends, the actor Morris Carnovsky and his family were invited to live in the coach-house apartment overlooking the entrance to the property.

It is possible Carnovsky knew of the house some years before the Coulouris's moved there and recommended it as a place to stay. In 1931 Carnovsky and around 40 other actors, scriptwriters and playwrights opted to leave New York's Broadway for a town in a remote part of Connecticut called Brookfield. Their aim was to form the structure of a new type of theatre which eschewed the 'star' system, performed plays which dealt with the real problems people faced, and was not dependent on the 'hit or flop' commercialism of Broadway. They also regarded the current way of acting as being 'too artificial and fabricated.' They called themselves '*The Group Theatre.*'

Their enterprise – coming as it did shortly after the Wall Street crash and the onset of the Great Depression – coincided with the rise of far-right politics in Europe which gave the scripts they developed a pro-labour and anti-fascist content. At any rate, the distance between Brookfield and Port Chester was less than an hour's drive, and Carnovsky may well have spotted 'Hill House' on his travels around the area. He may even have harboured a dream of some day turning it into a centre for 'The Group Theatre.' 'Hill House' was certainly big enough for the job!

Whether Carnovsky helped Mary Louise's father much with paying the rent was largely irrelevant when set against the fact that he was as passionate as George Coulouris was about playing Shakespearean roles. From the mid-1950s onwards he was to focus his career on such roles and playing major parts in several of the Greek tragedies such as 'Medea.' His presence at 'Hill House' must have been welcomed by Coulouris who would regard him as a kindred spirit.

Moving his entire family away from California was a pretty clear signal that Hollywood no longer fulfilled the promise it might once have had for Mary Louise's father. Although he'd been cast in 26 Hollywood films by this point, he was never again to appear in any motion picture made there. And by this time HUAC had begun its investigation of those in the movie industry suspected of holding views contrary to what the committee considered to be the American way of life.

The government, now led by President Harry S. Truman, had begun talking about taking oaths of loyalty to the country, and had ordered the American Department of Justice to draw up lists of organisations seen as harbouring communists and subversives, especially those seen as influential in shaping the thoughts and ideas of ordinary people. People producing and taking part in Hollywood movies were an obvious target. This soon extended itself to individuals regarded as being in 'sympathetic association' with any organisation on the list, and people in Hollywood – like those before them in teaching, local government and the trade unions – became a focus for investigation.

Lacking any coherent definition of what constituted an 'un-American activity' (for some people laws restricting child labour and registering women for the vote were seen as being 'communist plots'), people summoned to appear at HUAC hearings had to face unsubstantiated accusations based on inconclusive and questionable evidence relating to their political beliefs. Amongst those blacklisted, fined and imprisoned were several of George Coulouris's friends and acquaintances including actors such as Edward G. Robinson and Orson Welles, the black singer Paul Robeson, screenwriter Lester Cole and playwright Arthur Miller. Charlie Chaplin left the United States in disgust.

Largely oblivious to most of these developments however,

Mary Louise was soon contemplating her own list of priorities among which was the matter of her education. A short car ride away across the border with Connecticut lay Edgewood School where Mary Louise and her brother, George, were soon being enrolled as junior-school pupils. In Los Angeles, the children had attended several schools turning in some pretty useful report cards. Their new school in Connecticut however, which was run on quite different lines from what they'd been used to, energised them in ways they'd never experienced before.

Edgewood School operated on principles that were known in the United States as 'organic education'…the belief that all children should be motivated to learn by natural, free-development, rather than by competing with each other. The school – one of several Edgewood schools dotted across the United States – was the result of implementing the ideas of a respected educationalist, Marietta Pierce Johnson, who ten years prior to Mary Louise and her brother going there had been Director of Edgewood School in Connecticut. '*A child should be active in all their learning,*' she'd insisted. '*Not only do we learn to do by doing, but all learning is accomplished through experience.*' As a result, activities such as creative-play, arts and crafts and technical subjects like woodworking which didn't figure much in most schools at the time, were a significant part of Edgewood's child-centred curriculum.

For many suburban middle-class parents, Edgewood schools were beacons in America for what they regarded as 'progressive' education: and although their popularity had peaked in the 1920s and they were now in slow decline, Edgewood schools still put a high premium on assisting the growth of the whole child, physically as well as mentally. Exams didn't exist, no homework was set, and no child was ever regarded as having failed. In most cases a pupil never went near a text book until reaching the age of nine. Nature walks which taught children to understand the propagation of trees and wildflowers, to investigate the habitats of wildlife species and appreciate the cyclical nature of the seasons were given an emphasis in what primary-age pupils were expected to learn. All had abiding effects on Mary Louise, both in terms of her human development and later in her chosen career as a professional artist.

Yet ironically Edgewood might also have been a factor in what eventually decided her father to leave America. Years later George Coulouris was to say his reason for quitting the United States and returning to England was that he didn't want his children growing up saying things like '*Aw gee, Pop.*' But perhaps there were deeper, more-unsettling trends developing in the school especially amongst the senior pupils that persuaded him it was time to return to England. That decision, however, was still a couple of years away.

Outside of school, life for Mary Louise at 'Hill House' settled into a pattern that in some ways had changed little since her days in Beverly Hills. This included continuation of the usual range of childhood maladies such as measles and chicken pox and removal of her tonsils and adenoids in March, 1947. One of her eyes – the left one – had given her parents concern since birth, and early in 1947 it was diagnosed as having only 6% vision. Although having been prescribed glasses as early as 1942, she now required to have her left eye 'patched' – a bothersome situation for an active, growing child who persevered with patching for only three months before tossing it aside.

With her husband absent at rehearsals for '*Bonanza Bound*' Louise Franklin Coulouris continued to carry the main responsibility for raising their two children. Whether this was a factor in her drinking too much isn't clear: but alcohol might well have been the reason for her falling over one day outside 'Hill House' and breaking several of her ribs. Mary Louise's anxiety for her mother expressed itself in anger, provoking her to accuse Louise of being 'befuddled' and 'not all there.'

But there were more edifying events to record and participate in. During their first summer at 'Hill House' the Coulouris's agreed to host a political fundraiser for a man who was seeking to become President of the United States. He was leader of the recently formed Progressive Party, Henry Agard Wallace.

Wallace was from Iowa farming stock, and was about to turn 60 when he stood for the highest office in the United States. He was regarded by many as a sincere and intelligent individual, the author of a stream of publications on how to improve agriculture which in the early years of the Great Depression had seen him appointed Secretary of State for Agriculture by Franklin D. Roosevelt. From there he went on, via the Democratic-ticket, to be Vice-President of the USA until the end of the Second World War. But Henry Wallace was also someone determined to introduce new ideas that would change America, ideas that were eventually to bring his career to an abrupt end.

Throughout the Depression, Wallace had seen what was happening to his fellow-countrymen and women, amongst them reputable business people whose politics were far from being 'un-American' but who, nonetheless, had been ruined by the economic collapse. Being an innovative individual, he had begun developing new strategies that would avoid repeating the pain. Like a growing number of people he believed the worship of money and the venal politics which accompanied it lay at the heart of the country's troubles. Perhaps there were too many 'rented' politicians in Washington, he suggested. Perhaps too many senior businessmen and 'captains of industry' had been revealed as nothing but robber barons.

Contrary to advocating the revolutionary overthrow of the United States Wallace represented a desire to introduce better ways of managing the country's economy, of introducing permanent social welfare programmes, and co-operating with other countries in the world instead of dominating them. In many ways the same issues are still at the forefront of American politics today. People holding to these views in the latter part of the 1940s were known as 'progressives', although that soon became a pejorative term on the lips of their detractors, who portrayed them as subversives. Wallace himself was often portrayed as such, and after accepting nomination as the presidential candidate for the Progressive Party he was to be derided as a 'mystic and idealist', and someone living in a time warp. As the presidential election approached he had to go in search of the money needed to further his campaign. The fundraiser at 'Hill House' was one of several held on his behalf.

On a lawn that had the proportions of a football field, several hundred people gathered at 'Hill House' to listen to speeches, re-affirm their commitment to progressive politics and, of course, donate their money to Wallace's campaign. Among them were a fair selection of actors, writers and other creative figures including some teachers from Edgewood School. No record exists of how much the 'Hill House' fundraiser contributed to Wallace's campaign budget, but it was enough to occupy a couple of hours of Mary Louise's time after the party was over. The money donated by those who'd attended was spread out on the kitchen table and she and her mother set about counting it, making separate piles of the notes and cheques and emptying the buckets of more slender contributions. All history tells us is that Wallace ran for president with the support of what he described as 'Gideon's Army' – that small number of Progressive Party members whose convictions carried them through much abuse and racist attacks, especially in the south. When the ballot returns were counted however, it showed Wallace had amassed barely a million votes. It was the signal for him to retire from politics and return to his farming interests. He died in 1965 at the age of seventy-seven.

In several ways though, the fundraiser proved to have more lasting effects than collecting money for Wallace's failed presidential-bid. Progressives continued to hold to the belief that the economic system of the U.S. was seriously flawed and in need of reform, and 'Hill House' became one of several places where they met to discuss what they should do next. In between school, swimming and continuing to explore the great outdoors, Mary Louise would hear snatches of these group discussions that would eventually find their way into shaping her own political ideas.

Those ideas, however, were still a long way off and although she didn't know it, her time in America was quickly moving towards an end.

One afternoon as he waited to collect his daughter from Edgewood School, George Coulouris fell into conversation with some senior pupils there. Although the ethos of the school was quite different from that existing in mainstream institutions, Edgewood was never entirely free from the pressure to provide its students with an education that would enable them to survive in the highly competitive country America had become. Increasingly, as a child moved through the school, tensions developed between Edgewood's guiding principles and what was seen as the demands of a wider, harsher society. Unaware of these tensions and how they could influence the minds of older pupils, Mary Louise's father began engaging the youths around him in a debate on progressive ideas. To his surprise, then shock, Coulouris found himself under challenge in a heated discussion that ended badly with one of the Edgewood students telling him, '*If you don't like it in America, go back to where you come from.*' The remark, with its overtones of racism, probably contributed much to what he decided to do next.

Almost a year earlier, the musical *Bonanza Bound* had been premiered in Philadelphia to what critics described as a less than enthusiastic audience. In 1962 during a series of talks broadcast by BBC radio in England, Coulouris referred to his singing part in the musical as the most frightening experience in his life. '*I lost all sense of what I was doing,*' he said. '*I could see the conductor was going mad by the way his baton was waving so strangely in the air.*' The show closed after just a few performances taking over quarter of a million dollars of business sponsorship money with it.

The disappointment and recriminations which follow in the wake of a theatrical flop were assuaged a little for Mary Louise's father by his return to the New York stage for a while, linking up again in one instance with Jose Ferrer in a play called 'The Alchemist.' He got little money for these appearances but as he said, '*It was exciting after Hollywood (and you) had the feeling that you were doing something not just because of the money, but because you liked the plays and liked the parts.*' It was a comment that confirmed Coulouris's continuing commitment to the stage and the roles he most wanted to play.

By this time, however, the man who shared his enthusiasm for the classical repertoire, Morris Carnovsky, had already left 'Hill House' and returned to Hollywood to work as an actor and become director of the Actors Laboratory Theatre there. It was a step closer to playing the Shakespearean roles Carnovsky wanted to perform. Coupled to this was Coulouris's disappointment with the failure of progressive politics to make any substantial impact on the American people as evidenced by Wallace's poor showing in the presidential polls: and at a local level the hostile reaction of students at Edgewood – a supposed centre for enlightenment - to any ideas of supporting reforms to the way their country was run depressed him. Added to this was the increasing number of acquaintances in the media industry who were receiving summonses to appear before HUAC, or had already been put on a blacklist. To Mary Louise's father, it didn't look like a time to sit tight and see how things might shape up in the future.

Leaving his family behind, he made a solo trip to England that lasted for a number of months. During the visit he made contact with the Shakespeare Memorial Company at Stratford-upon-Avon, in particular with its recently appointed director Anthony Quayle. The two men seemed to get on well together, sharing many things in common including, of course, their love of performing Shakespeare. Quayle appeared to be a fairly straight-forward individual – an ex-army major, and during the Second World War an intelligence agent for the Allies in Nazi-occupied Europe. He was also a popular actor, on stage and in film, appearing later in classics such as Battle of the River Plate and The Guns of Navarone as well as being part of Laurence Olivier's Academy-award winning film production of Hamlet.

Of more significance to Mary Louise's father however, was

the fact that Quayle was laying the groundwork for founding the Royal Shakespeare Company at Stratford, something George Coulouris was keen to be part of. He returned to his family at 'Hill House' fairly certain he had done enough during his time in England to put himself in line for becoming part of an exciting new development in British theatre. But as time passed and he heard nothing from across the Atlantic, Coulouris became agitated, then dejected. '*I don't think Tony is going to send for me,*' he told Louise morosely as they sat one evening in 'Hill House' debating the possible reasons for Quayle's silence. What he'd been anticipating was a contract making him a member of what was to become the world's leading theatre company: but the contract failed to materialise.

Being the individual he was however, disappointment was soon subsumed by a strong feeling he needed to do something: and although there is reason to believe Coulouris was preparing to sue the RSC for breach of what amounted to a verbal contract, what he decided to do turned out to be infinitely more important for Mary Louise and the rest of his family. He made up his mind to leave the United States and return to the country where he'd been born and where he'd acquired and honed his stage skills.

Perhaps he calculated that becoming part of an actor's network in England would strengthen his prospects of doing what he most wanted to do in the theatre. Perhaps too, now that he'd been in Hollywood, he thought his reputation would carry more weight than previously and that his chance of succeeding against the old boy clique which dominated the theatre was greater than in previous times. After all, the country was grappling with post-war change of which the plan to establish the Royal Shakespeare Company was a part. In that context, his wish to rid himself of the '*Aw gee, Pop*' culture played only a small and inconsequential role.

When, in due course, the carriers arrived at 'Hill House' to take the Coulouris's luggage to the shipping terminal in New York, they found 12 packed trunks awaiting them. It could have been more, but by this time the baggage belonging to Taz had already gone with her back to Los Angeles. She had been like a sister to Mary Louise and her brother, and leaving her was a big wrench. Although her whereabouts and what she did after leaving Connecticut was never firmly established, the Japanese maid was never to be forgotten.

More than a few of the family's friends were on the quayside to wave the Coulouris's off after they'd boarded the Queen Mary bound for Southhampton. And as the giant liner shrugged off her moorings and headed for the open sea, the cheers and customary tickertape farewell began. Ahead of the family lay a five-day voyage – a time Mary Louise would pass playing deck quoits, having dinner at the captain's table, and experiencing her first bout of seasickness after marvelling at the size of the waves. In mid-Atlantic the Queen Mary hove-to for a while in response to a mayday-signal from a freighter in the area that was shipping water. But that apart, the voyage proved to be straightforward and uneventful.

As parents, George and Louise must have turned their thoughts from time to time to what their children would make of living in England. They'd both proved how adaptable they were to moving within the United States: but how would they take to moving countries? How would they respond to the need for fitting in to a different culture, to finding their feet amongst people still coping with the aftermath of the Second World War with its food rationing, bomb sites and the continuing dislocation of what had previously been everyday life? These were questions soon to be answered - in some instances through quite traumatic experiences, especially for Mary Louise. But as the Queen Mary rounded the tip of Britain and pointed herself directly at the port of Southampton, there were few clues to what the future had in store. A thickening fog hung over the English coastline, and even from the upper-deck of the ship it seemed what lay ahead was determined to remain unclear.

CHAPTER 5

The amorphous crowd gathered at the beach now draws itself into some semblance of order and begins moving off towards the centre of town. In contrast to the overnight rain, spears of sunlight now smote the Portuguese resort of Estoril adding their energy to the festival atmosphere that is rapidly engulfing the entire area. As the crowd wheels and enters the first main thoroughfare, more people join in, lifting its mood even higher like the balloons and bunting rising on the mild breezes coming from the ocean. Which Saint's day is being celebrated appears not to matter: more temporal pleasures is what the increasingly noisy participants seem to have in mind.

On a hotel balcony overlooking the route of the parade, Mary Louise is also in the grip of a curious exhilaration. The sound of firecrackers and the natural brio of a makeshift band only serve to heighten the sense of anticipation in the eleven year-old: and as her family relax beside her in the sun she cranes over the balcony rail as if willing the approaching cavalcade to make more speed. At times the restraining hand of her mother seems to be the only thing stopping her vaulting the rail and becoming part of the celebrations.

It is the Coulouris's first trip to mainland Europe since leaving America and settling in London. They've no sooner unpacked their bags however, than Mary Louise's father is offered a part in a film, scenes of which are to be shot in Portugal. The film is 'Kill or Be Killed' starring Laurence Tierney, and the deal is George Coulouris can take his family with him to Portugal, basing them at the Atlantic Hotel in Estoril. With its banks of mimosa and eucalyptus trees sweeping down to an ocean fringed with golden sands, Estoril is living up to its reputation of being the jewel in Portugal's 'Sun Coast.' It is certainly a wonderful place to spend a few weeks in 1950, especially on a festival day: and as the parade passes below her balcony, the few solemn clerics at its head engulfed by the animated crowd, Mary Louise says to her mother, 'Oh Mum, I wish I could

33

paint this! If only I had the materials I could make a picture!'

Next day, true to her promise, Mum drives to nearby Lisbon returning with enough materials to stock a small art store. Then she watches as her daughter sets to work, recreating the festival scene in all its vibrancy and colour. The picture doesn't survive long after the family's return from Portugal and few regard it as anything more than a child's first earnest attempt at making art. Only later will it be seen as a marker on the road to what she'll become and what will constitute the subject matter of her early artwork - street scenes enlivened by colour and the movement of people. In no small way Estoril will link with her earlier experiences in Hollywood's film studios..............

Before that ever came to pass, however, Mary Louise had to pick up the threads of her general education in England. This began with her parents placing her in several private schools within reasonable travelling distance of their home in the Putney district of London. On arriving from America the family had moved into a detached property at 15 Genoa Avenue, partly because the house was near to Putney Heath - a sizeable track of open land that did its best to compensate for the loss of liberty enjoyed in the acres surrounding 'Hill House.' But it seemed little could be done to compensate for the loss of other sorts of freedom Mary Louise had grown used to at Edgewood School. By contrast English private schools were like closed societies run strictly by rules which many children failed to understand but were obliged to abide by. Mary Louise was one such child.

At an interview for one school the headmistress remarked, 'I hope you'll wear something quieter if you start here.' She was referring to Mary Louise's red dress and the equally bright jacket she had on. At another establishment the girls were expected to wear white gloves and were marched to lunch, military fashion, in double-column formation. The same school insisted on skirts being worn at the stipulated 14-inches from the ground. On the day the Queen Mother was due to pay a visit, each girl was taken to a basement room to have her hem-line measured before being allowed to curtsey when introduced to the royal personage. After the liberties enjoyed under the relaxed regime in Connecticut, it was all too much for Mary Louise and she dug her heels in refusing to attend any of the schools who'd offered to enrol her.

Her brother George fared better, although after the first day at his new school in Putney he returned home greatly distressed at witnessing one of his classmates being caned. At Edgewood, inflicting such punishment on a child would have been unthinkable and young George broke down and cried. Soon he was on his way to another prep school in Wimbledon where he prospered enough to succeed in passing the entrance exam for Westminster School. At Westminster he settled to his studies, played cricket, and being a big lad built like his father, quickly dealt with any potential ribbing he might have attracted on account of his American accent.

During this period Mary Louise's father had begun networking with other actors in London, and was soon to appear in productions at the Bristol Old Vic. He had a long run as Tartuffe in Moliere's play 'The Imposter' and made the acquaintance of Dorothy Tutin, who also performed at Bristol and who became a frequent visitor to the Coulouris family home at Genoa Avenue. Tutin established her reputation as an actress in the early 1950s and later played Goneril in the internationally syndicated television production of 'King Lear' with Laurence Olivier. Her talent as an actress was recognised eventually by awarding her the title, Dame Dorothy Tutin.

But many of George Coulouris's theatrical contacts lived in or around the north-west London area of Hampstead. Like New York's Spuyten Duyvil, Hampstead hosted a hefty proportion of people with connections to the creative arts. In its time the writers Agatha Christie and H.G. Wells had taken up residence there, as had the architect Walter Gropius and artists such as Henry Moore and Ben Nicholson. They'd enjoyed living in a location close to the centre of London but which still retained a village atmosphere with narrow streets lined with trees and charming houses. It was a place George Coulouris could see his family taking to even if it meant uprooting them yet again. He began thinking seriously of moving to Hampstead and discussing the possibilities with his wife: but where were they to find an affordable property in an area high on the list of desirable places to live? The answer soon presented itself in the shape of 'Chestnut Cottage.'

'Chestnut Cottage' sat in a hollow on Hampstead Heath immediately below Whitestone Pond, and was accessed by a narrow road that wound itself around a small collection of houses that occupied a part of the area known as the Vale of Health. In the 18th century the place had

Chestnut Cottage, Hampstead. Mary Louise's room was directly above the door on the right overlooking the garden.

been a malarial swamp until it was drained and made safe for people to live there. In an effort to convince people of its new, disease-free status what had been previously known as 'Hatchett's Bottom' now changed its name to the Vale of Health. House building soon got underway, and among the first properties to be erected around 1808 was 'Chestnut Cottage.'

In the early 1950s 'Chestnut Cottage' was put up for sale but failed to attract a buyer. In keeping with some of the Vale of Health's first residents who'd ran businesses there in trades such as harness-making and tanning animal hides, the house was owned by a chimney sweep who operated his business from it. It had no inside lavatory, the bath was in the kitchen and one entire room of the property was used to store soot. The roof leaked in several places and the walls – some timber clad, others made from material that resembled little more than wattle and daub – were in need of major renovation. As a consequence when 'Chestnut Cottage' was put up for auction, it didn't find any bidders willing to pay the price. Having been made aware of this, the day following the auction George Coulouris offered to buy the property at the reserved price and had it accepted. It cost him £7000 to have the deal done in his name. Shortly afterwards the family said goodbye to Putney and headed for North-West London.

Moving to Hampstead saw Mary Louise enrolling in yet another private school, this time in nearby Highgate which she enjoyed more than any of the others she'd attended. But coping with an education system she was still adapting to, and which measured academic performance mainly through tests and examinations, proved too much for someone who had a natural desire to learn but in her own way and at her own speed. When she was due to end her primary-school years she was put forward for the compulsory 'Eleven-Plus' examination and failed. Like other children who faltered or fell at this watershed moment in English education (and this meant the majority of them), her options narrowed as to what type of secondary schooling was available to her. The 'Eleven Plus' was designed to separate the 'thinkers' from the 'doers', to filter-out the relatively small number of children seen as being academically capable of eventually reaching the standards set for university entrance. The rest were expected to serve out the remainder of their schooldays at 'comprehensives' before leaving at sixteen and getting jobs.

With hindsight, however, failing her 'Eleven Plus' might have been one of the best things to happen to Mary Louise. It meant her attending a comprehensive school within a short walking distance of her home in the Vale of Health: but more importantly it was a place she took too immediately and where in a more-relaxed atmosphere she was to take giant steps in developing herself both academically, and eventually in realising her potential as an artist.

The school was a girls-only establishment called Parliament Hill School, and its catchment area for recruiting pupils contained a good balance of middle-class and working class families. Being a comprehensive funded by the local authority it was free of the competitive pressures on private schools to raise finance by selling themselves to parents. And it was less hindered in applying its energy to pupil-learning by making discipline and 'proper, lady-like behaviour' appear like major items in the curriculum.

In this less-stressful environment Mary Louise quickly made friends, two girls in particular, who became especially supportive of each other so that all three began turning in good results to the extent of winning prizes for the progress they were making. There were still exams to be got through, but now they were looked on more as a challenge than a nightmare awaiting them at the conclusion of each school year. In her second year at Parliament Hill, Mary Louise came top in her form for examination successes and scored above 90% in mathematics and music. When she finished her formal education at sixteen she left with a fistful of '0'- Levels – something that would have been inconceivable a few years earlier. In the fullness of time, when she won a French government scholarship to study in France, her name would be inscribed on a roll of honour still displayed in the entrance hall to Parliament Hill School.

On the other side of the Heath, however, Chestnut Cottage was undergoing a strict examination of its own. To no one's surprise it failed and some major refurbishment was decided on. With the help of an obliging neighbour who offered to accommodate them, the Coulouris's moved out to allow the builder's to move in. An inside loo was the first thing to emerge from the chaos followed by conversion of the soot room to George and Louise's bedroom. Above this two further bedrooms were upgraded – one for Mary Louise, the other for her brother George – and a low-beamed living room, with a large window overlooking the garden, became the place where the family would gather after meals and visitors would be entertained. In earlier days the living room had been part of an area used for stabling the chimney sweep's horses and storing his carts. Outside, a new lawn was seeded and the garden put in order with privet hedges separated by cinder paths: and below the giant chestnut tree that gave the cottage its name a ramshackle structure that had seen various uses in its time was eventually to become a studio for Mary Louise.

By this time the idea of being an artist had begun moving upwards in the list of the things Mary Louise felt she most wanted to do. The idea appealed to her mother for obvious reasons: after all, this had been the route she herself had started out on as a young woman in Philadelphia before illness put an end to it. Oddly though, visits to art shows and museums hadn't been a feature of family activity at any point in Mary Louise's life. Giving art books as presents on birthdays and at Christmas was about as far as it went. And school didn't help much either in fostering an interest in fine art. Taking pupils in a group to art galleries was a rare occurrence and not seen as a necessary supplement to their general education.

At Parliament Hill, however, the teacher of the art class began recognising Mary Louise's developing talent in drawing and had spoken to her and other teachers about the possibility of her applying for a place at art school. But Mary Louise, now in her mid-teens, wasn't someone who found taking major decisions about her future easy to do. Her life had always been family-focused, and unless she was with them or a few selected school chums she reverted to appearing shy and, outwardly at least, somewhat indecisive. She was also awkward when dealing with people outside her fairly tight circle of friends and acquaintances, and attempts to widen this circle generally ended in failure. Friends of the Coulouris's, for example, had a daughter the same age as Mary Louise but of an entirely different disposition. It was hoped the girl would help Mary Louise to be more-outgoing and self-confident: but the girl's personality, which amongst other things led her to keeping assignations with boys on Hampstead Heath, was impossible to keep pace with and although the friendship remained for several years afterwards its mission was never fulfilled.

Another factor in her life was the matter of staying in school and getting 'A'-Levels, these being the basic requirement for university entrance in England. Her performance at

Parliament Hill in several academic subjects suggested Mary Louise stood a good chance of obtaining sufficient 'A'- Level passes to be accepted into a university: but that meant staying on in school for a further two years in which art would be just one subject among many that would demand her attention and concentration. As decision time approached one reasonably sound solution began emerging from the confusing number of options that were being considered.

For pupils who showed signs of having an aptitude for creative work, there was an opportunity to leave school and be enrolled in certain institutions which over a two year period enabled them to determine where best to apply their talent in terms of a job and an income. One of these institutions was London's Chelsea College of Art.

Chelsea's provenance stretched back to the late-19th century when changes in the British economy called for vocational education that was more relevant to employment in the burgeoning areas of trade and commerce. In the art world the old academies and their schools were impervious to such changes, and creating colleges like Chelsea was seen as a shot across their bows and a threat to their elitist values. Chelsea represented a new departure in training artists, a polytechnic that offered courses ranging from illustration to the design of textiles, from lithography to architecture. At various points in its existence it employed Henry Moore and Graham Sutherland as teachers and its alumni included Edward Burra, Elizabeth Frink, and the actor Dirk Bogarde. It wasn't until the late 1950s, however, that it founded separate departments for both sculpture and painting.

The award made to students who completed their two year course at Chelsea was an NDD – a National Diploma in Design. This was in keeping with its origins and its reputation as a centre of excellence for what was called 'commercial art' – a term of some disparagement which was only dropped when 'commercial artists' like Andy Warhol began exhibiting their work in fashionable galleries. For a time at least, the dividing line between fine art and that used in advertising and product labelling was largely ignored if never quite erased.

With the active support of her art teacher and the approval of her parents, Mary Louise submitted her portfolio of drawings and other pieces of artwork to Chelsea. The college took time to respond. The demand for places had increased in line with its growing reputation, and applications were always threatening to outstrip available resources. Among London's new, post-war generation were school-leavers already reacting to being seen as 'factory-fodder', and instead looked to finding spaces for themselves in non-traditional areas of work where the ethos of mass production and the assembly-line didn't exist. It was also the time when consumerism began to return after being disrupted by war. The design of products, allied to their wider distribution, was being associated with 'taste' and individual choice, bringing aesthetics and utility closer than they'd ever been before. In this changed environment many young people sought places at art colleges as a means to greater personal expression and satisfaction.

But dealing with an increasing number of applicants like Mary Louise was a headache for the colleges. And although they attached importance to an applicant's school achievements along with the essay they submitted saying why they wanted to be an artist, the portfolio accompanying these was regarded as the defining thing in offering places. Although each college claimed to adopt different approaches, reviewing an applicant's portfolio usually coalesced around certain fundamental things. Did it demonstrate an individual approach to drawing and painting? Did it show diversity in subject matter? Did it indicate a candidate's self-confidence in their drawing skills, in their handling of colour, in the composition of their work? In the dozen or so images making up a portfolio, colleges looked for a student's potential to develop. Did it suggest they had the wherewithal to improve their skills and increase their ability to represent 3-dimensional objects in a 2-dimensional space? Needless to say, portfolio days were pretty long days for the college staff involved in reviewing them.

While she waited to hear from Chelsea, Mary Louise saw out the last few months of her time at Parliament Hill School and spent the rest of the summer wondering what her future would be should her application be rejected. She continued taking her drawing pad with her wherever she went, scribbling notes across the sketches she made about colours and textures – details that would help if she decided to make a painting from them. And, of course, there was always someone or something happening at Chestnut Cottage to add to her interest.

Now that the renovations were complete visitors to the house grew in number. Walter Hudd, whose career spanned directing Shakespeare at Stratford to entertaining factory workers during the war, was among those who came to sit in the garden and talk. The actors Wilfred Hyde-Whyte, Peter Copley and Robert Morley were others who often arrived on Sunday afternoons for tea, as did John Gregson who'd already appeared in several popular films including Genevieve and The Lavender Hill Mob. Gregson also had a part in Whisky Galore, a film about a beverage which was usually dispensed in generous amounts to guests arriving at Chestnut Cottage. The 'tradition' established in Beverly Hills had carried over the Atlantic and consuming alcohol was an indispensable part of anyone's arrival at the Coulouris home. This was to remain a feature of the hospitality extended to guests at Chestnut Cottage, although eventually Mary Louise's parents agreed to give up alcohol for the sake of family accord. In a stand-up row with his father, George Jnr insisted he and his Mother quit boozing entirely. They didn't come to blows but their son's defiant stand on the matter eventually did the trick, even if total temperance was still a little way off.

A fortifying drink though, might have been welcomed by staff reviewing student portfolios at Chelsea College of Art. After eliminating those that failed to show the desired qualities, the rest were gone through again and a short-list of potential candidates was drawn up. Applicants on the short-list were then invited for interview and a few days later informed of their fate. Awaiting the verdict was just as nerve-wracking for art school hopefuls as it was for those pinning their futures on getting accepted at the university of their choice.

As 1956 got into its stride Mary Louise began transferring some of the tension she felt on to the pages of a diary she'd been given as a gift the previous Christmas. None of these entries referred directly to her hopes of becoming an art student, or if that failed what her fall-back plan might be. If anything she filled many parts of her diary with what you would expect a fifteen year old to do – the problems encountered in meeting and forming relationships with members of the opposite sex.

In the run-up to sitting her final exams at Parliament Hill School the real issue, or at least the principal one, was boyfriends and how you went about acquiring one. It seemed her school chums were making headway in such matters: so why wasn't she? She ran through a list of likely causes. She was overweight: she was too shy and lacking in courage and confidence: it was down to the rubbish quality of the boys she did meet – dumb, monosyllabic, uninteresting. At some points it seemed realising her ambition to become an artist paled to invisibility alongside the issue of finding a boyfriend. 'It will be Valentine's Day soon and I know I won't get a single card,' she wrote in the first week of February, 1956. 'Discussed the fact that I must meet some boys quite openly at dinner. Didn't like doing that….' On the big day itself she confided that her worst fears had come to fruition. 'Will I, won't I?' she speculated, early in the day: then later 'Of course I didn't get one single one. Depressed me terribly. Made me bad tempered and lonely.'

Other parts of her teenage diary recorded less miserable events such as going to concerts at London's Festival Hall and visits to the cinema with her brother and some of her school chums. In one week she watched 5 movies in as many days, all screened at the much-loved 'Everyman' cinema near to Hampstead Underground Station. But thoughts of romance were rarely left in the cinema foyer. Despite expressing her dissatisfaction with the rather shallow content of the film 'Court Jester' she left the 'Everyman' completely in love with the film's leading man, Danny Kaye. 'I liked it only because there was a gorgeous love scene in it,' she admitted afterwards.

Throughout this period of adolescent fluctuations in mood she continued to draw and paint, experiencing further oscillations in accomplishment – a familiar state of affairs for artists throughout their careers. But there was never a hint of her ever considering doing anything else with her future. Parallel with the quixotic circumstances of her love-life was a heart-felt devotion to art:

> *'Oh the tension, the agony, and the bliss of painting, the joy of copying a beautiful highlight perfectly, and oh the despair in one second the whole painting seems ruined - a blotch!'*

In the rather ramshackle structure under the chestnut tree which later became her studio she started several paintings, focusing on just two in the early part of 1956. One was a portrait of her father, the other a view of the Vale of Health which had intrigued her on her way to and from Parliament Hill School. Both were finished in the late-winter of that year, although she was never sure if the portrait (one of the most difficult challenges for any artist) was a success. 'Is it any good?' she confided to her diary. 'I'm scared to show it to anyone in case they criticise it.' Her father's thoughts on it were never solicited.

The landscape though, proved to be a much a greater accomplishment. The mother of Mary Louise's best friend at school was the actress Aileen Way, and Aileen with her husband Doctor Felix Brown were regular visitors to Chestnut Cottage. They spotted the picture hanging on the studio wall and offered to buy it. It didn't take long for Mary Louise to accept. At 16 she had made her first sale. And more good news was to follow. She was summoned to Chelsea and told she'd secured a place

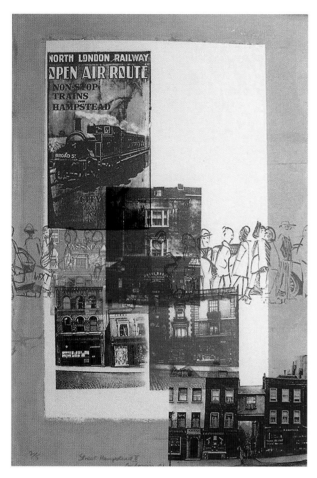

One of Mary Louise's early works of London street life.

beginning that autumn. 'Had a wonderful day!' she enthused in her diary on returning home. 'Loved the whole atmosphere of it. Everybody makes eyes! Headmaster (sic) nice. Work very good.'

Lots still had to be done, of course, including the challenge of final exams at Parliament Hill and dealing with periodic discord within the Coulouris household due in some part to her parent's continuing consumption of alcohol. In addition, Louise Coulouris had fallen victim to a malfunctioning thyroid gland – perhaps a recurrence of the condition that had blighted her earlier life - which brought her very low and she was hospitalised for several weeks. With Mother missing, the mood within Chestnut Cottage became even more fractious with clashes of temperament, sulks and banging doors inserting little more than a semi-colon in the continuing narrative.

Still, there was much Mary Louise could look forward to in a more positive light. A couple of months following her 17th birthday – on the 24th September, 1956 – she closed the door of Chestnut Cottage behind her and instead of taking the familiar path across the Heath to her old school, turned her feet in the direction of Hampstead Tube Station. A change of trains and one hour later she was walking through the gates of Chelsea College of Art. It was seminal moment…a turning point in her life which brooked no return. From here on, the vicissitudes of life as a professional artist would need to be faced and dealt with. But already the young girl who'd watched the parade go by in Estoril had come a considerable way.

CHAPTER 6

Between arriving in England and Mary Louise's enrolment at Chelsea her father was obtaining much gainful employment by appearing in plays and films, and on occasions in that new-fangled thing beginning to spread its influence in the early 1960s - television.

As the prospect receded of joining what was to become the Royal Shakespeare Company, George Coulouris set about earning his corn by appearing in productions at the Bristol Old Vic, the Citizens Theatre Glasgow (*King Lear*) and taking prominent roles in other plays such as Julius Caesar, As You Like it and the Admirable Crichton. Towards the end of the 50s decade he'd toured Ibsen's '*Enemy of the People*' around England with his friend Sam Wanamaker after its premiere at the refurbished Cambridge Festival Theatre - the place where George had his first off-stage role with Louise Franklin, soon to become his wife. The youngest of Wanamaker's daughters, Zoe, had become a friend of Mary Louise's and was often around Chestnut Cottage.

But film roles, where contracts offered higher levels of

Sharing a joke with Dad during a break in an early British TV programme. Left to Right: George Jnr. George Sen. Mary Louise, Louise Franklin Coulouris.

remuneration, enabled the actor to provide for his family in a way theatre work couldn't. After completing the jaunt to Portugal for '*Kill, Or Be Killed*' he played roles in fifteen films up to 1956 and appeared on television in a detective series called '*Colonel Marsh of Scotland Yard*' alongside another old friend, Boris Karloff. More than anyone Coulouris knew the parts he was offered were mostly rubbish for a serious actor. And who would argue with him despite looking down the list of credits and finding such luminaries as Ralph Richardson, Trevor Howard, Peter Finch and Dirk Bogarde all recorded there. It's hard to believe any of them appeared in stuff like the '*Doctor*' movies (pre-cursors of the fatuous 'Carry On' films) for anything other than the money and the exposure.

Occasionally, a more thought-provoking production would emerge from British film studios such as *Outcast of the Islands* (1952) and *The Heart of the Matter* (1953) both of which featured Coulouris in leading roles. They were separately nominated for a Bafta Award. In most other cases, however, they took their place in the '*Oh, missus, I seem to 'ave lost me trousers!*' genre of British film making, pandering to what was considered the taste of mass cinema audiences in Britain the same way Hollywood had seen their audiences expectations being strong family values and happy endings. Throughout his career, however, George Coulouris never gave less to any role than he believed a good actor should. Major role or minor part, it didn't matter to him – he gave them all thoughtful consideration and no one watching his screen performances from that era could ever doubt his commitment to what he believed acting should be. He may have done it for the money, but his experience and loyalty to acting never failed to show through.

Born the only child of a Greek migrant father and a Lancashire-born mother, Coulouris was tall and strongly built with deeply-recessed eyes which gave him, when required, an air of menace. For these reasons alone casting directors saw him as having the looks needed for starring in film roles as a villain, and

many of his subsequent movie appearances consisted of precisely
that. In Hollywood he worried about being typecast in villain
roles which would lead the studios to regarding him as a 'ham'
and stop offering him parts. He told his agent to pass on to him
any rumours to that effect, immediately. At other times though
his acting gave rise to more illuminating comment regarding
his talent. This was what one theatre critic, Russell Davis of the
Observer wrote about one of George's performances in 1976:

> 'Decades of strong, undervalued acting have left Mr.
> Coulouris with a face of monstrous tribal wisdom,
> an agreeable focus of interest for once, amid reeking
> plagiaristic trash.... '

Mary Louise's father never gave up his aspiration to play roles
in the theatre's classical repertoire. As a youth he'd tramped the
streets of Salford and neighbouring Manchester, reciting speeches
from Hamlet, Macbeth and other Shakespearian tragedies from
memory. When he finally overcame his father's objection to him
becoming an actor by running away from home and entering
drama school in London, the first lesson he was taught there was
how to get rid of his Lancashire accent. He promptly set about
doing so, but perhaps the obligation left its mark on him in less-
than obvious ways.

Throughout his professional life Mary Louise's father railed
against the way English actors like John Gielgud and Laurence
Olivier performed Shakespeare, draining it as Coulouris saw
it of its power and relevancy by an over-emphasis on the way
the speeches were intoned. He told me several times how, like
Orson Welles, the English establishment in acting 'destroyed'
Shakespeare by over-riding its content with 'The Voice.' He
followed this with examples of what he meant which were often
hilarious, although the point never got lost in the laughter.

His view on this and other criticisms he voiced regarding

English theatre was a resumption of what he'd told the New York Times back in the days at Spuyten Duyvil. They didn't exactly endear him to the elite who ran England's most prestigious theatre company. To some of Coulouris's actor-friends this might have been the reason why he'd failed to secure a contract with it. After all, he'd returned from Broadway and Hollywood as someone known and respected for his acting and experience, and there was no apparent reason why he should not have been considered for employment at Stratford. However, it is just as likely that Coulouris didn't understand enough of the topography of Shakespearian theatre in England at the time: had he done so he may well have seen his failure to land a contract as constituting a lucky escape.

Long before he arrived on the scene what was described as 'close reading' of Shakespeare's work had become the domain of academics, Shakespearean scholars and theatre critics alike. The gist of what they believed was that Shakespeare was 'too big' for the theatre, and his work should be read as long dramatic poems which discouraged putting too much emphasis on content and the historical context of the plays. People were urged instead to concentrate on intrinsic matters such as language tone, image and rhetorical patterns, word play and the internal rhythms of the speeches. It had a parallel of sorts in fine art where people were encouraged not to respond to the artist's vision as much as assess things like the quality of the brushstrokes, the 'architecture' of the picture and the 'painterly quality' of the finished work.

The outcome to this in Shakespeare was to reveal 'close reading' as an academic and rarefied aesthetic. Though several successful playwrights challenged it seeing modern topical issues in Shakespeare's works, 'close reading' which began in the late 19th century continues much as always to the present day. Characterisation and plot are still sacrificed to the 'poetry and deep symbolism' of Shakespeare's work.

To Coulouris's fiery passion for Shakespeare this would have been anathema had he fully understood what he was intent on achieving with the future RSC. Stage plays are, of course, subject to much varied interpretations: it's what makes the theatre what it is. But '*creating it anew with each production*', which was the stated practice at the RSC under Sir Peter Hall, created much dissension among playwrights and audiences alike leading to a drift away from Shakespeare's abiding themes into a province which seemed governed by a narrow and conservative elite.

No doubt the polemics of this entered family life at Chestnut Cottage and occupied much of the conversation at Sunday get-togethers in the re-modelled living room, or if the weather permitted in the garden. It linked directly with politics which Mary Louise's father took a keen interest in though he never joined a political organisation or party at any stage in his life. In a way this freed him to castigate political figures with as much vigour as he did the theatre establishment. This was the era of hapless Anthony Eden: of Harold McMillan who told the British people they'd 'never had it so good', and somewhat later the rather cadaverous-looking Sir Alec Douglas-Home who looked as if he'd never had it good at any point in his life.

Sunday afternoon gatherings at Chestnut Cottage generally began with discussing the Machiavellian manoeuvrings of the current government, then spun out to observations on just how awful a country Britain was becoming. Few were as vocal on the subject as Mary Louise's father, but few who listened were abashed by it. Several continued making visits to Chestnut Cottage for many years afterwards. Among these were former acquaintances in Hollywood like Perse Harris of 'Motley' the film and theatrical costumiers, Betty Box and Ralph Thomas the film producers, and the very first victim of the Hollywood blacklist, the screenwriter Lester Cole. After serving a year in prison and paying a hefty fine Cole left the US for England settling near to the Coulouris's in Hampstead where he set about picking up the threads of his career. Eventually he returned to America to write under an assumed name the screenplays for several successful movies, including the much-remembered '*Born Free.*'

Between jobs and the Sunday afternoon gatherings, Coulouris presided over a Chestnut Cottage which Mary Louise for one found less than comfortable at times. Family altercations often fuelled by her parent's consumption of alcohol were not infrequent. In the aftermath to one particularly wounding affair over something now long forgotten, Mary Louise noted in her diary:

> *'It's awful, Daddy got drunk again today, gradually each day after the big row he has been different degrees of drunk. Tonight he was belligerent. I could see it coming before we went out that he would tell Mummy off before the end of the evening. He did, even when she is so ill. She looks like death. That is what drink does to him. What can we do? Even when he stops he starts again soon. '*

Anyone who has experienced alcohol abuse within the family will empathise with the pain and desperation recorded by the sixteen-year old in that short entry. But at other times calm restored itself along with a measure of positivity to the household perched on its corner of Hampstead Heath:

> *'I had a feeling I accomplished something in the discussion with Daddy tonight, he seemed to see reason and it seemed to be me who brought the conversation on to a logical basis. He promised to be better (although) he has done this so often before....'*

In a BBC radio talk he gave in 1962 called 'Hollywood and Back', George Coulouris gave some idea of the pressure actors come under to be successful and keep the work and income coming in. Often there's a link between this and alcohol consumption. In Coulouris's case a similar pattern of behaviour existed in Hollywood when weekend boozing at North Roxbury Drive was a regular feature. You might say there were some things Mary Louise's parents brought with them on the Queen Mary that didn't require a trunk to carry them.

But according to their daughter similar stresses brought about by alcohol assailed other families too. The home of her best chum at school – the daughter of actress Aileen Way – was a place she visited often:

> *'It's funny to watch a whole family at work. Aileen personally is what decides the mood of the Brown family. She can be so sweet and ferociously teasing or she can be angry, very unreasonable! Felix* (Way's husband) *is sweet and affable and stupid all the time. I like him…..'*

To their credit Mary Louise's parents finally decided to banish the demon drink, or at least eliminate it permanently from their daily intake of fluids: it remained on offer, of course, to any visitor fond of a tipple. The decision to abandon alcohol had not a little to do with worries over Louise Coulouris's health, which wasn't being helped repair itself by consuming immoderate quantities of drink. Whatever the root causes for their decision, they stuck by it and when I came to know them in the 1960s they had been tee-total for several years past. Not that George was reduced in any way by it: his passion for political debate continued unabated, and fulminating against a theatre establishment which continued to keep him at arms length grew in intensity. These were things that were to last for the rest of his life.

Little of what he watched in the way of television drama met with his approval. He viewed other actor's performances with a jaundiced eye seeing television as the new vogue which would soon oust cinema as the most popular media-form in the 1950s. In 'Hollywood and Back' he described how film and TV made no demands on the actor at all:

'You go into make-up in the morning sometimes not having read the script. You say, 'What is it today? Yes, I see, I go in, I say hello, how are you?' And you get so that it's second nature without any (need to) study.'

Anyone regarding this view as being contradictory to Coulouris's unwavering belief in what constituted good acting, are failing to see how it represents the way he saw his profession as being in danger of declining into mediocrity. Was he right in thinking so? Or is it the perennial complaint that things ain't what they used to be in any profession? Granted television is often less exhilarating than a night out at the bingo, and when something half-memorable in the way of drama does get a showing people actually talk about it in the way of a rare occurrence. In the age of soap I suppose we get used to a lot of froth.

One of the shows on television I recall watching together with Mary Louise's Father was the detective series 'Kojak' featuring Telly Savalas – another actor with Greek associations, although that wasn't what attracted George to the show. It was more Kojak's blunt approach to dealing with issues, in being less than respectful of higher authority and following his own hunches whatever the threatened consequences might be for him. I believe this was what appealed most to us both. '*Who loves ya baby*' was a Kojak-ism which soon found it way into the language – a wry, rather than an angry Coulouris-type response to the changeable fortunes and challenges of professional life.

Chestnut Cottage, despite renovation, was still an old house in need of constant maintenance and repair. When time allowed George set about jobs that needed doing around the place, applying his faltering technical skills as a handyman. It isn't uncharitable to say duct tape and similar products were the mainstays of his efforts to make things whole again. When nails, screws, or other fixings failed, strong sticky tape came to the rescue on many occasions. It baffled me a bit until Mary Louise and I started visiting Greece.

There, exactly the same approach prevailed presumably because of a shortage, or the expense, of the appropriate materials. At any rate, these days I can't see sticky tape connecting together two bits of electrical cable or holding a household object to the wall without a smile and a fleeting remembrance of my father-in-law stooped over his labours. I guess as a Greek it must have been in the blood..................

CHAPTER 7

Mary Louise's first year at Chelsea seemed to pass in the blink of an eye. This was due in no small way to the characters who made up the class she was allocated to - an eclectic mix of young and not-so-young students who hailed from various parts of the United Kingdom and shared the excitement of having the chance to become artists. Among them was a Welshman (rather lamely nicknamed 'Taffy') whose sense of fun was the catalyst for helping everyone else relax and get along with each other. There were also a couple of older men and two London 'debs' who regaled everyone with gossip from the world of upper-class English society. But it was the friendship of two other teenagers – much as it had been at Parliament Hill School - who really made Mary Louise's life at Chelsea get off to a confident start.

The first of these was Bridget McWilliam the daughter of the Irish surrealist sculptor, F.E. McWilliam: the other was a girl called Jenny Lousada. Being outstandingly attractive, Jenny got lots of attention which shortly led to her appearing in an experimental film, 'The Rocking Horse', with Drewe Henley who was later to marry the actress Felicity Kendal. But perhaps it was the theatre connection that brought her and Mary Louise closer together, beginning a friendship that lasted for many years afterwards.

Jenny's mother was the stage designer, Jocelyn Herbert, whose appointment by the Royal Court Theatre in London boosted her career just at the time her daughter was about to begin her studies at Chelsea. Described as a 'spare, unfussy innovator' in stage and costume design, Herbert was just what the Royal Court wanted as they sought to rid English theatre of its stuffy 'anyone for tennis' reputation. This they proceeded to do in staging works by Beckett, Brecht and Genet, and in particular John Osborne's play 'Look Back In Anger.' The Osborne play, which coined the phrase 'kitchen-sink drama', is still regarded as the one which heralded the beginning of modern British theatre.

Exciting developments of a different sort were also taking place on the uppermost floor at Chelsea School of Art. It was here Mary Louise's first-year group of students had their own room but most days, at set intervals, they moved out to various other parts of the building where exposure to a number of specialist subjects awaited them.

With Liz Frink as their teacher, they learned about figurative sculpture by building up metal layers of wet plaster on metal armatures. This followed the life-drawing class where nude models posed surrounded by easels and the sound of pens and charcoal sticks scratching across paper. The 'debs', understandably, went mostly for the screen-printing classes which transferred images and patterns from a silkscreen on to bales of fabric that could eventually be used to make uniquely-fashionable items of clothing. On the other hand those unafraid of getting their own clothes soiled practised the techniques of lithography, which meant drawing with greasy crayons on sections of stone or metal plates then coating them with a mixture of acid and gum before inking them over and taking them to the printing press. Only the class on typography failed to elicit the same degree of enthusiasm as the other subjects. Described as the art of printing, typography put too much emphasis on exactness in the arrangement of letters drawn from a seemingly-endless variety of fonts. It was a discipline that came as close to commercial art as the group would ever get, and as a result didn't sit well alongside the more-romantic idea of becoming an artist. As a reaction to the typography class, Mary Louise wasn't the only student who rushed to doing 'real art' afterwards – in her case producing a solemn portrait of herself that stared out rather darkly from the canvas.

Lunchtime for students at Chelsea was often spent in the local pubs, or hanging out on the nearby Kings Road which was already beginning to establish itself as an area offering much of what the rock 'n roll generation went in search of. But traditional jazz and quirky bands like the Temperance 7 continued to provide the music for the Friday night hops at the Art School. Soon, the Temperance 7 were to enter the hit parade with whacky numbers like 'You're Driving me Crazy' and 'Home in Pasadena', arrangements which were piloted at the hops and made for a variety of instruments including a sousaphone and a pangolin sadolin…whatever that was!

At weekends there was usually a party taking place somewhere to which all were invited. Bridget McWilliams's family home in Chelsea was one such venue, as was a place at Durham Wharf in the London Borough of Brentford where Jenny Lousada's step-father, George Devine - artistic director at the Royal Court – was often to be found now that her mother had and gone to live with him. Mostly though, parties took place aboard a river barge which had once carried merchandise to various parts of London from over 4000 wharfs which peppered the banks of the Thames in the heyday of river traffic. The barge was probably owned, or at least rented by the playwright John Osborne whose professional relationship with Devine at the Royal Court was now being firmly cemented. Mary Louise remembers meeting Osborne for the first time aboard the barge. '*Of course, he was regarded by everyone as a genius,*' she recalled '*but the awe soon dissipated in what never failed to be drunkenly enjoyable evenings.*' Her own enjoyment, however, had to be moderated quite a bit when it became apparent she had an allergic reaction to alcohol, particularly red wine, and from that time on she became fastidious about what beverages she consumed.

And there were other equally agreeable events the art school scheduled-in at intervals throughout the year, the main one being a boat trip on the Thames to Cookham, the home town of the artist Stanley Spencer. Not that anyone spent all that much time looking at his art. Spencer's work was admired and held in high esteem by everyone who ventured close to his canvases and was well known to art students. Before returning to London they sat around outside Spencer's old studio munching through the contents of the picnic hampers they'd brought with them.

But there were other things to be digested during that first year at Chelsea. Her arrival at the school coincided with the founding of C.N.D. – the Campaign for Nuclear Disarmament. She joined CND, and soon the first protest marches against Britain's possession of nuclear weapons were being organised culminating in the spring of 1958 with a four-day march to Aldermaston, Britain's research centre for developing the country's nuclear arm. Many students at Chelsea participated in anti-nuclear protests, and Mary Louise also joined the British Peace Committee where she designed leaflets and banners that called on the government to unilaterally renounce the production and stockpiling of nuclear weapons. For many young people, joining what the media labelled the 'Ban the Bomb' movement signalled the beginning of their political education, radicalising them in ways unheard of in the past. Aligned to this was a growing awareness of the direction in which Britain was headed in terms of the country's return to consumerism after the austerity of the Second World War. Taking their cues from the anti-conformist stance of America's Beat Generation, young people in Britain including many of those attending art schools sought to distance themselves from the consumer-led values of mainstream society. In questioning these values they laid the basis for the 'counter-culture' which was rapidly emerging, beginning with Britain's version of the 'Beatniks.'

On long protest marches to places like Aldermaston, there was plenty of opportunity for people to get into discussions and work out where their own political sympathies lay. On one march Mary Louise met Liz Piratin, daughter of Phil Piratin, one of only two communist MPs ever to sit in the British House of Commons (the other being the Scot, William Gallagher.) Talking to Liz and others like her helped Mary Louise to make more sense of what she'd only overheard in America when progressives met at 'Hill House' to discuss politics. Even more likely though, the roots of her growing political awareness lay closer to home in the life-experiences of her father, George.

At the time when her father was growing up in Salford he was verbally abused on occasions by some of the locals. He often spoke about being called a 'Greasy Greek' and a 'Dirty Dago' by people in the Lancashire town, and remembered being chased by a gang of children and their mothers calling for his 'dago' blood after he'd ejected them from his father's business premises for loitering with intent to steal. Added to this, of course, was his more recent experience with pupils at Edgewood School and his perennial angst over the elitism of the English theatre world.

As Mary Louise saw it, however, her father seldom, if at all, did anything concrete about his political beliefs. He'd never joined a political party and had taken part in few public protests. To his daughter this was irksome to say the least: so her membership of CND and the British Peace Committee showed a commitment to what she believed in, and offered a way of avoiding becoming what she saw as an armchair critic like her Father and many of his friends. If such was the case then what she did in the summer of 1957 was entirely in keeping with these sentiments. With money provided by her parents (perhaps her father's awareness of his own inertia played a part here), she took off for Moscow and the World Youth Festival.

It was a time when the newspapers were describing the Soviet Union's changing position on foreign policy as a 'thaw' in East-West relations. Nikita Khruschev, the Soviet President, was the main moving force in this new and more-conciliatory approach to the western powers, and it was he who spoke in ebullient terms of the Soviet Union 'opening its doors' to the world. The World Youth Festival with its motto, 'For Peace and Friendship', was one of the centre-pieces of this open-door policy, and during the month of July, 1957, 34,000 young people from around 130 countries descended on Moscow to participate in what the Russians claimed to be the biggest youth event ever held. *'It would take you nearly a hundred years to attend every event during the festival'* declared the festival organisers, giving some idea of the scale of the thing.

To give her a chance of absorbing as much of the entire experience as possible, Mary Louise chose to travel free of attachment to any particular group, making her way to the Festival on a train chartered by the British Peace Committee. The train left London with hardly a seat or bunk left unallocated. She took the three-day journey in her stride. Perhaps those journeys as a child between New York and Los Angeles were now proving useful in terms of her endurance and stamina. The passengers were all under 25 and en route seemed to live mostly on cakes and sweets as they listened to songs and music provided, amongst others, by the folksingers Robin Hall and Jimmy MacGregor. As they rolled through Germany and Poland and then crossed the frontier into the Soviet Union itself, the train made frequent halts to allow local people to pass bouquets of flowers through the open windows.

'*It was exciting and different and just utterly amazing!*' Mary Louise recalled many years later. '*At home we'd been told the Russians were grim-looking people living under the yoke of a totalitarian regime. Yet here they were smiling and making us welcome.*'

She was put up in a dorm with half-a-dozen other girls in a building that was on the site of the Festival's agricultural exhibition in Moscow. Not that she spent much time there. Her first call was on an artist's club in Gorky Park, followed by a tour of established galleries and printmakers studios. In between times she made friends with a Russian family, went to a performance of the Bolshoi Ballet and attended a ball in the Kremlin. '*I don't remember dancing there,*' she said '*because so many other things were going on and I was just mesmerised by the surroundings.*'

As if to test the paranoia about foreigners being followed everywhere by KGB agents, she took off alone on Moscow's metro system and went as far as Smolny and back without encountering anyone remotely like a Russian security man in dark glasses and long gabardine coat:

'Whatever went on in the Soviet Union in later times, the Youth Festival lived up to its promise of allowing foreigners the freedom to go wherever they wanted.'

Despite this, however, people still viewed the rather formidable ladies posted outside the dormitories with a suspicious eye. They sat at tables positioned at the end of each corridor giving everyone who came and went a great deal of close scrutiny. To some they were…just had to be…hirelings of the KGB, or connected to the country's spy and surveillance systems. Only after the Youth Festival had finished did the real purpose for the ladies being present surface. Early in 1958 the birth-rate in Moscow gave an uncharacteristic jump. Babies appeared whose ethnicity wasn't immediately recognisable as being Russian. It seemed the ladies who'd been instructed to keep any shenanigans in the dorms to a minimum, would have been better deployed elsewhere when Russian girls freely mingled with the many foreigners flooding Moscow's Festival hot spots.

Students from countries who'd recently freed themselves from colonialism were a source of excitement and curiosity for Russian people. Together with traditional jazz music – never heard live before in the Soviet Union – and exhibitions of avant-garde art, these proved a heady mixture for many local females who took the 'Friendship' element in the Youth Festival's slogan to significantly deeper levels of intimacy than was intended. Mary Louise herself received several proposals of marriage, most of them from Iranians and men from other Middle-East countries. Instead of exchanging rings, however, she settled for exchanging badges, returning home with dozens of brightly-coloured enamelled memories of Moscow pinned to her jacket.

Her second year at Chelsea passed as quickly as the first. John Berger, painter and author and oft-times described as 'the art critic with a social conscience' came on his motorbike to hold seminars, talk to the students and review their work. It was the year Berger – himself a former student at Chelsea - published his first novel, 'A Painter of our Time', which was withdrawn after a month due to pressure by a CIA-based group called the Congress for Cultural Freedom. The theme of the novel is a fictional account of a Hungarian artist who goes missing in London: but its essence is the struggle for the minds of post-war Europeans between the competing ideologies of capitalism and communism. Berger's own political beliefs and his skills as a writer made readers think the story was true (some present day catalogues still list it as non-fiction) and the book was taken out of the market. It stayed beyond the reader's grasp for several years afterwards until the real function of the Congress for Cultural Freedom – funded by the Ford Foundation and active in 35 countries – was revealed. Despite a change of name in 1967 to the International Association for Cultural Freedom its influence faded, unlike Berger's who went on to write many more novels and challenge a whole generation's way of looking at art through his essays, books and television appearances.

As the end of her second year at Chelsea approached Mary Louise was obliged to look at some major things affecting her future. The first was to get through the end of term exam that would be decisive in her continuing for a further two years at the school and obtain her full National Diploma. To achieve this meant producing a large painting that would demonstrate most of the skills she'd acquired up to that time – something that with enough preparation didn't pose too many problems for her. The other less-tangible issue, however, was whether or not to stay on at Chelsea or consider moving to another institution where the qualification was a Diploma in Fine Art without any reference to its commercial applications.

'*I loved Chelsea,*' she always told people '*and after being at an all-girls school it was great doing things in a mixed-gender group. It really gave me the chance of becoming a young woman, but I was still into the romantic thing of being a professional artist and Chelsea didn't inspire me in that direction.*'

She wasn't alone in expressing such feelings. As the end of the college year drew ever nearer both her friends, Bridget McWilliam and Jenny Lousada, began talking about applying to the Slade School in London which offered the prospect of gaining the much-cherished Diploma in Fine Art. All three girls began putting together portfolios that would be the cornerstone of their application to become a student at the Slade. In Mary Louise's case the portfolio consisted largely of sheaves of drawings fixed together at the edges and slid inside a purpose-made leather folder. They all trooped down to Gower Street where the Slade was located, both to make sure their submissions were delivered safely and to take a closer look at what they hoped would be their home for the next two years. After that there would be nothing much else to do but tidy up at Chelsea, say an interim-farewell to the school and its teachers and, of course, organise an end-of-session party.

Like Chelsea, the Slade rarely gave any student a place at the school without interviewing them first. And in Mary Louise's case the interview was to take place with the Slade Professor of Fine Art himself, William Coldstream, later to receive a knighthood. Emboldened by the fact that her portfolio had been interesting enough to get her to the interview stage, she was nevertheless extremely nervous as she made her way to Coldstream's office perched high above the Slade's main life-drawing studio. Inside, she found Coldstream sat amidst a clutter of things that contrasted vividly with the appearance of the man himself. Slim and impeccably turned out in suit, tie and waistcoat Coldstream motioned her to a chair then began questioning her on her application. Although reputed to be a brilliant conversationalist, he often spoke to students in clipped tones and you had to be quick to recognise the irony in some of the things he said. An example of this came close to the end of his interview with Mary Louise when he snatched off his specs and looking directly at her said, '*Well, are you absolutely sure there is nothing else you could do instead of art?*' Without stopping to draw breath, Mary Louise replied loudly, '*No! There isn't anything I want more than becoming an artist!*' Coldstream twitched the corners of his mouth, and gathering up the contents of her portfolio handed them to Mary Louise from across his desk. '*I'll let you know shortly,*' he said '*when all the interviews are completed.*'

While she waited for the Slade to decide on her application she put her time to good use by continuing to draw and paint, and in a sudden burst of self-confidence went down to the headquarters of London County Council to apply for a student grant based on a firm conviction that the Slade would give her a place on their Diploma course. As events proved, she was right. A few weeks after her interview with Coldstream he wrote telling her she had been given a place at the School. And as if the School was in a benevolent mood dispensing good news, she was soon hearing from other fellow-students at Chelsea about their applications. To her great joy both Bridget McWilliam and Jenny Lousada come October 1958 would be joining her at the Slade.

Chapter 8

As the end of the 1950s hove into view the prevailing 'you've never had it so good' view of British society was predicated on the end of food rationing and other post-war austerity measures which had characterised much of the decade. These had now begun giving way to more affluent times and to a revived optimism which was to hallmark the advent of the 'Swinging Sixties.'

Around three-quarters of British families now had television sets and car ownership was growing exponentially at the expense of public transport. At other levels, hire-purchase agreements were fuelling a consumer boom; syrupy pop music had been overwhelmed by the tsunami of rock and roll; and in almost every town and city centre preparations were in hand to tear down fine old buildings and replace them with what looked like grim fortifications. A lot more changes were in the offing yet only at the Slade School of Art it seemed, did things look set to continue in much the way they always had.

As Mary Louise stepped over the threshold of the Slade for the first time in the autumn of 1958 her dream of becoming an artist was as strong as ever: but it would have to face what William Coldstream and others emphatically claimed to be a proper education in art. '*Even at the time I thought it was dry and objective and far too analytical,*' is how she would come to describe much of her time at the Slade. In a way this might also have been a pretty accurate portrait of the man who presided over the institution – William Coldstream himself.

To understand the ethos which prevailed at the Slade during Coldstream's reign you have to know something about its past and how it came to be. You also have to be aware that Coldstream – an artist well-connected in the art world – was the man, who in the early Sixties at the request of government, wrote the Coldstream Reports which for several decades thereafter was to provide the framework for art education throughout England and Wales. In this sense the future Sir William was an unusual hybrid of professor and politician - an artist who was an administrator of the government policy he himself had drafted. How this became so goes back to the origins of the Slade itself.

Felix Slade was a Victorian lawyer and philanthropist, who died leaving money to set up professorships in fine art providing the posts were created in what was called 'liberal arts institutions.' The universities at Oxford and Cambridge were chosen to be beneficiaries of Felix Slade's wealth as was University College London, which was to become home to the Slade School on the city's Gower Street. But the insistence of the Slade bequest on 'liberal arts' was to colour what the schools taught their students and influence the methods they used in teaching them. If you run an eye over what is generally defined as a 'liberal arts education' you will probably spot what's missing, especially if you like looking at art or have ever wondered what it must be like to go to art school.

A liberal arts education is quite specific about what its objectives are. It is designed to impart knowledge, encourage social responsibility, develop rational thought and avoid narrow specialisation such as is considered necessary in vocational and technical education. These are noble aspirations, of course, and as relevant today as they were when liberal arts courses and institutions were being established all over Britain. But for someone nurturing the idea of becoming an artist something important was palpably missing from the 'liberal arts' continuum. Where, for example, had 'creativity' gone? Whither 'imagination?' And what, to quote Wordsworth, has happened to 'the visionary gleam?' Shouldn't these also figure prominently in the curriculum of an art school? Well no, not at the Slade, or at least not at the time when the teenager Mary Louise was walking through its doors to begin her studies in the final years of the 1950s.

In her first year at the Slade she was expected to follow the route mapped out for her – a route well-worn by previous generations of Slade students. First, she was obliged to focus on drawing from the antique, this being drawing done from plaster casts of classical Greek and Roman sculpture. These were located on the ground floor at the Slade, interspersed with plants such as aspidistra and giant fern which also figured much in what students drew in the antique-drawing class. There was nothing much wrong with this, of course. Artists should be able to draw: indeed most people would be surprised if they couldn't, although in later years when the art world made celebrities out of those who showed how poor they were at drawing, the public response was to find something better to do with their time than go to art galleries. Nevertheless, to concentrate on little else but drawing over a longish period was a drag for any new student at the Slade, especially when their application portfolios already displayed how much promise they showed in this area – a factor in them becoming Slade students at all.

Added to this was the cramped conditions in the Slade's antique-drawing room where talking to your fellow-students was not encouraged and in some instances, forbidden. All the talking was expected to take place with a student's personal tutor in between classes, although in Mary Louise's case the gentleman concerned – a world authority in the rules of perspective – had problems relating to female students:

> *'My tutorials with him usually followed a familiar path. He just couldn't relax in the presence of females and this made him nervy and jumble his thoughts. Eventually, he'd pick up a matchbox or another object from his desk, hold it in the air and say something like, 'everything is interesting to draw, isn't it? It just depends on how you perceive it.'*

Nonplussed, she would leave her tutorial little wiser than she had been when entering it.

Alongside drawing from the antique was yet more drawing, this time in the life-class. The Slade prided itself on being the first art school in Britain to admit women to life-classes, although this fact has been a little distorted in the telling of the School's history. In fact, women were never allowed anywhere close to the male nude, only to the draped model: and even when there was license to draw the naked figure they were often manoeuvred away to form their own group where the draped-model was invariably female. All that had changed by the time Mary Louise joined the Slade, however, and students of both sexes now drew from the nude: but it didn't do much to meet the expectations of students who still buzzed with the idea of becoming painters. '*Painting was never even hinted at during my first year,*' Mary Louise said '*and anything imaginative in terms of subject matter and the treatment given to a picture was hardly ever mentioned*'.

In a curious about-turn in the progress of the Slade since its foundation, life-drawing for students now came in roughly equal parts with drawing from the antique. Yet the very first Slade professor of Fine Art in London, Edward Poynter, had insisted on life-drawing taking precedence over other forms of drawing practice. In his day new students spent much of their time in the life class following which they moved on to the antique. Poynter was quite clear about this progression, stating in his inaugural lecture to students that preference would be given at the Slade to working from the living model. Study of the antique, he said, would come *after* that had been accomplished. His insistence on this was probably due to the fact that unlike artists in mainland Europe, especially France, English artists were poor at drawing the human figure: and leaving skills-development in this area until after students had mastered drawing from the antique wasn't the way to improve matters. Whether it was Sir William Coldstream's decision to change this process is unknown, but changed it was and changed it stayed throughout Mary Louise's time at the Slade.

But no institution is free to do exactly what it sees fit with its students. And art school students are probably the most difficult to keep in line. In an attempt to break away from the organised discipline at the Slade, Mary Louise took to the streets of London armed with a drawing pad and pens. Life as it was conducted on nearby Tottenham Court Road became a regular place where she drew: and she found plenty of interest further afield in construction sites, working-men's cafes and street markets – all places where people met and moved around, interacting with each other and their surroundings. It is not unusual for present-day art students to follow a similar route, but for Mary Louise these experiences were to provide enduring images which she drew on for much of her career afterwards. Later, they were to take her into shipyards and docks, down into coalmines and other places where people did work that was often dirty and dangerous but always necessary for the continuation of life. You could say these early experiences of observing street-life and people in the workplace were formative experiences, which together with the formal instruction provided by the Slade, went a long way in shaping her career.

Back at the Slade another opportunity to break with the routine came in the form of what in today's education-speak is known as 'an elective.' This was the choice given to all first-year students to choose something outside of the mandatory subjects which appealed to them. Mary Louise opted for stage design which was led by a lecturer called Peter Snow with help from Nicholas Georgiades. In this period Georgiades (known to Slade students as 'Nico') had already forsaken painting to become a stage designer where he made himself famous by working on ballet sets for Nureyev, and during the Fifties and Sixties formed a close working partnership with the choreographer, Kenneth MacMillan. Joining her on the stage-design elective was someone else, who in the fullness of time was to make an international reputation for herself as a sceneographer – the modern term for someone specialising in the 'aesthetics of the stage.' She was Pamela Howard who became professor emeritus at the University of the Arts, London, and a world authority in 'setting' contemporary opera productions and musical theatre.

But although she liked stage design to begin with and was inspired by projects that included making maquettes for Ibsen's 'Hedda Gabler' and Prokovief's 'Love of Three Oranges', Mary Louise's interest eventually waned: *'I don't think I was cut out to be a stage designer, and I found myself getting bored by the need to pay so much close attention to detail. It was too practical for me and in the end I decided to give it up.'* Of course, there is a lot of complex optical science in stage design which she presumably didn't connect with, or else the Slade failed to show her. In any event in giving up stage design she also had to forego the privilege of free tickets to opera productions and stage plays in London which was a difficult perk to relinquish.

Though talk may have been discouraged in the Slade's drawing classes it couldn't be stopped elsewhere in the establishment where students gathered. On one of the upper floors of the building a widening in the corridor provided space for a few students to set up their easels, do some unscheduled painting and talk to each other. Down in the basement where a cloakroom sink was used to clean paint brushes the chat increased in tempo and became a veritable information exchange. Here, matters of real importance were discussed such as where the weekend parties were taking place and which member of staff was having an affair. Coldstream, for example, was reputed at one point to be having a relationship with one of the female life-models. This, it was rumoured, was why his office door was sometimes found to be locked. Speculation on the matter ended in 1961 when Coldstream married Monica Hoyer, who was indeed a Slade life-model. She was 30 years his junior, and at a stroke the daughter of a fairly anonymous provincial journalist became Lady Monica.

One amusing tale concerning Lady Monica's employment as an artist's model relates how she posed undraped for an amateur artist who displayed the finished work, as artists were allowed to do, on the railings at Whitestone Pond in Hampstead. The image caught the eye of a man who later became leader of the British

Labour Party, Hugh Gaitskill, who bought it and hung it on the wall of his London home. Commenting on her past career as a life-model Lady Coldstream explained *'It was just a job that gave me interest and pleasure for a number of years,'* And the artist who sold his picture of her to Gaitskill was adamant that it was no more than an *'Oh, I'm shivering because it's so cold'* rendering of the now ennobled lady. *'It's not a nudey-nude,'* he opined in language not accustomed to being heard in art-loving circles. *'It's a side view, really a very discreet affair.'*

One door Coldstream never locked though was the one opening on to a little balcony he had built outside the rear of his office from which he could look down two floors on the life-drawing studio. Perhaps this was how he first spotted Monica in her in-flagrante state, although it was meant to provide the professor with a bird's eye view of how students were progressing without the need for him to walk down several flights of stairs. For years after Coldstream had retired the little balcony remained in place and was only bricked-up, then demolished, a few years ago.

As she entered her second year at the Slade, an opportunity for Mary Louise to begin putting an end to the shy teenager she still was presented itself. Elections to the Slade's student union were due and with the encouragement of her peer group she put herself forward for the unlikely position of social secretary. She won the vote and along with her fellow student, Patrick Proktor who was elected president, they took their seats as representatives of the Slade on the larger Student Union body which spoke for all students at University College. President of the Student's Union at the time was the Labour M.P. and former Cabinet minister, Jack Straw.

As was his custom, Sir William Coldstream invited the two new office bearers to lunch at an Italian restaurant in Soho where over the pasta he sought their views on a range of topics which would influence life at the Slade in the forthcoming period. As well as organising social events Mary Louise was also responsible for planning with Coldstream those in the art world who might be invited to give guest-lectures at the School, and what artists with established reputations should be asked to review students work. Out of this came an invitation to the Sicilian artist Renato Guttoso – friend of the two Pablo's, Picasso and Neruda – to come to the School and talk about his work. Guttoso was a popular choice for students at the time, an artist who had been part of the anti-fascist resistance in his Italian homeland, and whose still life's crammed as they were with everyday objects appeared to some as being a comment on society's growing propensity for mass consumerism. His allegiances to 'realism' in art, which depicted scenes of daily life in Italy, also did much to increase his popularity and spread his reputation internationally.

Another artist who was invited to make an assessment of student-work hailed from a very different world than Guttoso's. He was Lancashire-born L. S. Lowry whose interview with Mary Louise she remembered well:

> *'He struck me as someone you could relate to immediately. He wore a dark suit and waistcoat, but his personality was warm and even a bit hesitant as if he wasn't sure what he was supposed to say, or why he'd been invited to the Slade at all. He took my portfolio of work and slowly turned each piece over, peering at them from behind the tiny specs he wore. Then he said 'Eh lass, you can draw. I've got owt to teach you about drawing.'*

If Coldstream had been present in the room he would have given himself a little pat on back. Soon, Lowry's canvases of life in the industrial towns of northern England would be finding wall space in some of the most-prestigious London galleries, and today are bought and sold for prices he'd never have believed.

Every Friday afternoon, just about every student at the Slade stopped what they were doing and got ready for their five o'clock lecture on the history of art. The history of art was something else

Coldstream had introduced after his appointment at the School, and it was now a compulsory subject for every student enrolled at the Slade. But it was the eruditeness as well as the charm of the man giving the lectures that drew students to his lectures. He was Ernst Gombrich, a Viennese-born academic whose approach to art history was grounded in psychology, on how people perceive pictures rather than understanding the reality on which pictures are based.

To Gombrich a painter didn't examine the nature of the physical world he produced in his work, but the nature of our reactions to it. This approach led the way into some pretty complex hypotheses which Gombrich tried to explain in simple terms in a book he wrote called 'The Story of Art'. The book was soon being bought by over two million adults and became a standard textbook in many schools and universities.

'The Story of Art' helped boost Gombrich's career and in time he followed in the footsteps of John Ruskin by being appointed Slade Professor of Art at Oxford: and in the years 1961-63 he filled the same post at Cambridge. During this time he wrote many essays and dissertations on art history and another book, 'Art & Illusion', which demonstrated what some described as his 'ruthless logic' in perceiving art and enabling people to look at artwork in new and different ways. Two decades later, deploying the same ruthless logic, he was to assert that commercial interests and attention-seeking lay at the heart of the new 'fashionable art' now being produced. Much of the contemporary abstract art being exhibited, he claimed, amounted to nothing but a 'fad.' One fad, however, which Gombrich himself turned into a fairly long term commitment was leaving a pile of ripe, freshly picked apples from his garden in the Slade lecture theatre for his students to grab.

When Gombrich was indisposed or engaged elsewhere his place at the Slade lectern was taken by a variety of other luminaries from the world of art history and criticism, principally Sir Anthony Blunt who was later to be disgraced and stripped of his knighthood under the government of Margaret Thatcher. Mary Louise remembers Blunt more for his appearance and deportment than for his lectures on Renaissance art in which he was an internationally-recognised specialist. Her memories of the man remained clear:

> 'I used to think he had problems in communicating with people outside his circle of academic colleagues. He seemed aloof and distant from his audience as if he found life difficult away from his peers in the senior common room. He would hold his head sideways and look up at some point above our heads like he was peering from underneath a canopy. You couldn't have got anyone more different from Gombrich. We students didn't care for him much as a lecturer. We'd look down from the window when he and Coldstream were returning from lunch and say 'Sorry people, its Blunt today.' That put a bit of a dampener on things......'

At the time Blunt was Director of the prestigious Courtauld Institute and Surveyor of The Queen's Pictures. In 1964, however, he confessed to being part of a spy ring at Cambridge which included Kim Philby, and in helping the spies Burgess and MacLean to escape Britain for Moscow. His confession was made after being given assurances that he would be granted immunity from prosecution. But in 1979 his activities were made public and the press branded him the 'Fourth Man' in the Cambridge spy case. Blunt's reputation was ruined and his knighthood taken away after a lengthy campaign by the media to have him branded as a traitor.

Facing somewhat lesser charges, however, was Mary Louise who also found herself arraigned before a criminal court. Her continuing commitment to the peace movement went beyond her participation in the annual protest marches to Aldermaston, and during her second year at the Slade she was arrested for using a loud-hailer at a gathering in Oxford Street called in support of CND. After some hours in a police cell she appeared a few days later before a magistrate charged with causing a breach of the peace. The case attracted attention from the press, and the public gallery at the court was crammed with CND supporters including Patrick Proktor and other students at the Slade. The Guardian reported she was bound over to keep the peace, a sentence that was welcomed by no less an individual than Sir William Coldstream who was amongst the first to offer her his support.

Despite the best efforts of her Father, who introduced her to people working in television, Mary Louise decided to stick by her decision not to continue with her studies in stage design. This meant a gap appearing in her schedule at the Slade which she used to some advantage:

> 'I began liking being at the Slade despite having to put up with its stuffy traditions, but it was a relief sometimes to shake off the art school environment and get outside for a bit. I went on drawing life on the London streets, but there were other things to focus my thoughts on. The CND meetings were always interesting, and my role as social secretary for the Union was another way of putting art aside for a while. I helped write a satirical review that was performed by Slade students at Christmas, giving myself the part of a chorus girl. Satire was all the rage at the time and we poached a lot of material from a TV show called 'That Was the Week That Was.' Other than the title though, that's about all it had in common with what went out on telly.....'

In this period, however, amid the warren of narrow corridors and closed studio doors that constituted the interior of the Slade, she stumbled almost by accident across the etching department and embarked on a phase in her career that was to influence her work for many years after. 'I was intrigued by what you could do with the spidery-line involved in etching,' she said 'and decided on the spot that this, rather than stage-design, was something I wanted to explore.'

Etching, which was a technique practised by goldsmiths and metal workers in mediaeval times was something artists down through the centuries had made use of. Rembrandt, Goya and Durer had been among those who'd mastered the skills of producing images from etched plates, using them to illustrate manuscripts and books, including the Bible.

For those with an interest in the technique, etching begins with coating a metal plate with waxy material which is then scratched through using a needle-like tool (called a burin) where the artist wants a line to appear. The plate is then placed in a bath of acid which bites into the metal where it has been exposed by the needle leaving lines etched into the plate. After removing it from the acid bath the waxy ground is cleaned off and the plate is inked all over. When the ink is then wiped off it leaves traces of itself in the etched lines. The plate is then put through a high-pressure roller press together with a sheet of paper which picks up ink from the etched lines making an image, commonly called a print. Several prints can be made from the same plate and usually the artist will write the number of the print edition at the bottom of each sheet.

Part of Mary Louise's excitement at discovering the possibilities of etching, lay with the character and reputation of Anthony Gross - the man who was head of printmaking at the Slade:

'I saw his work and could tell immediately we were on the same wavelength. At the time he was doing images of people going about their daily lives…exactly what I was interested in! So, there was never any doubt about me applying to be one of his students.'

'Street Musicians.' Another early work. To achieve the effect Mary Louise wanted the etching plate was left in the acid bath where it dissolved until only the figures were left to be printed on paper.

Gross was already established as an artist and printmaker when he joined the Slade, and many of his almost four-hundred catalogued prints have since been taken into public collections. He died in 1984 but his work is still to be seen at galleries like the Ashmolean in Oxford, the Victorian and Albert Museum, London, and in collections held by MOMA in New York.

Joining Gross's etching classes meant Mary Louise linking up with a new cohort of students at the Slade. But her union duties kept her in contact with the student body as a whole so she was still surrounded by familiar faces. Among her closest group of friends were two people who stood out from the pack if only because they seemed to be entirely immune from the ego-tripping that tends to characterise many artists and those who have the potential for succeeding in the profession. They were Dehta Hsuing, whose family was from Thailand, and the girl who was later to become his wife, Thelma Lambert.

Ironically perhaps, Dehta is better known for his books and recipes on South Asian cooking than his artwork, although Thelma went on to make a reputation for herself as an illustrator – her children's book 'The Adventures of Little Brother' inspired by stories of her husband's homeland being among her greatest successes.

Also among those who met to talk and exchange news at the brush-washing sink in the basement were Eliza Hutchinson, daughter of the actress Peggy Ashcroft, Euan Uglow whose preciseness in composition (he often took the best part of an hour to pose his life-model before starting to paint her) made him one of Coldstream's star pupils, and Anthony Green who was amongst the first breed of artists to engage with what might be called the 'autobiographical school' in art. His later depictions of middle-class domestic life drawn from experiences within his own family brought him many admirers and collectors, and encouraged the likes of Tracy Emin to follow in his tracks. Painting on large irregularly-shaped canvases, Green ignores the normal conventions of perspective and produces scenes (in which he invariably appears) that spread out in every direction so that all four corners of a room, for example, can be seen in the finished work. At the start of the 21st century he was made a Royal Academician and currently lives in Cambridgeshire with his wife, Mary Cozens Walker, herself a talented artist who was also a Slade student in Mary Louise's time.

Towering, literally, above everyone else however was Patrick Proktor. Estimates as to Proktor's height vary, but he was at least six feet-four tall which along with his lean angular frame made him impossible to miss as he moved through the low-ceilinged corridors of the Slade. He and Mary Louise shared many ideas in common, including involvement in the politics of peace and nuclear disarmament. Irish-born, Proctor moved with his family to London at an early age after his father died. His widowed mother spent the little money she had on educating Proktor's younger brother thwarting Patrick's ambition to go to art school, and he eked out an existence as a merchant seaman followed by several dead-end jobs before accumulating enough cash to enrol himself at the Slade. He was older than most students when he joined the School, five years older than Mary Louise.

Coldstream helped him by negotiating the rental of a flat he himself had once occupied, which settled Proktor sufficiently to allow him to concentrate on developing his talent as an artist. Although he was said to have 'risen' with the likes of David Hockney and Bridget Riley, the dark figurative style of Proktor's early work and his later pop-art influences never brought him the fame accorded to his more-illustrious peers. And although outwardly he struck people as being a highly-entertaining and amusing extrovert, inwardly he was tortured by hesitancies regarding his sexual orientation. Outside of the Slade he socialised within a gay circle that included David Hockney (Proktor and Hockney were seen as the 'dandy twins of the art world'), and attended parties wearing a fez, velvet slippers and green fingernails. Among the crowd he circulated in was the future film director Derek Jarman, playwright Joe Orton and fashion pace-setter, Ossie Clarke. The Queen's sister Princess Margaret and her photographer-husband Armstrong-Jones were also regular guests at Proktor's flat.

Although Patrick was eventually to marry a woman who owned the restaurant where he sometimes traded his pictures for meals, he could neither deny his homosexuality nor reconcile himself entirely to it. Made a member of the Royal Academy in 1996 he produced one piece of work many younger people today may recognise – the cover of an Elton John album called 'The Guardian Readers.' Most of his other work perished in a fire at his flat in Manchester Street, London, in 1999. It was also the year he was held on remand pending charges of trying to kill his mother. Prokter himself perished in 2003 from a blood clot, although drink and drugs couldn't be discounted in his early demise. Appropriately, his chums saw him off from a church in Piccadilly which on the day was described by one newspaper as having been 'transformed into a shimmering orchard of pink cherry blossom.'

As her second year at the Slade unfolded, Mary Louise was still not fully-conscious of what it would it take for her to become a full-time professional artist:

> *'The boys got very serious about building careers and were making contact with galleries with the idea of being given one-man shows. But I hardly thought of that at all. Like a lot of the other girls I suppose I was just too caught up in doing art and relishing the opportunity of trying*

out new ideas and techniques. I think I was still infected by the art bug. Art was all I wanted to do, and it never really occurred to me what I would probably have to do in order to make a living from it after leaving the Slade.'

Two options within her reach presented themselves as the year wore on. One was to apply for a Catherine Maude Pearce scholarship which was granted by University College London to students who had demonstrated an ability to take a specialist subject (in Mary Louise's case, etching techniques) to greater depths. She submitted an application for the Pearce scholarship and was told in due course that her bid had succeeded. Hard on the heels of this success came news of another opportunity, this one from farther afield.

It was customary at the Slade to make students aware of two scholarships abroad they could apply for. These were located in Rome and Paris, and were long-standing arrangements which saw value in broadening horizons and enabling students to experience living and working in a different cultural environment. Both scholarships were essentially funded by their respective national governments, and to her delight the French agreed to fund Mary Louise through a two-year programme based at L'École des Beaux Arts in Paris.

But now she faced an embarrassment of riches – two offers, each of which held out exciting prospects. Which offer would she accept, which would she regretfully put aside? She was still awash with the youthful energy and enthusiasm that had taken her from Parliament Hill School to Chelsea, and from Chelsea to the Slade. But these had been part of a progression that would end with the completion of her Diploma course in Gower Street. Now choices had to be made, choices that would doubtless have a huge influence on her future career. *'My life was all about art,'* she was to say later *'which meant that in most other respects I was still immature. Taking decisions about what pictures I wanted to paint, or what images I wanted to turn into etchings came easily enough. But now I had to decide what course my life was to take. Was it to continue in the familiar surroundings of the Slade, or move to somewhere substantially different and far from home?'*

As things were to pan out she did both, and her life took another significant turn towards the future.

CHAPTER 9

It is the interval at an Offenbach concert in central Paris and a group of art students including Mary Louise, is having a noisy discussion about the Can-Can. Well, it's just the sort of thing we all do at Offenbach concerts, isn't it? Anyway, convinced she knows how the vigorous, high-kicking dance should be performed Mary Louise sets about giving the others a practical demonstration. Unfortunately, a *folie a deux* between the tight skirt she's wearing and a slippery marble floor gets in the way and over she goes.

'I'll never forget the painful thump of that floor on my bum,' she'll recall forever afterwards. 'I don't know what the others made of it, they were too busy giggling.'

Though the incident may have caused some temporary damage to her derriere, it was never allowed to threaten Mary Louise's life-long love of dancing. If fine art was her chief passion, that didn't mean other forms of self-expression were to be ignored. Throughout her life dance and movement was a source of pleasure for her and it wasn't long before they began showing in her pictures.

The reason she was in Paris in the autumn of 1962 was to take up her French government scholarship which saw her become a student at the city's L'École Des Beaux-Arts. More important than that though, was her admission to the renowned Atelier 17 owned and overseen by a one-off individual called William Stanley Hayter. Her experiences there over the next two years were to leave rather different marks on her than those occasioned by a wayward Can-Can.

The scholarship had been awarded subject to her beginning her studies the previous year. But because her application for the Maud Pierce scholarship had also succeeded she'd begged a year's postponement from the French and spent the academic year of 1961 continuing at the Slade deepening her skills in the techniques of etching and printmaking. This she did under the Head of Printmaking, Anthony Gross, assisted by his Spanish-born assistant Bartolemeo Dos Santos. In both men she couldn't have had better tutors.

Gross, a former student of the Slade, had also spent time at the L'École des Beaux-Arts. Perhaps what helped make him the ineffably-patient individual he was lay not in his secured reputation as a talented artist but in his origins which showed him to be of Hungarian-Jewish, Italian, Anglo-Irish descent. Whatever it was that formed Gross's personality, Mary Louise took to him immediately. Most people did.

As a war artist Gross was remembered for his presence at the D-Day invasion of Normandy in 1944, helping to establish the beachhead landings with his easel strapped across his shoulders. Post-war he was forever on the move travelling mostly between England and France where he established contact with an impressive range of institutions and people which were of help to fledglings like Mary Louise. Renowned for the wealth of detail he put in his pictures and the vivacious movement of his work, he was seen by many in the art world as one of the most famous British artists of the 20th century. '*I was tremendously impressed by him,*' Mary Louise recalled '*not only because we shared the same interest in what we wanted do in art, but also because he was so willing and pleased to teach students how to do difficult things in etching.*'

By the summer of 1962, however, Gross and the Slade School were coming to an end for her. The French scholarship meant bidding farewell to the cramped accommodation at Gower Street, to William Coldstream and his staff, and to the wafting odours of oil paint mixing with the smell of printing ink and acid baths. It was also goodbye to Chestnut Cottage for a while and her little room perched above the garden. Before leaving for Paris the garden provided Mary Louise with the subject matter for a picture she subsequently sold to Lester Cole and his wife. It was of an iris at the peak of its splendour growing near to her studio.

Any lingering regret at leaving Hampstead for Paris was

easily subsumed by the excitement felt at the prospect of moving to one of the greatest capitals in the world for art. Many of the artists the city had opened its heart to had become legends, and its bohemian life-style had been copied in many other parts of the world. It was a place that seemed to have been meant for artists, sculptors and architects. In the way of proof it had even named some of its streets after them!

As sometimes happens though, pre-conceptions of a place can be dented at the point of first acquaintance, taking time to resile and begin meeting expectations. Something of the sort happened to Mary Louise. In the first place Paris was gathering itself for a social upheaval that would have a permanent place in its history – the mass street demonstrations and accompanying violence would draw the world's attention to the city for a sizeable chunk of the Sixties. In the second place, she was allocated living accommodation in a place distant from the arrondissements most associated with art and artists. This was in the Franco-Britannique building at Cité Universitaire which sat in the 14th arrondissement. Mary Louise's opinion of it didn't take long in forming:

> 'I didn't like it from the start. It was boring because of the stuffy, English atmosphere that existed. But, of course, it was a magnificent building and overlooked the Parc Mont Souris which I did several paintings of. But I couldn't get settled there and luckily I grabbed the chance of moving to another part of the complex called the Fondacion États-Unis where you were given an individual studio to live in. The Fondacion was close by so I stayed within the Cité Universitaire but in much more interesting surroundings and people.'

Within a few days of arriving in Paris she was out with drawing pad and pen recording life on the streets of the capital. Some of

Her beloved
Paris. The streets,
squares and
parks of the
French capital
were a constant
source of wonder
and delight to
Mary Louise
during her French
scholarship there.

these were turned into finished artwork – a kiosk where an old lady sold toys: a vendor selling griddle pancakes on the corner: chess players under the trees at the Jardin du Luxembourg. One sketch that eventually became an oil painting showed a worker passing a flower shop, contrasting the delicate blooms on display with the roughness of the man's clothes and his grim appearance.

She teamed up with others studying in Paris to visit churches playing organ music, to visit the chanteur Jacque Brel backstage at a theatre on the Rue de la Gaité (*'what a wonderful name for a street that is!'*), and to use the windows of a room belonging to the American artist Ariane Berman which framed more views of the Parc Mont Souris. A tall, lanky English girl called Alicia, was her guide to the city, she being the daughter of a wealthy London businessman who'd given up hope of Alicia doing anything other than being an artist and playing her guitar. She was a lovely person who I was to meet often in the years to come after she'd returned to her family home broke but unchanged, quietly maintaining her view as to how the gift of life ought to be spent.

Built into Mary Louise's scholarship agreement was free attendance at the École des Beaux Arts which was situated on the Left Bank of the Seine. Her scholarship demanded she develop further her skills in etching, but it also helped widen her command of the French language which led to her being virtually adopted by an ordinary Parisian family, who she visited regularly for meals. She must have welcomed that alternative to having to queue for a meal ticket at the Cité Universitaire as all students there had to do.

Her mentor at the Beaux Arts was a M. Clarin who was soon heaping praise on her progress and the work she was beginning to produce. 'Genius' was the word he used as Mary Louise told her parents in one of a regular flow of letters home, although her more modest self suggested Clarin was being a little extravagant with his use of the *English* language. Nonetheless, the sculptor Ossip Zadkin who had joined the staff of the Beaux Arts the same year Mary Louise arrived was also complimentary about her work. '*It succeeds because you are remembering it is not enough to just represent a scene,*' he told her '*but to ask why you are doing it*'

Zadkin was a printmaker as well as a sculptor - a small snowy-haired man with prominent grooves running from nose to chin. A Russian who'd studied art at various centres in England he spent most of his life in Paris where many of his public sculptures are to be seen in the streets around districts such as St. Germain des Pres. But his best known work is unquestionably '*The Destroyed City*' – a memorial to the destruction of much of Rotterdam in 1940 by the German Luftwaffe. It stands at the entrance to the port of Rotterdam and shows a man with a void where his heart should be, arms raised dramatically upwards in a gesture that might be read as both defence and supplication, or perhaps anger and frustration. Described by some art critics as melodramatic, it is Zadkin's leitmotiv - seen again and again in his dramatically expressive sculptural forms made from metal which has been torn into jagged shapes.

But despite Zadkin's addition to the staff at the Beaux Arts the School appeared to Mary Louise as having become 'degenerate.' I think she might have meant in 'decline' rather than depraved or debauched. But it was true the place was now becoming a shadow of its former self. Fewer students went there anymore which in a way was great for those who did. It meant more space in the studios and workshops, and a greater chance of bonding with the teachers as well as your fellow students. On the top floor was the Lithography Department – lithography being a close relative to etching but often using a stone in preference to a metal plate. Here work was supervised by M. Clarin supported by a small army of brawny men who had the muscle to move the lithography stones to the printing presses. However, it may have been evidence of the low morale at the institution that Clarin appeared only at midday to review the students work then went home: and the workers enjoyed a two-hour lunch break which saw them gather round a long trestle table in the main studio, dressed in their blue dungarees, to eat their food and polish off more than a couple of bottles of wine. Needless to say activity, not to mention productivity, tended to tail-off a bit in the afternoons. Bored by the regime adhered to by staff at the institution, Mary Louise did what you might expect – she drew the workers at their repast and afterwards produced a painting from it.

At Atelier 17 however, the culture could not have been different. Owned and run by an Englishman called William Stanley Hayter, it was located on the Rue Campagne Premiere a short distance from the Metro station at Denfert Rochereau. Mary Louise's successful bid for French government funds was based on her attending Hayter's atelier for the simple reason it offered to teach students how to produce coloured etchings in virtually one operation instead of having to use different plates for each individual colour as had been the case up to the time Hayter appeared on the scene.

The term used to describe this method was 'viscosity' printing and Hayter had invented it. He'd worked out how printing inks of different viscosities (their relative thinness or thickness) would prevent them from mixing so that a piece of art containing up to as many as six different colours could be run off the press using just one plate. It was a discovery of momentous proportions which revolutionised printmaking and returned it to the status of being a fine art form. News of the viscosity method soon spread around the art world, and shortly Hayter's premises was playing host to such as Picasso, Chagall, Joan Miro, Hans Arp, Yves Tanguy and Giacometti. In return for what he learned there Picasso bought several of Hayter's own artwork. Later, when the occupation of France by Germany during the Second World War forced Hayter to move his atelier to New York, a further bunch of artists including Jackson Pollock became habitués of his atelier in that city. In many respects Hayter was Britain's most famous art export, exceeding by far the reputation of any artist of the same nationality.

But less-accomplished artists - still in their student days - gradually became Atelier 17s bread and butter. For a slice of their scholarship grant Hayter accepted students like Mary Louise for development training although it would be quite wrong to think that the purpose of the studio was simply to pass on techniques in colour etching, as Hayter explained in a 1940 interview. *'I want artists to try the impossible,'* he told the New York Sun *'to try different, unusual methods. If they want advice or information I'll give it. I'll teach them technique. I'm not teaching art first of all, it can't be done....if I give my ideas to anyone they'd become second-hand. That's no good....the test whether a piece of work is good or bad is whether it's dead or alive, and that you can tell (only) by feeling.'*

On arrival at Atelier 17 Mary Louise like all new entrants had to do a small practice plate in the traditional manner which was then printed and put before the proprietor himself for assessment. In her case he went ballistic because she'd done a figurative piece of work and Hayter was far from being an admirer of figurative art. This didn't mean her place at the atelier was now in jeopardy, only that she was on the first of many collision courses with Hayter as were many of his students then and later. The philosophy of the studio was said to be based on Hayter's subscription to egalitarianism and his co-operative approach to labour and technical discoveries: in this way it broke away from the rigid structures and attitudes of most French traditional studios. But if such was the case then new students like Mary Louise failed to find it much in Hayter's behaviour at times. He was sceptical about anything that departed from his earlier involvement with the Surrealists and later his approach of letting the unconscious mind direct the artist's hand. Consequently, aggressive outbursts directed at young students who didn't immediately conform to his views were quite frequent as Mary Louise recalled:

'He often came across as being very arrogant, someone who expected you to comply with his ideas and approaches to content. If you answered back and insisted on continuing with your view he'd call you '...a cheeky

little girl.' In time though I think he grew to accept that my approach to doing figurative work did have its merits, even if he never fully agreed with it.'

Often it seemed it was Atelier 17's technician, M. Messier, who restored calm and kept the workshop functioning. The workshop itself was large but 'rough and ready' although it held all the right equipment for doing colour-etching. M. Messier laid out the materials and tools students would need, helped in adjusting the rollers and blankets used at the printing end of the process and kept a weather eye on student safety especially when they used benzene – a highly flammable substance – to clean their etching plates after taking them from the acid bath. It was he too who tended the pot-bellied stove on the ground floor which was a favourite meeting place for students on winter days in Paris.

Arriving at Atelier 17 early in the day Mary Louise would prepare her etching plates along lines now very familiar to her. The most exciting and stressful part of the whole business came towards the end of the process when the protecting blankets and paper used in the roller press were stripped away and the image revealed. In the age before heated racks the final prints were hung to dry in the air usually on strings stretched between the studio walls. This would be their first exposure to the public gaze – of interest to other students and any artists present and, of course, to the gimlet eye of Stanley William Hayter himself. Any evidence of slap-dashery never mind the choice of subject for the print, would certainly elicit the caustic comments of Atelier 17's proprietor.

Of course, at every stage of the etching process things can and do go wrong. And in colour-etching the viscosity of the inks have to be just right if the final print is to satisfy the artist's objectives. Hayter had developed quite detailed procedures in this respect even down to the number of drops of oil that should be used in the inks rolled on to the plate. He also showed how an etched plate could be treated with different coloured inks to create variations of the same print.

If anyone deserved the designation 'genius' it was Hayter who in addition to an OBE was given a Légion d'Honneur by the French in 1951 and made a Chevalier des Arts in 1967. It isn't clear if he was given these honours as a result of his revolutionary discovery of how to produce multi-colour prints, or for his output as an artist. Certainly he had exhibited with the surrealists in 1929, and his artwork had been chosen to represent Britain at prestigious art exhibitions abroad. But he had also written two books based on his unrivalled knowledge of the technicalities of printmaking, and his reputation in this field positioned him not just as an international authority on the subject but in a class of his own. Not having access to the citations which bestowed the honours on Hayter it is not possible to say which way they leaned, or if they leaned at all. Perhaps they were an acknowledgement of his excellence in both.

At any rate, the end of each term at Atelier 17 was always marked by Hayter throwing a party for his students and invited guests. In among the acid baths, the roller presses and the workbenches strewn with tools Hayter would be at his boisterous best. His belief in '...*realising the necessity of collective work in a group in order to develop possibilities...*' would seem a more tangible philosophy at such moments than it did at other times when the proprietor was at his intractable worst. Mary Louise was to recall her presence at these get-togethers with a lot of warmth and affection: but there's no record of her being requested to demonstrate the Can-Can. I daresay if she had been she might well have gracefully declined and found something else to do.

CHAPTER 10

The two 'Bills' – Coldstream and Hayter – both had very different but lasting effects on Mary Louise. There is no indication the two ever met in a formal setting to exchange views on major art issues, although it is hard to believe their paths didn't cross at several points before and after the Second World War. Anthony Gross and a few others would, of course, keep both men updated on the other's current activities, Gross being one of Coldstream's department heads at the Slade and, in his journeying between London and Paris, a frequent visitor at his old alma mater, Atelier 17. He had also been a fellow-student of Hayter in the mid-1920s.

But even if Gross's personality had enabled him to be a friend to both men, it's doubtful that would have been enough to bring about any meaningful bond between them. How could it? They were polar opposites in just about everything except being artists of the same generation and heads of their own establishments. Coldstream was a planner, a measurer, a man who sought to put on canvas the precise relationship between one thing and all other things around it: Hayter on the other hand didn't as much '*draw a line, but released it*' from his unconscious mind, granting it the freedom to move as it wished so that later he could consciously shape it into abstract forms and images. The two 'Bills' could not have approached the making of art from such different starting points had one been from Muckle Flugga, the other from the Moon. Both men had their followers and supporters however, and in their lifetime were held in high esteem.

I corresponded with several people about both men during my preparations for this book, people who'd had direct contact with them mostly as students. Coldstream emerged as a less-easy character to come to grips with than Hayter, although the inventor of viscosity printing and colour-etching was far from being an uncomplicated individual. You could say Hayter was the more-consistent personality to handle, paradoxically because he allowed less of his rough edges to be knocked off. Regrettably, I never had the opportunity to meet him but did encounter Sir William on a couple of occasions.

The first was at the Slade some years before he retired from being Professor of Fine Art there. When he heard Mary Louise had brought her husband to see her old stamping ground he came down from his eyrie overlooking the life studio to greet us. My first impression of him therefore was a positive one. Here was a man who remembered his students and was keen to keep track of their progress after graduation.

After being introduced to him and exchanging the usual pleasantries I began to understand better why one of his former students had told me she was in awe of him, finding herself more or less dumbstruck in his company to the extent that she would avoid crossing paths with him at the Slade, or even later at functions such as private views and exhibition openings. Coldstream stood looking at me expectantly, waiting I thought for me to say something a bit more interesting than how the Slade was quite different from how I'd imagined it. He had on his suit and tie and was a bit stouter around the middle than I'd imagined. But I hadn't managed to make more than some boring comments about how narrow the corridors were and how cramped the studios before he sighed 'Ah yes, we all have to make do these days with what we are given.' Then after updating himself as to Mary Louise's current plans and few more exchanges with me he exited back to his office where work, and perhaps Monica, awaited.

Afterwards, I thought maybe he had been listening to my Scottish accent since he'd originated in Northumberland, not so far from the English/Scottish border where the accent is different from that encountered in London and the South. In shades of Mary Louise's father, Coldstream had no doubt been prevailed upon to ditch any idiomatic words and phrases from his vocabulary and adopt Received Pronunciation as his lingua franca. This would be entirely fitting, of course, for somebody who one commentator described as 'not just a pillar but a colonnade of the Establishment.' My only other encounter with him was at a private view of one of Mary Louise's exhibitions in London after he'd retired where he pressed the flesh of many old acquaintances, including Patrick Proktor and left early before I'd had a chance to say very much to him. I didn't think he looked at all well and he died soon afterwards in 1987.

More than his art, Coldstream is arguably best remembered for producing the reports to government which proposed wholesale changes to the way art education was delivered in England and Wales. These set a new agenda for people like Mary Louise making the history of art, for example, a compulsory subject and offering film studies as an option for those who wanted to strike out in that direction. Overall though the Coldstream Reports sought to raise art school qualifications to the level of academic study which merited awarding students a degree. The pressure put on Coldstream in producing his reports resulted in him having what was effectively a nervous breakdown shortly after completing them. Uncharitably, some suggested it was his misgivings about the consequences of what he recommended – subsequently accepted by government - which caused his mental illness. Can making art ever be seen as an academic discipline? Many critics of the Coldstream Reports thought not.

According to the novelist Emile Zola art is '...a corner of creation seen through a temperament.' If this is the case then Coldstream's temperament according to one art critic was not perhaps made of the stuff Zola had in mind. 'His crises...' the critic averred, 'were familial, domestic, amatory and bureaucratic.' The 'bureaucratic' bit could be taken as read due to Coldstream's role in the reform of art education: but the others? Certainly he'd divorced his first wife, and his dalliances with other women were well known until Monica Hoyer appeared on the scene. Altogether he fathered five children. Outside of his duties as Professor of Fine Art at the Slade, Coldstream was for periods also a trustee of both the National Gallery and the Tate,

Director of the Royal Opera House, Chairman of the British Film Institute (a position one assumes which had some bearing on him introducing film studies to the Slade curriculum), and a member of the English Arts Council. Perhaps this gives a better indication of his temperament than anything else – one more suited to arts administration and the politicking that invariably goes with it.

Yet it shouldn't be forgotten that Coldstream was also an artist whose work is to be found in various national collections. Described by some as 'austerely naturalistic' his art hardly fits Ernst Gombrich's view that 'a painter does not examine the nature of the physical world, but the nature of our reactions to it.' Personally, I like some of his work though I can see how they won't necessarily have people collapsing breathless on the gallery floor having looked at them. His studies of the female nude – measurement marks and all - are arguably his best works, but their precision and objectivity drains them somewhat of vitality: and Coldstream's use of colour hardly has the emotional impact colour is expected to have.

Just prior to the Second War Coldstream was appointed to a post in an organisation called 'Mass Observation' which was a social research project aimed at recording the everyday life of ordinary people in Britain – an 'anthropology of ourselves' as its founders described it. Coldstream and a photographer were both dispatched to the industrial town of Bolton in the North of England, where Coldstream set about fulfilling his remit of painting scenes of the place. However people viewing the outcomes to his labours were less than impressed. '(Bolton) *looks deserted, hollow, lifeless, yet all the chimneys are smoking!*' one local woman declared. '*There's something I don't like about them,*' she went on. '*We're dead, we are. Our people are dead.*' Coldstream's response was never recorded and he never again visited the town. Later, an early supporter of him, Sir Kenneth Clark – an art historian and one of television's first arts-presenter - came to describe Coldstream's approach to making art as 'dismal rectitude.'

For all that, many still remember Coldstream as someone

who could be witty and in a tight-lipped way, a brilliant conversationalist. He could make a joke and share a joke, so maybe like all of us he had his good days and one's which weren't so great.

'I remember him being a fast mover and a bit buttoned-up,' Mary Louise said. *'And he could be pedantic at times. There was one thing he did which students at the Slade didn't appreciate much and that was taking the paintbrush from your hand and explain what he meant by using it on your canvas. But apart from things like that I learned a lot from Coldstream.'*

To get a picture of what the other 'Bill' looked like, he being Stanley William Hayter, you could do worse than compare him to a slightly smaller but craggier Jonathon Miller the well-known English humourist, opera director and television presenter. If that doesn't help then form a photo-fit of Hayter from these elements supplied by Mary Louise – a face dominated by a nose like an eagle's beak: eyes of indeterminate-blue with large dark circles under them: strong chin: deep lines incised in both cheeks: and a great mane of greying hair falling over his forehead which he frequently has to brush aside. Add to this large hands permanently stained with printing ink and a mouth which refuses to close unless for sleep and you have a fairly decent image of what the proprietor of Atelier 17 looked like. And oh, don't forget the burning cigarette which hangs from his lips – French, of course, most probably a Gauloise. Despite the fags and the acid fumes in his studio though, Bill Hayter kept himself reasonably fit by playing tennis and he seems to have been attractive to women as Mary Louise remembered:

'Yes, he did appeal to some women and he always seemed to have one on the go most of the time I was a student at his workshop. Mostly he talked in a slightly-desperate, worried tone and he was aggressive to younger students, arrogant at times. 'You people who come here from a welfare state who supply you with everything, all the

materials and equipment you need,' he would snarl. 'So you expect the same here…...'

If this was a remark fired at students from Britain, then he was quite wrong of course. Students at British art schools had to fund a lot of consumables from their own pockets, or else from that of their parents. To get to Paris at all Mary Louise had had to use up just about all of her own savings.

Compared to Coldstream, Hayter was described to be like a tightly-coiled spring – an incendiary device primed to go off at a moments notice. The trouble was it didn't give people time to run for cover. The best thing to do was to meet his outbursts stoically and hope the flames wouldn't take long to extinguish themselves. In a way he may have reminded Mary Louise a little of her father who created his own cyclonic zones at times, but fulminating mostly at people outside of his immediate vicinity. Certainly she was more used to displays of temperament than perhaps most of her fellow-students at Atelier 17.

Maybe the reason for Hayter's mood swings lay in an inner-conflict between him being an artist and his reputation for having invented the colour-etching process. *'Oh, I am a scientist, of course'* he said to Mary Louise on more than one occasion. *'I have a degree you know, in chemistry.'* This was obviously important to him and he would know that without his background in chemistry the discovery of viscosity, printing would have had to wait, and the art world's reinstatement of the print as a legitimate art form would have been delayed. Yet his reputation as an artist was by the 1960s well-recognised. Did he resent having to continue teaching others his methods now that the big names like Picasso had learnt enough about the technique to be no longer in need of his guidance? Did the repetitive nature of teaching begin taking its toll as the years passed? During the occupation of France in the Second War Hayter had moved Atelier 17 to New York where it stayed for 10 years. Overall, the experience was devitalising for him. He was horrified by the American's taste in art seeing it as 'vulgar' and undiscriminating, and couldn't wait to get back to Paris – a move he completed in 1950. There may also have been illness to contend with: as a young man Hayter had contracted malaria on one of his assignments abroad as a geologist. Could the recurring symptoms of this have been responsible for his fiery outbursts at times? We can only speculate.

Hayter came from a family of artists, but it wasn't until he was in his mid-twenties that he gave up his career in science and turned to art. After studying under the respected Polish artist/engraver, Joseph Hecht, who also taught Anthony Gross he opened his own workshop in Paris which in 1933 he named Atelier 17 – one of many similar establishments in the city at the time specialising in different art forms. Before that he was intent on developing his own artistic endowment, coming under the influence of the Surrealists some of whom worked at Atelier 17.

When the Spanish civil war broke out it invoked a passionate response in Hayter who produced work that was seen as 'violent' by some but epitomised his revulsion of fascism. He organised a portfolio of prints to raise funds for the Republican cause in Spain to one of which Picasso made a contribution. He also collaborated with the poet Paul Eluard and the playwright Samuel Beckett, all of which provide clues to where both his political and artistic sympathies lay. But there were other areas of his life which lent their own drama to his existence. Not least of these was what had been said of Coldstream with respect to his 'amatory crises.'

The etching plate may have been to Hayter the arena where physical, chemical and psychological phenomena dramatically combined: but to the women in his life the action was being played out much closer to home. Mary Louise reckoned that his outbursts at Atelier 17 during her time there were due to his long-term girlfriend having left him. In fact Helen Phillips, an American sculptor, was Hayter's wife (the middle one of 3) and she may well have left him for a period in the early Sixties because of her husband's short-term affairs with other women, among them students and associates at his atelier.

Her marriage to Hayter was only dissolved in 1971 although whether this came at the end of a long separation period it isn't possible to say. What can be said is that Hayter in today's milieu would have been viewed as a bit of a sexual predator and exhibited many of a predator's chief characteristics. His technique was usually to invite a likely prospect to eat at his apartment – lunch of scrambled eggs was a favourite – then give her a guided tour of the premises which ended with him saying '...*and this is the bedroom, of course.*' He couldn't have made it plainer what he had in mind. One student, who was *not* a target for the proprietor, took offence at him asking her once if she carried any contraceptives with her, presumably because an unexpected opportunity had arisen which threatened to catch him out. Cheeky little girls, indeed......!

'*It was never easy working with him*' Mary Louise said '*but for me the biggest obstacle to start with was his dismissal of figurative art which was, and still is, my choice. I think in time though he came to recognise it could work. I'm not saying I converted him or anything, I just think he accepted it. Maybe he was secretly pleased the process he'd invented could be applied to any fine art form.*'

It would be nice to imagine the ghost of William Stanley Hayter still paying the occasional visit to his former premises on the Rue Campagne-Premiere (now named 'Atelier Centrepoint') where much of his life was spent. I can see him, cigarette burning, pausing to squint at what's in the acid bath, what finished work has been placed in the driers and if anyone today bothers much to acknowledge him as the father of viscosity printing. Modern methods using solar plates, electrolysis and non-toxic chemicals offer today's young artists a somewhat simpler and less-hazardous means of doing multi-colour prints.

In her two years at Hayter's Mary Louise acquired a superb range of skills and techniques which she utilised in her later work as a professional artist. Even when she moved on to oil painting, watercolours, murals and other art forms her 'formative years' at Atelier 17 proved of immense value. In some of her later work you can detect at least a little of Hayter's influence, her mosaics and images done on self-made marbled paper being examples. Coldstream also left his mark on her, of course. She was never a disciple of either of the two 'Bills': but she had cause to be grateful to both of them as her career continued to unfold.

CHAPTER 11

She goes out every day, often as dusk is gathering its veils, shaking off Hayter at his worst, Clarin at his most indolent, the studio-apartment at Cité Universitaire too cloistral for her mood. This is Paris after all and there isn't a second to be wasted.

She starts on one of the boulevards (less cars then, more people), but soon she is striking off into side streets lured by the sight of a little square which leads off to another little square then another until she's confused to where she is exactly. Nothing to worry about though: her French is excellent now. If she has to ask for directions she will: easily.

She enters a park with a fountain matching the fountain of flowers cascading down the old stone wall nearby, arbitrarily, untouched except with the eye, unmolested by people ever-mindful of its transient beauty. Here, old couples, meeting under the trees, exchanging gripes, motioning in the air, lips moving like little bellows, everything spoken as if through caramel, as if exhaled from an unfiltered cigarette, words running like smooth pebbles caught in the backwash of a wave.

A young girl walking with her Maman, arms linked, Maman frowning at times, tempus fugit, remembering when she was the one to let her teasing laugh drift in the moist air to where the boys gathered. Chess players under the plane trees, little accretions of solemn spectators building around them, heads angled, arms folded, eyes narrowed in concentration….might be a picture in that.

Then paved pathways ending, giving out as they approach the inner reaches of the park, relinquishing control, conceding to nature, nature reasserting itself here in the city with tangles of stunted trees, escaped shrubbery, weeds and wildflowers.

A busy intersection now, pavement cafes, restaurants, clink of glass, scrape of knife on plate, off to the left a glimpse of an amusement arcade, gaming machines, men playing roulette, filtering it all in, snapshots stored in the memory, scenes of low salience: but not to an artist. More strollers, more diners, reading the chalked menu boards, running an eye over what's being ordered, what's being eaten, chefs in tall hats, waiters in long aprons, insouciant, looking like out of work poets, affecting boredom, smiling only when bringing the bill, collecting the tip.

Up through a splurge of tourists around the famous church, people in ridiculous clothes, exhausted by their itineraries, resting on the steps, wondering if they dare sleep here for a bit before returning to their hotels. But beyond the sprawl of them the street of small, exquisite houses, this one only partly visible through the screening vegetation, that one where Susan Valadon painted in between rescuing her errant son, Utrillo, squabbling in the bar, too far gone to raise his hands if it ever comes to fisticuffs.

And then the only vineyard in the city, raised on high ground to be nearer the sun, heavily fenced, patrolled by guard dogs, uniformed men who peer through the railings at others playing boule on a patch of sandy earth folded between the giant plane trees. Need to remember. Should have brought a bigger drawing pad. Could be a picture there. Christ! All this rubbish in her bag and only a single pencil to be found!

Shortly, a large street market, drawing her in, swallowing her up, stalls sagging under the weight of produce. Who would have thought humble fruit and veg could engender such noise! Jews and Arabs commingling, the burkah rubbing shoulders with the tallit, the hijab and the yarmulka. Here, women resting on their haunches at the kerb, henna tattoos on feet and ankles, on the backs of their hands, under the hijab watchful eyes, glancing-brown, looking at what you're wearing, your shoes, your bag, your scruffy jeans, the ink and paint spatters: you might well be a hobo looking for discarded apples.

Higher up, the house, the door, the very step where Piaf was abandoned as a baby. Here the smell of cooking, Lebanese, Turkish, pastries from Tunisia, Algeria, coffee, always coffee, the aroma of freshly-ground beans at odds with the bitterness of the brew. Then *even higher up, the Butte, the park fashioned from a worked-out limestone quarry, flooded to make a lake. People lying on the grass, ignoring the 'forbidden' signs, catching the last rays of the sun, mothers, toddlers, boys dangling from a bridge, exuberant, daredevils, challenged by a menacing ten-inches of water overlaid by lilies. Limestone under her feet, dazzling white, Utrillo again, digging out a few handfuls for himself, taking it home, softening it up with linseed oil, using it in his art, pictures of Paris made from the city's naturally-occurring materials.*

Back now on the Metro, ionised air, smell of piss and electric flux, separate and combined, thinking things over, so many possibilities for pictures, children's play parks, Arab women, Chassidic Jews with their long side locks, men in blue overalls flooding the gutters, sweeping with long-handled brooms, fag ends swirling, Gitanes and Gauloises, green vines, 'Ouvre Rouge' on posters left over from the last protest march. Recalling the little squares, puzzling, why a tennis court in that one, why in that other a ruined house amid such elegant buildings? And who put the pot of brilliantly-coloured flowers on its crumbling window sill? Filtering-in, filtering-out. So many options, drawing pad crammed with ideas, seeing the finished work even before it's been started. Never satisfied with just one thing. Too many ideas, too many images tumbling before the inner eye. Must be more-selective, not start so many yet finish so few. Almost misses her stop for the Cité Universtaire.

Climbing the stair to her room, exhausted now, fruit and eau mineral for her supper, fresh sheets to sleep in, lying flat the way she always sleeps, staring at the shadows on the ceiling, listening to the rumble of distant traffic, recalling Cezanne's comment on first seeing Venice.

'Why did I take so long to get here?'

CHAPTER 12

Though in no sense a parallel universe, another Paris was emerging during Mary Louise's time in the French capital. It was one which a few years later would erupt in what was called the 'Paris Spring' of revolt and near-insurrection. Some of the people she began seeing on the streets of Paris in 1962 were quite different from those who appeared in her initial artwork. They were the political activists – the sentinel species of those who came to barricade the boulevards in 1968 as they challenged authority in a continuum of violent clashes which shook France and her increasingly-alarmed neighbours. They included a great many students whose numbers were to swell from around 170,000 at the start of the 1960s to well over half-a-million by the end of the decade. They had grievances of their own to add to the volatile mix.

The underlying causes of the unrest has been a separate battleground for historians and political pundits ever since. One thing they all agree on, however, is that the policies of the French government at the time were deeply unpopular. This had much to do with France's recently-formed compact with Germany – its erstwhile occupier and conqueror in World War 2 – which soon became the Common Market and is today called the European Union. The ramifications of this union were copious and diverse and struck the French as an attack on their national sovereignty, an issue which has remained the subject of heated debate as the EU has grown over the years to what it is now.

The French people's opposition to the Franco-German alliance was focused on the measures being taken to reduce the country's deficit by laying siege to the infamous French 'bureaucracy' which appeared to have too many state employees, and too much foreign borrowings to pay their salaries. If that strikes you as being familiar today then it's hardly surprising. *Plus ca change, plus ca le meme chose.* To reduce the burden, as

President Charles De Gaulle saw it, the 'bureaucracy' had to be whittled down by shedding public sector jobs despite many of these being necessary and contingent with a modern society's requirements. The outcome to this was not long in showing itself.

As Mary Louise explored Paris during her first year in the capital she encountered in no uncertain way the feelings of sections of the population towards the cuts being enforced on them. Strikes were called by the giant CIO-AFL trade union, and noisy often violent street demonstrations took place. As an indication of how high passions were running six people were arrested and sentenced to death for conspiring to assassinate De Gaulle. Adding to the turbulence was the challenge to French colonialism, especially in North Africa, where Algeria was in ferment over French rule. In a Paris demonstration on the Algerian question eight demonstrators were shot dead by police.

Needless to say, many among the burgeoning student population joined in the protests citing their own sense of injustice about overcrowded institutions, the lack of basic facilities in schools and universities and the pittance paid to them while they were studying. More than any other section of French society who aligned themselves with the protests – and they included health professionals, teachers and local government workers – the students were the ones to give the entire situation an ideological cast. The red flag, the hammer and sickle and the Internationale were to be seen and heard frequently on the streets of the capital.

In a clutch of letters home Mary Louise described for her parents some of the scenes she was witnessing up-close in Paris, and some of the rows these elicited within the purlieu of the Cité Universitaire. The concerns of her roommates had now shifted from mundane issues like leaving food to rot in the fridge, to how metro strikes and enforced cuts to the water supply were causing havoc. Added to this was a rather specious concern for their personal safety despite the increase of troops and riot police deployed on the boulevards. In a postcard to Chestnut Cottage Mary Louise made mention of the massive May Day demonstration of 1962 in Paris. For a girl who'd only experienced the Aldermaston marches the palpable fury in many a fiery speech added to the growing conviction that something fundamental was about to happen in France. There might even be a revolution!

But there were other less-sensational events to report on. For reasons unknown she was co-opted as a film extra in a movie shot in Paris starring the English actress Anna Massey, although if Mary Louise's scene did survive the cutting room floor it became like the film itself, lost in obscurity. She wrote more on her visits to the family of a friend Francine Vitry, and even if she expressed concerns about money she was able to give her parents the happy news that her French government scholarship, paltry though it was, had been extended for a further 12 months.

It could have been this was due in part to Hayter, who had liked a large coloured print of a Paris scene which Mary Louise had etched and put through the roller press at Atelier 17. In seeking a reference for the renewal of her grant Hayter might well have been willing to put his name to it. And there was another Hayter-inspired move which resulted in her being invited to visit someone who was known to the proprietor as lover of art and who, like her father, was already establishing himself as a Hollywood actor. He was Vincent Price, now remembered for his roles in countless horror movies and his radio series as 'The Man in Black.'

Price at the time was also an agent for the giant Sears-Roebuck company who were proud of their art collection which they added to most years by dint of Price's visits to Paris and other European art centres. On his way through he networked with those like Hayter who could point him in the direction of young, up-and-coming artists whose work suggested they had a future as collector's items. If this didn't turn out to be the way Sears-Roebuck saw it, then Price would buy artwork anyway for his own private collection. On leaving her appointment with Price at a hotel in central Paris Mary Louise's portfolio was much lighter than it had been on the way in due to him having purchased several of her works. The money he paid her she spent helping finance her extra year in Paris.

In return for her news her parents kept her updated on what was happening at home and how things were going with her father's career. Towards the end of 1962, George Coulouris had already been signed-up to work on the soundtrack of a film about Russia before and after the revolution which was to be made in Berlin with Stanley Foreman of Plato Films directing. Before that happened however, he was busy rehearsing every day for a big theatrical event in Richmond, Yorkshire, along with the actresses Dame Edith Evans and Sybil Thorndyke – Thorndyke along with her husband being responsible for the Berlin movie. At the opening of the grand theatrical event the Princess Royal was due to make an entrance to the accompaniment of six trumpeters and thereafter entertained by harpsichordists and singers from Sadler's Wells Opera Company. What Mary Louise's Father made of these arrangements, being the man he was, wasn't spelled out in the letter to his daughter but one can imagine it only too easily.

Startling for her parents though must have been Mary Louise's decision not to make use of her privileged pass to visit the studio of the French Cubist, Ferdnand Leger and a couple of other artists of equal fame. And even worse in the eyes of people then and now, she declined to join a student group from the Beaux Arts who had been invited by the people around Pablo Picasso to visit the great man in Antibes. '*I was too mesmerised by Paris,*' was how she later came to explain her action. '*I knew I had limited time to experience the place and taking time out to go on the trip south just seemed a waste.*' She never expressed regret at missing the opportunity although I think she'd have jumped at the chance had it arrived at a different time in her career. Hayter must also have been surprised at his pupil's decision although he said nothing on the matter directly. Perhaps he thought she was just being a conceited 'silly little girl.'

As her second year in Paris moved inexorably towards a close, she tried everything she knew to stay there. By now she was approaching her mid-twenties and couldn't go on living on scholarships and the sporadic income from selling her work. '*I would have done anything to stay in Paris*,' she said '*and if I hadn't been naïve about how to go about it I'd have taken a job serving in a café just to survive*.' But her love affair with the city was set to undergo separation, albeit temporarily, while she returned to London to consider what her next step would be. But there was still her swansong to come.

At the Beaux Arts there was an exhibition space known as the 'Maison' whose large wooden doors opened out on to the Left Bank and the busy river traffic passing along the Seine. The Maison Des Beaux Arts was, still is, available to students for hanging their annual summer show, or at other times to individual artists who had a connection to the institution and wanted a solo-exhibition. The exhibition area was vast but imaginatively partitioned into smaller sections all painted, as artists demanded, with white emulsion. Mary Louise assembled a number of prints – 16 works in all – and got very excited at the prospect of having her first ever solo show. In addition to working hard at producing what would hang on the wall she also made posters advertising the event and went around the streets sticking them on walls and any other available surface. It was a lesson in self-sustainability which Atelier 17 didn't include in a student's programme, but which was to stand Mary Louise in good stead at many points in her future career. If no one else is available to help, then do it yourself! Five French newspapers reviewed her exhibition as did the art reviewer of the then 'Glasgow Herald', Phyllis Jenkins:

'*I went (to this exhibition) in a spirit of duty: I came away quite besotted by this girl's work and one of her coloured engravings under my arm…..she has power, craftsmanship, appeal and a texture which sends shivers of excitement up your back….*'

Shortly after the opening to her show she'd sold every print. Word got back to Hayter of the success and he invited his contacts at the French Biblioteque Nationale to take a look at other work she kept at the Beaux Arts. They did and ended up buying two other prints by Mary Louise for the French nation's national collection.

The sales boosted her spirits even if artists will continue making art even if no one buys. And, of course, the proceeds from selling her work meant she had enough to pay for her return home and cushion her for a bit until she re-adjusted to life back in England.

After Paris though, that adjustment looked like being as tough as the one she'd had to make on arriving from America. There were old contacts to be renewed, new ones to be made and a family life to be resumed: and where was she to continue making prints when the process needed such a lot of infrastructure funding? But already she had become adaptable to leaving one place and looking positively at whatever came next. It was a hallmark of her character, a deeply ingrained part of her make-up which was to serve her well on many future occasions. Not even the wrench of bidding Paris farewell could alter that.

CHAPTER 13

Leaving Paris must have felt like having a glass of the best Bordeaux wine snatched away after sampling just a couple of mouthfuls. Not that there was any hardship in Mary Louise resuming her residence in London's Hampstead: there were few nicer places to live than in the semi-rural surroundings of the Vale of Health. After adjusting to being back home, however, there were several important matters to be addressed.

In setting her sail to becoming a professional artist meant she had to face two issues which had seen many talented individuals in the past holed below the waterline before even getting out of port. The first of these – the London art scene at the time - had an immediacy requiring close investigation and assessment: the other, much deeper embedded in art history, was an on-going issue which even today is largely unresolved. This was the position of female artists in a profession dominated by men. Banishing either to the wings with her enthusiasm for making art was not an option. They were likely to make their influence felt at some point, leading perhaps to personal disappointment and frustration no matter how short-lived these might be in someone of her nature and temperament. Much depended on her awareness of what she was getting into and how she managed to mould it to her own designs.

The state of the London art world in the mid-1960s was something she was obliged to know about. Out there was the competition, daggers drawn, vying for the gallery spaces that brought media reviews and with it a reputation and, hopefully, lots of money. If competition between academics and in the boardrooms of big business is well known, compared to the world of art it is like a squabble over who gets the last biscuit in the box. Among artists it was commonplace to watch egos soar and witness displays of arrogance, fits of pique, moodiness and petulance according to how things were going at the time with respect to their exposure in the media. Appearing drunk on television and using foul language in front of the cameras hadn't quite arrived yet: but artists with a nose for turning notoriety to their advantage were eventually to do just that.

The dynamic of the 1960s art scene lay in its protean nature where artists of many different stamps and producing vastly different types of work regarded themselves as being in the vanguard of what was labelled 'the counter culture'. This was a movement whose mission was seen to be that of overturning the social conventions of a country which still reeked of class divisions and the attitudes that went with them. The 'counter culture' could trace its origins back to the time of the Beatniks, and after re-fuelling itself with a decade of drugs and rock 'n roll had produced a range of disparate tendencies which just couldn't be synthesized into any sort of coherency no matter how much critics and art historians tried.

Spokesmen for the 'counter culture' claimed to be opposed to traditional values in art (in terms of art history there was nothing new in that), and dedicated themselves to destroying art as an elitist pastime of the wealthy. Art had never been entirely that, of course, but as things stood at the time they weren't totally off-target. What they proceeded to do, however, didn't get far in persuading others to believe them. Indeed, you could argue that over the period they managed to do more to alienate people from the medium than anyone did. Visits to art museums began falling faster than a single by Peter & Gordon in the pop charts. As she began looking closer at the world she was about to enter, Mary Louise might well have wished she'd found employment after all as a dishwasher in Paris.

Pop Art was about the first 'movement' to emerge in the late-50s quickly followed by Op Art with Fluxus and Minimalism hard on their heels. Alongside these at various times was New Realism, Magic Realism, Psychedelic Art, Graffiti Art, Junk Art, Post-Painterly Abstraction, Land Art, Environmental Art,

Art Photography and the beginnings of Installation, Video and Performance Art. They all staked their claim for attention along with a lot of other labelled goods whose shelf-life proved to be blissfully shorter as the 1960s unfolded.

'Conceptual Art' which traded on the rather arrogant assumption that it came closest to the purest form of making art, was predicated on the belief that the artist's imagination was paramount and it was perfectly okay to have your 'vision' given form by other people and not by yourself. In other words you did the creative thinking bit and other, less-celebrated souls turned your 'concept' into reality. This included 'works' which hadn't any physical existence at all, like standing in a room with an artist who attempted to communicate a work of art 'telepathically' in a flow of thoughts not connected to language or any sort of images. Bunkum? Hogwash? People made up their own minds usually preferring a night in with sausage and chips to accepting an invite to the opening of a 'conceptual art' exhibition. The fact that such 'art' continues being produced today can only be explained by dealers serving wealthy clients with investment portfolios. How it qualified as art at all will remain a mystery until the next weighty volume attempting to explain it hits the bookshops.

Indeed, many of the 'art forms' which appeared in the 1960s, though declaring themselves anti-establishment (one actually labelled itself 'Anti-Art') still insisted on being described as art, which inferred the artists producing it remained welded to a world they professed to despise. This was yet another conundrum to add to the growing pile which fledgling artists like Mary Louise found standing in their way.

The din and obscuring dust created by 60s art pulled the rug from under art historians and critics alike. The reason for their downfall lay in a reluctance to accept that the art they were expected to review and record arose directly from the re-birth of consumerism following the Second World War. Unable to cope with such a crass idea they hummed and hawed and kept their options open, tip-toeing around exhibitions fearful of misjudging what hung on the walls in case posterity held them up to ridicule for having missed something of seminal worth. Well, hadn't critics in the past done precisely that when the Impressionists came along? And the Cubists? And the Surrealists? Heaven forbid they should prove culpable on similar charges about present day art!

In most cases they hedged their bets leaving others in their peer group to wrestle with the ongoing shemozzle characterising the 1960s art scene. They wrote newspaper articles and exhibition catalogues, gave lectures and published books which lent credence to whatever was currently in vogue, in the process making stars of certain artists and making money for them and their dealers. Left with deciding, for example, which two works by different artists, each consisting of pieces of rotting wood slobbered-over with brown paint was adjudged to be better, bewildered critics with a living to make left the gallery mumbling something to the effect that the positioning of the mouldy wood in one case was preferable to its arrangement in the other. Well, at least they had something to look at unlike 'telepathic' art, or later attempts at referencing the vacuities of modern life in empty canvases and casts taken of concrete walls due for imminent demolition.

Histories of the London art scene during the period when Mary Louise was getting her career underway became as frequent in the bookshops as lorries shedding their loads at key points on Britain's motorways. Some of these, suitably updated, are still there: but few are likely to enable art lovers of today to make meaningful sense out of much belonging to the era. Because of their availability there is little point in making any appraisal of them here. Let's just say if you have an intense dislike of someone in your life, you might think of buying them one for their birthday.

Clearly, one thing we now know about 1950s- 60s art is that the prevailing influence on it came largely from the commercial world, specifically from product advertising in the United States. Who needs reminding of Warhol's soup tins, Roy Lichtenstein's comic strip evocations, Rauschenberg's Coke bottles, Jasper John's laboriously realistic beer cans and Tom Wesselmann's television sets? Some of these images have been given the status of icons along with their creators. Perhaps the most revealing example of this is a work belonging to the Fluxus group of 'avant-garde' art (of which Yoko Ono was one) in a piece of collage by the British artist, Richard Hamilton, who gave it the title '*What is it that makes today's homes so different, so appealing?*' Against a background of household items including furniture and modern electrical appliances you might easily hear the voice-over' to a radio or television advert. Of course, supporters of Fluxus maintained images like this were an expose of the modern acquisitive society we'd become, and its detractors just hadn't got the joke. The Tate Modern though, where they're always falling about laughing, bought many such artworks for their national collection.

'Business art is a much better thing to be making than art-art' Andy Warhol declared before going off to produce more of it. Some art critics pretended not to anguish over this, or think overmuch at what damage it might be doing to the relevance of art in people's lives. Others just got on with selling the stuff to those rich enough to pay for it. One of these was the man behind the promotion of Silk Cut cigarettes and eventually Margaret Thatcher and her Conservative Party, Charles Saatchi.

Saatchi, an erstwhile advertising copywriter, began collecting art at 26 by purchasing the work of a Minimalist from New York. Later, he purchased the entire show of another Minimalist, Robert Mangold, and 17 works by Warhol. In time he established a gallery with his brother and went on to sponsor the Young British Artists group of which the 'conceptualists' Damian Hirst and Tracy Emin were to emerge as leading lights. 'I am an artoholic' Saatchi frequently told people, just in case they misheard and attributed spirituous liquors to his penchant for art others wouldn't take seriously. Ultimately though he admitted to the 'emphemerality and superficiality' of much of the artwork he purchased. According to his biographer Saatchi concluded that 90% of what he'd collected would be worthless in ten years time.

As expected the art of the 'counter culture' had its opponents among them some critics, gallery owners and luminaries from elsewhere in the arts establishment. Unconvinced by the argument that artists in the past such as Toulouse-Lautrec and Salvador Dali had participated in promoting commercial products (Dali appeared in telly ads for Alka-Seltzer and Lanvin chocolates), they might have pointed out this came after their art had established their reputation, not as a vehicle or the central inspiration for it. They could also have added a rebuttal to the argument that resumption of consumerist society after the Second War had forged an affinity with an art which was only responding to it in its own way. And if it wasn't always coherent that also should be viewed as predictable in a society freeing itself from its former constraints. A lack of coherency was present in many things until all was explained by those who possessed a better understanding of them: that's why promotional advertising was an essential ingredient of everything, including art.

The story of one artist, Bridget Riley, might well illustrate the point about consumerism. An artist whose talent was never in doubt, Riley had been influenced early in her career by the work of the French Neo-Impressionist, Georges Seurat, who studied scientific dissertations to help him construct a hypothesis on vibrant colour effects. What the Impressionists had done almost unconsciously, Seurat gave a rational explanation to.

'He showed how by placing dots of pure colour side by side on a canvas greater luminosity was achieved than if the colours had been mixed together on an artist's palette beforehand'. This optical effect struck Riley as having endless possibilities and she began producing large-scale works in which the size, placement and shape of these dots caused them to appear as if they vibrated and dazzled. This made her the major figure in Op Art in the mid-1960s. The fashion, design and advertising agencies were soon after her services and her career thereafter never faltered for as long as her re-purposed optical abstractions were in vogue. Not everyone was overwhelmed though. 'Visually arresting and somewhat reminiscent of wallpaper,' was the opinion of one reader after an illustrated article on Riley's early compositions appeared in the Guardian newspaper. 'Nice…!' was the extremely brief response from another.

Across the Atlantic, in the country of Mary Louise's birth and whose consumer boom was ahead of Britain's, some American critics raised their voices above the din to remonstrate with what one, Harold Rosenberg, described as 'The Vanguard Audience' which he said 'was open to anything.':

> 'Its eager representatives – curators, museum directors, art educators, dealers – rush to organise exhibitions and provide explanatory labels before the paint has dried on the canvas or the plastic has hardened. Co-operating critics comb the studios like big-league scouts, prepared to spot the art of the future and to take the lead in establishing reputations. Art historians stand ready with cameras and notebooks to make sure every novel detail is safe for the record. The tradition of the new has reduced all other traditions to triviality.'

'I think Mr Rosenberg may well be right,' Ernst Gombrich said in reply to this scything criticism 'when he implies that we art historians have contributed to this change in the situation.' Why they had done so he later had a stab at explaining: but because this made no reference to consumerist society and how art by certain celebrity figures had become an investment for wealthy patrons and a source of profit for dealers in the 'free market', the results were feeble and unconvincing. Overall, it just reinforced the view that although the dogs barked at the caravan the caravan moved on.

Seeking to establish a reputation while all this was going on, Mary Louise quickly realised it wasn't for her. Instead, she took to the streets of Britain's capital city just as she'd done in Paris sometimes taking a prepared etching plate rather than a drawing pad with her to record what it was out there that intrigued and motivated her.

> 'I would sit in a café and scribble directly on to the metal plate. I was fascinated by other people's lives and collected overheard conversations along with their animated gestures and behaviour. There was richness to street life, especially in the open air markets. My favourite haunts were Queen Street, East Street, Portobello Road, Petticoat Lane and that market in East London where they sold birds in cages, pets and all manner of things that probably fell off the back of a lorry. I can't remember what it was called. Is it still there?'

The following year, many of these images after suitable development and a visit to the acid bath were inked and passed through her studio press to form Mary Louise's first solo exhibition at the Everyman cinema in Hampstead. The cinema, adjacent to Hampstead's main thoroughfare, was presided over by the vigilant but paternalistic eye of its owner, a local solicitor called James Fairfax-Jones, and the show attracted highly favourable reviews. About the 17 etchings on show, one reviewer said of Mary Louise's work: 'She has the two-fold ability to adapt colour to the mood of her work, and to adapt her style to the mood she wants to display.' It was recognition of how much she'd matured into her art and her mastery over what she wanted to say and how to say it. She sold several prints to a new cohort of exhibition goers intrigued by the process of colour etching applied imaginatively to figurative art work. Fairfax-Jones immediately set about fixing a date for a further exhibition. As things turned out, however, that exhibition was to consist of work depicting worlds as far from London street-life as anyone could ever imagine.

As far as the streets of the capital were concerned in the

latter-half of the 1960s, however, the crowds thronging the main shopping areas had now been joined by protesters expressing their disapproval on a number of issues the British government was supporting. To Mary Louise this must have carried echoes of Paris just a few years previously. Unarguably the foremost of these was the anti-war demonstrations against America's attempt to recover lost ground in Vietnam. In 1965 'Operation Rolling Thunder' saw the first U.S. combat troops sent to Vietnam: less than two years later they had half-a-million soldiers there in support of the puppet-regime. The recently elected Labour government under Prime Minister Harold Wilson, though refusing to contribute manpower to the conflict, backed the American position nonetheless. The bailout of bankrupt Britain by the USA in the wake of the Second World War and Britain's continuing dependency on American finance saw to that.

In several parts of Europe the anti-Vietnam war campaign was gathering strength, in London the focus being on the American Embassy in Grosvenor Square where riot police were frequently in action and detained protestors often ended up in the dock at the Old Bailey – England's highest criminal court. Among the protestors was Mary Louise. As dedicated to the protests as any around her she was at the same time taking mental snapshots of events which she later retrieved and turned into images on paper. And if this 'political' art failed in many cases to satisfy her – the issues involved tending to take precedence over the aesthetics – it was no less indicative of how she was developing as an artist. Her commitment lay within the broader society of people surrounding her in London and in other lands. What was happening in Vietnam was important to her and an image she made depicting Vietnamese peasants cycling through what was left of their bomb-shattered village and chemically-defoliated forests was bought by the veteran Labour MP, Emanuel Shinwell. The proceeds went immediately to a charity for medical aid in that stricken country.

In the summer of 1966 she was invited to be an artist-in-residence at the Pratt Gallery in New York. In between revealing the methodology of colour printing to patrons of the Pratt, she also exhibited in gallery space attached to it whereupon the New York Public Library purchased one of her works for their collection. In a starkly different location, East Berlin, she was invited to repeat the substance of her New York residency after making friends with a German couple (he an artist, she a book illustrator) at an international conference in London where Mary Louise acted as an interpreter for the French delegation. For a month she taught and demonstrated her specialist skills in Berlin, met dozens of East German artists, visited the totally re-constructed town of Dresden and, of course, took herself off, drawing-book under her arm, to record scenes of anything that would register her excitement at being on the 'wrong' side of a city divided by things beyond the physical presence of a massive concrete wall.

Back in London she became a founder member of the Printmakers Council, who then commissioned her to produce a print for a mixed exhibition at their Gallery on the south bank of the Thames. This attracted buyers from a range of institutions and soon other works of hers were entering the collections held by Hambros Bank, the Royal Bank of Scotland and the Nuffield Trust. But perhaps the most memorable sale to date was to a man who had only a short time to live, and was on a whistle-stop tour of Europe along with his wife. He was John Steinbeck, author of innumerable stories about the American people one of which, 'The Grapes of Wrath', had been made into a Hollywood movie starring Henry Fonda.

The Steinbeck's had heard from friends of theirs about the charm of Chestnut Cottage and during a conducted tour of the house which included Mary Louise's studio, their eye fell on one of her recent prints not yet removed from the clothes line where it had been hung to dry. Steinbeck lingered on the image for a little while before deciding to buy it. Rolled-up in a large cardboard tube he left Britain with the picture stored safely in his luggage.

After his death, another friend of the Coulouris's from their days in Beverly Hills, Bob Wallsten, collaborated with Steinbeck's wife Elaine in collecting the writer's written correspondence and publishing it in a single, large volume. A copy of it, signed and presented to me by Wallsten, has pride of place on one of my many bookshelves.

By now Mary Louise was thinking of finding a place of her own to live, but this had to wait for a little time yet until her personal funds accumulated. To supplement these funds she took on part-time teaching at a number of colleges offering art courses, several of them outside London where etching had been added to their provision. Meanwhile life at Chestnut Cottage continued much as before. '*Dad would rant and blast away at the state of things, and how the English were hopeless at everything from running a country to performing Shakespeare,*' Mary Louise would recall. '*I could see his reasons for a lot of it, but he still wouldn't do anything practical about it. I think frustration about his career in acting had a lot to do with it. His ambition to appear on stage in the classics was just as strong as ever. It must be awful when you are totally dependent on others offering you parts. Maybe my freedom as an artist just reminded him of his own entrapment.*'

One period in the day, however, guaranteed to lift any gloomy spirits arrived at four in the afternoon when tea was brought in for whoever was at Chestnut Cottage that day. Louise Coulouris served it on the dot and if it was delayed for any reason her husband tended to get a bit grumpy. Over tea and cake Mary Louise would hear about the latest developments in her father's career. Around this time he'd appeared in a number of films including '*Arabesque*' with Sophia Loren and Gregory Peck, and on television in episodes of '*Koroshi*' and '*The Prisoner.*' Sometimes fellow actors appeared in time for tea preceded by a glass or two of something stronger. Dinah Sheridan, described as the quintessential English rose, was one of these along with her husband Jack Merivale, also an actor. Merivale was afflicted by hereditary kidney disease and not expected to live long: but his eternal good humour and Sheridan's mastery of administering kidney dialysis at home stretched his life by at least ten years.

At these tea-gatherings Mary Louise's father would be at his best – by turn amusing, effusively critical, boisterous, and exceedingly well-informed due to him being an inveterate bookworm and newspaper addict. How he managed to return from the local lending library with triple the allowable number of books in his bag was a mystery to everyone but himself. Shortly, I'd be joining some of these get-togethers myself and often left with a copy from his own book collection in my bag. The novels of several forgotten authors (Lionel Merrick, for example) whose work I enjoyed hugely I can remember clearly to this day.

And, of course, political discourse was never far from the scene at Chestnut Cottage on most occasions. Possessed by at least some of her father's outspoken opposition to things, and her mother's wry, mild-mannered determination to add a humorous chuckle to any serious conversation, Mary Louise could move ahead knowing her family was behind her. In the push and shove of her chosen career, that was a valuable asset to have as the art scene continued on its capricious course heading towards the end of the Sixties.

CHAPTER 14

Within the babble and blare of the 'counter culture' other less-recondite voices were to be heard. One of these was seen as urging a return to an important dialogue which had had begun the previous century before being interrupted by two world wars. This was the position of women in society, and more-specifically in Mary Louise's case the recognition of women artists.

Since Renaissance times at least the world of fine art had been dominated by men. Surveying the workings of this world at close quarters seemed to support what one feminist writer, Tillie Olsen, described as 'the silencing of women's creativity.' To many people, both men and women, the negative impact of gender division on art history was something which continued to go unaddressed. Despite the emergence of a wider women's movement in the 1960s it was twenty years further down the line before this became a subject for further investigation and debate. If the artwork hanging on the walls of our national museums were instantly recognised as being by Rembrandt, Picasso, Cezanne and Warhol, where then had Berthe Morisot, Mary Cassatt, Susan Valadon and Frida Kahlo gone? Even more so, whoever bothered with the work of Gwen Raverat, Dame Ethel Walker, Audrey Flack and many other talented women artists?

In his best-seller 'The Story of Art' - translated into umpteen different languages - the historian Ernst Gombrich uses 415 images to illustrate his text: only one of these is by a female artist, Kathe Kollwitz. Well done, Kathe! But for you the score would've been 416-nil. As if to add irony to this huge imbalance in gender representation, Gombrich begins his book with the opening line '*There is no such thing as art history, there is only the history of artists.*' I wonder how many people are aware that this statement, word for word, was written by the Russian-born woman artist, Marianne Werefkin, who entered it in her journal for 1904 around half a century before the Story of Art was even thought of? It's hard to believe Gombrich arrived at the same opinion independently: however, he neglected to attribute it to the woman artist who first gave voice to it.

In what was admittedly a 'cod-survey' of on-going art exhibitions in London in the early 1970s, I scoured the columns of the art press trying to get a better fix on just how great gender discrimination might be. The first thing to emerge was that of all the artists exhibiting in galleries large and small, just over 5% were recognisable by forename as being female. On digging a little deeper I discovered that of this number many did not have artwork hanging on the wall but displayed such things as jewellery, ceramics and decorative glass work in cabinets occupying the galleries floor-space. In a way this could be taken as an indication of the non-linear approach women have to making art: but in consequence the figure for woman painters and printmakers and those who worked on canvas or paper sunk to below 2% - in line with what women in the art sector had previously claimed. In reviewing a major anthology of writings about modern art published in the early 1990s it was established that it included just 2 women artists out of 113, (1.8%).

Somewhere around the time when Mary Louise was getting her career going a group of women artists demonstrated outside the doors of the Metropolitan Museum of Modern Art (MoMA) in New York brandishing posters which asked '*Do women have to be naked to get into MoMA?*' This was a reference to the fact that although only 3% of the museum's works on display had been produced by women artists, 83% of nudes on the walls were female. Too often, when national collections did purchase work by women artists they went into storage faster than money put into an off-shore account. If you wished to see them an appointment had to be made with the museum to view them privately.

The treatment of women artists at one point gave rise to the 'Guerrilla Girls' who with a surfeit of irony produced around a dozen points in a public service message which identified '*The*

Advantages of being a Woman Artist working without the pressures of Success.' This included 'having an escape route from the art world in your 4 freelance jobs', 'not having to choke on big cigars and paint in Italian suits,' and 'knowing your career might pick up after you're eighty.' They also offered advice on how a woman artist might get herself into the art magazines by having her picture taken in a gorilla suit. Gorilla suits? Guerrilla Girls? Has to be a connection there somewhere!

In her final year at the Slade Mary Louise had noticed how 'the boys' at the School had been doing business with dealers, collectors and museum curators with a view to obtaining exhibition space, or at least getting together the beginnings of a network that would serve them advantageously in the future. The girls on the other hand just went on being 'dreamy' about becoming an artist. Perhaps though, the picture of an art world where men dominated had already begun revealing itself and the odds against making a breakthrough looked stacked against them. More importantly, maybe the 'silencing' of their creativity was also becoming evident brought about by their relative isolation including isolation from other artists and the constraints imposed by social conventions and expectations on women generally. There was also the perennial view that come marriage and child-rearing a woman had to do something less creative to support any art she still managed to produce.

Yet there was a growing belief that although 'artist' equated with 'male', women approached the making of art in distinctively different ways from men. The image of the lonely outsider subject to depression and attacks of doubt in between bouts of drunkenness and sexual promiscuity didn't sit at all well with most women artists despite some of them adopting these features of the male artist's persona in years to come. Examples to the contrary were there to be seen if you bothered to look. The sculptor Barbara Hepworth, for example, who was as surprised as her doctor when she gave birth to triplets still produced work amid the noise and clutter of a studio invaded by children: a floor strewn with toys, window sills stacked with baby clothes and corners incapable of restraining balls and spinning tops, all sat alongside the stones which she'd eventually shape into memorable pieces of art. Gwen John, seen by many as more gifted than her acclaimed brother Augustus, also lent currency to the view that women artists could adapt to less-structured environments for making images. '*Doing housework and doing painting*,' John said '*are about the same, only sometimes I learn something from painting.*'

Faced with the need to establish her reputation amid the hullabaloo of late-Sixties London, Mary Louise stuck with her vision of making art which meant something to the broad spread of society irrespective of whether it was made by a man or a woman. In finding her 'inner voice' and expressing it through a medium that would communicate her experiences to those who lived outside the bubble of the current art scene, she never considered the risks of being ignored or dismissed as just another minor female talent. Her oeuvre would always contain pictures that 'hadn't worked', were over-wrought, or would be seen as just plain 'bad art.' The first person to recognise this would be her, and if she still had doubts someone else would be asked for their opinion. The antithesis of this, of course, was what she accomplished in exhibitions and sales, in commissions and positive reviews in the art press. No small part of this was what people left in the way of comments in the visitor's book at her one-woman shows.

It is fair to say that the gender issue didn't seem to over-bother her much, or at least didn't show outwardly most of the time. She adopted the view that women's liberation in all spheres of activity could only be accomplished along with the liberation of society from unfairness, bias and injustice. That included men too. Perhaps though she didn't dwell long enough on gender discrimination in art to see how iniquitous it was. Perhaps also she didn't see until later (although she practised it) that women eschewed the linear approach to making art which was a characteristic of male artists, moving from oils to watercolours to etching, montage, illustration and lino-cut among others. Only now and again do we recognise what a tremendous asset women artists possess in this respect.

In any case, there were certain other things beginning to pre-occupy her besides the next steps in her career. The main one was a fairly longstanding matter which she'd first given voice to in the journal she'd kept as an adolescent. '*I am getting desperately in need of someone to love me*,' she wrote. '*I am frustrated now and don't know how to look at a man straight...*' As she grew into her twenties her ability in this latter respect obviously changed for the better, and she'd been dated by several men including a Bulgarian artist in Paris who'd proposed marriage. This she'd rejected: but being back in London saw the return of her old longing for a relationship which had the prospect of becoming permanent. At 26 just about all her old chums had got themselves married and were planning families. But where was this man who *she* could look confidently in the eye and glimpse a future there?

Well, in the words of the old song love was just around the corner: or if you insist on being more precise it was less around the corner than about to vault over the parapet of a bridge not so very far from where she lived.

CHAPTER 15

The young man in a donkey jacket and denims, casts a speculative eye over the gap in the fence. It is too narrow for him to squeeze through: but there again the corrugated-iron sheet alongside looks decidedly wobbly. He lifts one of his bright-yellow desert boots and gives it a thwack. The sheet growls angrily back. He gives it another boot, this one harder than the first. In slow motion the sheet of metal begins moving sideways increasing the gap before coming to rest tremulously on its last remaining rusty nail. With a triumphant grin the man levers himself through the gap and on to a surface he's been trying to access for some time now. It's the gravely-towpath of the Regents Canal which runs through London all the way to Limehouse and the docks.

Although 24-years old, the man – a Scot born and bred - has only recently become a full-time student. 'Not saying much for a grammar school education, then!' he has a habit of telling his mates. 'I was expected to go to university, but I must have got on the wrong bus.'

What he means is that after leaving school everyone around him, including his working class parents assumed he'd head straight for an apprenticeship in one of the engineering trades just like his brothers before him. Sure, it was good he'd managed to collect a few certificates before doing so, but now real life was about to begin and for the vast bulk of Scottish school-leavers at the time this usually meant passing through the factory gates. He'd avoided that by joining the building industry, initially as a painter and decorator then on arrival in London working as a builder's labourer. Shortly after settling in the capital, he heard that for the first time ever in the history of the British parliament the Prime Minister and the Leader of the Opposition were both ex-grammar school boys. Presumably they'd caught the right bus and knowing them had probably not even attempted to dodge the fare.....

Once on the towpath he turns his feet in a direction opposite to the sluggish flow of the coal-black canal water. He berates himself for not having brought his camera. Photographs would have enhanced the college dissertation he's putting together on the Regents Canal – a proposal his college tutor had met with a lukewarm response.

'I know you want to go on and be a civil engineer,' the tutor had said 'so shouldn't you target something a bit more relevant than a piece of infrastructure originating back in the early-eighteenth century?'

They'd reached a compromise eventually. The man said he'd add a somewhat new dimension to his dissertation arguing that canals, particularly those running through urban areas, should be opened up to the public as places for sport and recreation. 'As much chance as bringing back horse-drawn barges,' his tutor had sniffed. 'And anyway how are you going to go about getting access to these industrial relics? They're strictly out of bounds to the public.' It was true, but obviously his tutor had never been apprised of the latent power contained within a pair of desert boots.

Nonetheless, as he walks the towpath the man keeps a weather eye out for patrol-men, though mostly he focuses on the dereliction and decay surrounding him. It reminds him a little of Scotland – an industrial giant now grown old, stooped to semi-recumbence in advance of receiving the last blessings from ruinously indifferent policy makers. What he ought to be concentrating on, however, is the political meeting he is scheduled to take part in, something not unconnected to his anxieties about Scotland. The meeting is bound to be tense. It has been called at short notice because everyone in attendance is threatened with expulsion from the organisation they have belonged to for several years. That organisation is the Young Communist League – the youth wing of the Communist Party of Great Britain.

For the moment though the young man's mind is entirely engaged with the past. On the opposite bank of the canal an old wooden wharf tilts drunkenly towards the water as if seeking its own darksome reflection. Above him a couple of gulls who have long forsaken the sea circle indolently, killing time. Blinking at them through its shattered windows towers an abandoned warehouse. If the canal is ever to function as a recreational area for the public the young man thinks, there's a lot of cleaning-up which will have to be done first.

When he comes to a bridge he glances at his watch which suggests his brief sojourn on the towpath should now really be at an end. He is uncertain as to where he is exactly in relation to the venue for the meeting. It's like that on urban stretches of a canal – it's a narrow corridor sunk in the earth and fenced off from familiar landmarks. Faced with the choice of retracing his steps to where he began his walk, or searching in vain for another gap in the fence he decides neither will do and he should clamber up a steepish-incline to the stone wall forming the parapet of a bridge. This he does grabbing hold of the tall weeds and stunted bushes growing there. When he reaches the top he turns himself around and with a mighty backwards lunge manages to get his backside resting on the parapet wall. From there it's a relatively simple matter of swivelling round and jumping on to the pavement of the street beyond.

Trouble is when he lands with an almighty thud he finds himself within a few yards of a woman standing in a shop doorway. She blinks in surprise at his sudden appearance almost dropping the crayons she's been drawing with on a large pad of paper. 'I'm the old man of the canal come back to haunt it!' the young man says, opening his arms in an overly-expansive gesture. 'Prince Regent himself,' he adds, now feeling slightly silly 'the man who gave his title to that there waterway.' The woman stops blinking and smiles. Their eyes make contact for a second, but she says nothing. The man leaves her and strides away in search of his meeting venue.

Luckily, he finds he has landed within a few hundred yards of the basement premises where the meeting is to take place. When he arrives others have already gathered, sitting round a large table which fills two-thirds of the room. When all twenty or so people have assembled the chairman opens the proceedings by saying there is only one item on the agenda – the group's expulsion from the YCL unless they stop challenging the party line and agree to support it, unreservedly. The discussion on what is seen as the issues leading to this position ranges far and wide. A lot of mention is made of Karl Marx, Lenin and Mao Tse Tung. When it comes his turn to speak, however, the young man decides to concentrate on the experiences which moulded his political views as a teenager in Scotland, primarily among the Lanarkshire miners.

Just as he's about to begin the door to the room cracks open a fraction revealing the features of a woman, who blinks rapidly before apologising for being late on account of her losing track of time. As she edges into the room self-consciously seeking an unoccupied chair, the young man recognises her as being the person he might easily have collided with when he jumped from the parapet of the bridge. How would she now regard his views on political class struggle after introducing himself earlier as the old man of the canal?

The meeting lasts over two hours and would have lasted longer had not the person caretaking the premises appeared rattling keys. It is the signal to adjourn and catch last-orders at a pub across the road. The young man sits with a Cockney girl who the group consider as being his girlfriend, although being the era it is – the 1960s – relationships tend to be fitful at best and not noted for their permanency. From time to time he makes eye-contact across the pub with the woman he'd encountered earlier. She blinks when this happens: he comes to the conclusion she blinks a lot, mostly from shyness he thinks rather than any visual impairment.

Eventually, coming back from the gents he veers off in her direction and finds a seat beside her. He asks to see the content of her drawing-book after saying his interest in art was cultivated by the kind of school he once attended. Shyly, she shows him her sketches which she tells him she will later work on until they become finished work. Their conversation is a welcome relief from the politics they've been discussing for most of the evening. In the works of Marx and Lenin art is as likely to get a mention as the lyrics to 'Always the Bridesmaid Never the Bride.' They are still talking when the bell rings and the pub proprietor starts yelling 'Last orders, please!'

When she stands up to leave the man sees someone around five-eight in height with long, darkish-hair scraped back from a high forehead and fastened behind with an array of brightly-coloured clips and clasps. Beginning from between brown eyes flecked with green, her fleshy nose runs straight down to slightly-flared nostrils below which sits a mouth with strong teeth and a delicate chin which looks as if it might easily fracture if she talked too much. She wears no makeup of any sort, her cheeks being naturally high-coloured: under the taut skin her cheekbones are noticeable in the overhead lights. But it's her hands which the young man keeps returning to, especially her fingers. Long and graceful, they hollow inwards above and below the middle knuckle ending in the soft pads of rounded tips. He notices that she keeps her nails in good order despite traces of crayon and charcoal still adhering to them. As she leaves the pub he follows her, oblivious to the daggers being thrown at his back from his 'girlfriend' across the room.

He walks with her to the nearest Tube station learning she lives just one stop away and close to where he himself lives. 'Maybe we could meet somewhere in between,' he jokes 'or take a walk if the weather holds out.' It's more a question than an offer, but she agrees. They arrange it for the next evening. Leaving her at the entrance to the Tube station he watches her walk away in the direction of the escalators before striding after her. 'It's stupid of me I know, but in case you didn't catch it my name's Gordon...Gordon Wallace.' She blinks and smiles, wordlessly indicating she was probably already in receipt of such worthless information. 'And just in case you've forgotten,' she says ever so sweetly 'I'm Mary Louise Coulouris.'

CHAPTER 16

Looking back 40 years later, Mary Louise was to describe herself as a 'late developer' with regard to the opposite sex. In a short memoir she recalled the circumstances which led to us meeting in the pub that night and the effects this had had on her. '*Meeting Gordon was a cataclysmic event for me: it was the catalyst to a change in the course of my life.*' These are her words I rush remind you, not mine! She also explained why she'd joined the YCL having become '*bored listening to my father and his friends talking about politics very passionately, but with no intention of doing anything about it*':

> '*I have always had a strong impulse to match word to deed and deed to word if possible. This conviction came into other parts of my life as well. The compulsion to put down in a visual form what I saw was part of it, as was my impulse to respond to music with dance.*'

We spent the early days of our relationship getting to know each others background and views, although having both been expelled simultaneously from the YCL was as strong an agent as you could get in cementing a relationship. It was though, despite the politics, a very romantic time for us both. Mary Louise recalled:

> '*We walked in Regent's Park and Primrose Hill. We went shopping together met people from around the area, and did all the things you'd consider mundane but had suddenly become special and important to us. I took Gordon to see my parents and I don't think they were impressed. I think they would have preferred me to have a boyfriend different from him, someone whose social*

status was on a par with their own. But it didn't matter to us. We just laughed at how ridiculous this was. Falling for someone doesn't take account of such trivial things...'

By this time her brother George had married and moved into a rented flat near Primrose Hill. It was an attic conversion in an elegant Georgian-style property accessed by many flights of stairs. When he and his wife decided to start a family the inconvenience of this among other things prompted them to look for more-appropriate accommodation elsewhere. This meant their flat becoming available and with a bit of skilful negotiation George had the rental agreement transferred to his sister. She was overjoyed and within days had moved her belongings down the hill from Hampstead to number 4 Chalcot Square. Though reluctant to see her go, Mary Louise's parents helped with the removal.

But if our relationship developed in spaces ruled mainly by commonplace everyday things, there was no hint of that in what happened next. In the winter of 1968, three trawlers from the English town of Kingston-upon-Hull sank within three weeks of each other in the icy waters of the Artic Ocean. All together 58 trawlermen lost their lives. The tragedy filled the front pages of the newspapers and was detailed on television feeds direct from the scene. No one with a heart that beats red will ever forget the last call made by Phil Gay, skipper of the Ross Cleveland as she sank: 'I am going over...we are laying over...help me...give my love and the crew's love to the wives and families.'

Mary Louise and I discussed the disaster which reminded me of my teenage days among men who did a similarly dangerous job – the coal miners. Thank God, I'd never been present at a major pit disaster: but I knew only too well of individual deaths and the incapacitating injuries to men 'working the coal.' After being noted in the local press, such cases vanished into the obscurity of the mining companies records. I told Mary Louise

Workers
manning the
presses at the
'Scotsman'
newspaper.
Pictures
depicting the
Durham miners
and the trawler
men of Hull were
to follow.

that the Scottish miners had a saying that there was no such thing as 'an accident', that all 'accidents' were preventable if the proper safety measures were in place and observed. True enough, in the investigation following the Hull disaster it emerged that it was not a legal requirement to have a trained radio operator aboard fishing vessels. One of the ships which sank, St. Romanus, had no one capable of operating a ship's radio when she left port for the last time.

In time the impact of the Hull disaster faded from the media: and it was superseded also in the conversations Mary Louise and I continued to have during our perambulations around London NW5 and elsewhere. But unknown to me it had found a permanent lodging place in her mind. One day, when discussing her plans for the next step in her career, she told me she had decided to go to Hull and make drawings which would form the basis of a series of etchings about the fishing industry. I was to hear her later in life referring to this as 'Gordon's idea': but I always doubted it. I knew little of Hull and its dependency on trawling apart from the fisher lassies from Scotland's east coast who journeyed there every year to gut and box the herring. To me Mary Louise's plan was entirely in keeping with her desire to represent in her art the hidden achievements as well as the hardships of ordinary people in their everyday lives. It also represented *doing* something instead of just talking, except now it was in terms of artwork rather than hard-edged political activity.

So, in the late-summer of 1968 she travelled with her art materials on the relatively short rail journey from London to England's east coast city of Hull. Once there she became a familiar figure on the broad flagstones of St. Andrews dock. When exhausted by the expenditure of the creative energy needed to record what she saw, she would wander away to the Hessle Road – the city's biggest community of trawlermen-families for the past 150 years. No one in the Hessle Road area didn't have a family member or relative working at sea. It was no surprise then that one of their number Lillian Bilocca – or 'Big Lil' as she was known locally - took a leading role in bringing the grievances of trawlermen to the doors of government and those with a powerful vested interest in the riches drawn from the ocean.

Returned to London, Mary Louise went into top gear working-up the masses of drawings and sketches she'd made in Hull. Out of this came 13 prints and 2 paintings. I didn't see all that much of her during this time unless I went to the studio she still kept at Chestnut Cottage. Covered to the elbows in rubber gloves I'd watch her removing zinc plates from the acid baths, washing them clean before inking them over and passing them through the star-wheeled press she had bought shortly after returning from Paris. Ranged above her head were the finished prints hanging on a clothesline to dry.

As I viewed the results of her efforts I got as excited as she was. There were images of men repairing, cleaning and scraping boats in dry dock, hunkered-down on their haunches welding steel plates and staring through their visors at the spray of sparks caused by their blowtorches. In other places it was the fish-filleters, bobbers and kit washers who formed the subject matter. Even the quay-side auctioneers got a look in. There was nothing merely representational about these images: nothing photographic. She let colour define the form in most cases, turning the images into a spectrum of the whole environment which lifted them away from any danger of being simply documentary.

Soon her work based on Hull was on exhibition, first at the Oxford Gallery in Oxford then in August 1969 it transferred to perhaps its natural home at the Ferens Gallery in the centre of Kingston-upon-Hull. The exhibition was the backdrop to an opening event organised as a fundraiser for the efforts of 'Big Lil' and the women campaigning for greater safety aboard trawlers. There was music, songs and poetry about the fishing industry delivered amongst others by the playwright, Alan Plater, a native of Hull whose work at the time – principally scripting the highly-popular police drama, 'Z-Cars' - was being regularly featured on BBC television.

From a green mountain top people release a bird which carries their hopes for peace on its powerful wings.

The Ferens Gallery wasn't at the opposite end of the Earth from some of its counterparts in London: but it might well have been. Displayed on the walls of the main galleries in London was work which separated fine art from any hint of social relevance. Warhol's business art was busy eclipsing 'art-art': at least that was how a lot of critics and dealers saw it. Due to its origins in consumerism it was an art that reflected the individualisation and separateness – at times the loneliness – of a society being atomised and heading for the 'free market' in which the money value of an artwork in terms of an investment was replacing the real value of what it meant to someone seeing it. In that way the *invention* of modern art was fast replacing *imagination*.

Nonetheless, there were a few galleries in the capital and beyond who saw Mary Louise's work as being more than capable of selling to their clients. The Curwen in Central London was one, and the Perry Gallery in Brighton another. At times I thought the man from the Perry was a more-frequent visitor to her studio than I was! He'd arrive with an empty portfolio which he'd proceed to fill with Mary Louise's prints. He must have had interested buyers somewhere in the Sussex town because I was never to set eyes on any of them again.

Over a cup of tea he'd describe the art market as he saw it, advise the artist on the prices for her work and then turn to what Mary Louise planned to do next. It was during one such visit that I first got an inkling of what that might be. Blinking a little and letting the colour rise in her cheeks, she glanced at me and said, '*I want to extend the Hull idea to other industries, and since Gordon talks often about the miners I thought I might enquire about going down a pit.*' Now it was the turn of the man from the Perry to blink. As it turned out it wasn't too long before she was putting her idea to the test.

CHAPTER 17

The old bridge looks too narrow, too lean in the spine to take the large crowd about to set foot on it. There again, among the crowd are men who are used to treading narrow places, who spend much of their days crouching, kneeling, barely able to turn around. Here though, at the bridge, Elvet Bridge in County Durham, at least there's air to breathe that isn't salted with dust, and limitless light free from deep shadows. Above the noise, if they cared to listen, they'd hear the sound of water running below the bridge to the sea instead of pouring, oily and dark, over the steel toecaps of their boots.

'E Tenebris Lux.'

'Light from Darkness'

This is the inscription on one of the first banners to appear on the bridge. The people carrying it bend on its poles as a sudden gust fills it out like a sail before the wind. Like all the banners to follow, red will be the predominating colour. Red like the flames from burning coal: like blood spilt in the ceaseless quest to making a living.

A brass band, then a silver band, then the pipe band of the Trade Union Congress, all march in formation on to the bridge.

'Gresford' the miners hymn.

'Hold Me Lord in the Day Now Dawning'

Handel's 'Royal Fireworks'

'The Bonnie Lass o' Fyvie, O'

As one tune fades another capriciously takes its place: another hymn: something from Gilbert & Sullivan: 'Freedom Come All Ye' set to the tune of 'Bloody Flanders.' The people grouped at the far end of the bridge including Mary Louise tap their feet and take a trial-squint through the viewfinder on their camera.

As the crowd enters the bridge proper it thins of necessity, allowing some brave members of the local television station to stand on top of its parapets wreathed in cables and sound equipment. Along come three people typical of the whole on this day. On one side a stout woman looking a bit weary and carrying the day's shopping in a plastic carrier: in the middle her twelve year-old son, a chubby lad in tracksuit-bottoms looking pleased but a little self-conscious at being filmed. To the left of him a small, sinewy man of retirement age wearing a safety helmet and orange overalls and carrying a miner's lamp. More than he will be in similar attire today, the second Saturday in July, the day the old-timers still refer to as the day of the 'Big Meeting' but is now known to everybody else as the Durham miners Gala Day.

At one time this area of the Yorkshire coalfield had over a hundred pits employing 170,000 miners. Today, in 1969, though estimates vary one thing looks certain: before too long there will be less and less men checking in their lamps at the pithead. They don't know it, but by 1994 they will be all gone.

'Production For Use Not Profit'

'Suffer The Little Children To Come Unto Me.'

The straggly line of people at the far end of the bridge are becoming trigger-happy. As the head of the parade swings towards them they click and ratchet-on to the next frame, ducking into shade to reload in the days before the dawn of digital cameras. A flower seller snakes among them: she might have done a brisker trade by adding Kodak or Fuji film to her wares.

'Education is our Future.'

'Education: Organisation: Emancipation.'

The banners belonging to union branches from across the country appear, clasps of vermillion and gold, some frayed with age, others engaging in their first battle with the weather, all packed tightly together with the values they represent. After all 'Unity is Strength.'

Chilton Lodge, Seaham Lodge, Lumley Lodge, Easington Lodge, Sacriston Lodge, Harraton and Blackwell Lodge.....behind them a group of around eight young miners, a few pints taken, dancing in a circle, led by an accordionist, fumbling to remember how to do a jig, a hornpipe, arms extended upwards in the clear air without fear of bruising them on low ceilings and heavy pit-props. From the bridge parapet the TV cameras roll dumbly on.

Thornley Lodge, Browney Lodge, Monkswearmouth Lodge, Murton Lodge, Blackhall Lodge, Wheatley Hill Lodge, Lambton Lodge…… on every banner an image of some sort. On Chopwell Lodge: Marx, Lenin, and the pioneer Labour leader, Keir Hardie. On Boldon Lodge: the portrait of a miner, the pithead winding gear, the dignified front elevation of a working man's institute.

'Socialism through Education'

'We Take Up the Task Eternal, the Burden and the Lesson.'

Most of the parade has now swung off the bridge scattering the snapshot takers, leaving the rear echelon and the stragglers to follow. Older people, slower on their pins, women pushing baby-buggies, schoolchildren, a couple of mounted police side by side, chatting to each other. But there are still a few banners left to be seen. The Workers Educational Association ('The Right to Learn'): 'Justice for Working People' (sponsored by a local solicitor): a school banner showing a playground surrounded by trees and other greenery – 'The Community Garden.' In the end, all of them will make it to the Racecourse Ground where the 'Big Meeting' will soon get underway. The parade will finish in a rally addressed by the main union leaders and senior Labour politicians of the day.

As she stows her camera and heads in that direction herself, Mary Louise is satisfied with her afternoon's work. She's talked to a few people, exchanged smiles with others, and suppressed the usual anxieties about whether the film she's shot will later reveal its contents clear and unblemished. No one will have guessed that just a few days previously she'd travelled in a cage deep down into the earth and then travelled a mile and more under the seabed.

Unrecognisable now in slacks and a tight jacket with suede panels, she had donned brightly-coloured waterproof leggings, laced-up her boots with the steel toe-caps, crammed her long hair into a safety helmet and adjusting the miner's lamp she'd been allocated, set off on her journey through the boorish, sour-smelling intestines of the earth. She had mentioned this to one of the blokes next to her on the snappers-line, but he'd looked back at her bemusedly. Mining was men's work; a pit was a man's workplace. It was like letting a woman into the main area of a pub!

As she takes a last look over the bridge at the Elvet flowing seawards, she catches a snatch of a song she's heard before, carried on a gust of wind from the direction of the Racecourse Ground. Perhaps it's the seemingly-inexhaustible group of dancers now adding a song or two to their repertoire, spurred on by being below the vault of clear sky above their heads. She arches her neck and listens hard in an attempt to recognise the song.

Ah yes, of course… 'He's a fine lad, a canny lad the miner….'

CHAPTER 18

The officials at Hobart House - headquarters in London of the National Coal Board – were a bit nonplussed by Mary Louise's proposal. 'Why would you want to go down a coal mine?' they had asked more than once during their conversation with her. It brought back memories of Sir William Coldstream at the Slade – '…are you sure there's nothing else you could do?'

'Because I'm an artist,' Mary Louise repeated *'and my work is based on people. Miners are people whose jobs interest me, and I would like a chance to draw them. I can only do that satisfactorily by going down into the places where they work.'* Her voice rises as does the colour in her face as she makes this declaration. She sounds to herself a bit like one of the speakers at the Racecourse Ground on Gala day.

It wasn't easy sometimes explaining what artists did to people who didn't know any and relied on others to guide them through the madcap world they seemed to inhabit. Artists were a bit rum, weren't they? Odd-balls who cut off their ears and ended up spending time in the loony bin. And anyway, she's a woman for God's sake! Didn't they just do pictures of flowers and stuff usually in a sunhat?

Eventually, one of the officials came up with an idea. Let's send her to Jack Redding: he'll probably know what to do. Mary Louise was escorted through several corridors, up a broad staircase, and shown into an office which by the usual standards prevailing at Hobart House was anything but luxurious. Sitting at a desk was the small, slightly-woebegone figure of John (Jack) Redding. Unlike his colleagues he was immediately on the case.

Redding was an openly-gay, middle-aged man who lived with his more-youthful partner in a flat near Lords Cricket ground. It was a place over-furnished with antiques and Victorian bric-a-brac, including a stuffed owl in a bell-jar. Later, Mary

Louise and I would have dinner there sampling the delights of his partner's cooking. I can still recall that cooking: it provided some of the tastiest meals I've ever sat down to. First on the menu though was the small matter of a pit visit.

'*I don't think I ever fully understood what Jack Redding's actual job was,*' Mary Louise was to say '*but he was the person who made things happen for me. He'd not seen my exhibition at the Ferens, but he'd read about in the art press: so that would mean part of his job at least at the Coal Board had to do with cultural things. Anyway, he understood straight away what I wanted to do and was very supportive. It's great when you meet someone like that, someone who offers practical help to get things done.*' Though Redding didn't mention it at the time, his help was to range much further than simply organising Mary Louise's trip to a coal mine.

When asked what coalfield she had in mind Mary Louise was stuck for an answer. The state-owned NCB had pits all over the country so the choice was a very broad one. Whether Jack Redding suggested the Durham coalfield or somebody else did, isn't clear: but Durham it was to be and the only question then was…which pit? Though by 1969 the number of pits in Durham had shrunk it still left a lot of choices. Several options suggested themselves and in the end Horden colliery – sunk in the early years of the 20th century – was decided on. The pit with its massive winding gear stood on the edge of the North Sea close to the mining village of Horden which had given it its name.

Before being assigned to the tender mercies of Jack Redding, his colleagues at the Coal Board had gone on the assumption that Mary Louise would be satisfied with a brisk walk around the pit-head followed by a visit to the bottom of the shaft where there was enough headroom and activity going on to enable her to draw standing up. Now she informed Jack that she wanted more than this: she wanted to travel along a roadway taking her deeper into the pit workings and closer to the coalface. Even Jack was a little taken aback at the news. '*I hope you realise that at Horden,*' he said '*the workings stretch at least five miles under the sea. What you'll have is not just rock and earth above your head but a big part of an ocean!'*

Sitting across the desk from him the young woman with the pink cheeks blinked and summoned up her resolve. If that was the case then miners had to face that fact every shift they joined, every day of their working lives. So, why shouldn't she? It was slightly foolish to make all these arrangements to go there, she reckoned, if she was to be held back from viewing what essentially the place was all about, and what the men there had to do to earn their pay and meet their production targets. There was no question really of not travelling as close to the coal face as possible: the North Sea would just have to behave itself, that's all!

A few weeks later she was on her way to Durham and having wangled accommodation at Van Mildert College – part of Durham University – was soon preparing for the visit to Horden. Before that however, there was a chance to explore the areas around other pits in the coalfield. Drawings she made in Hetton-le-Hole and around Easington colliery would eventually be turned into prints covering a wide spectrum of subjects which in many cases related to the palpable sense of decay and deliberate abandonment of the people there.

The government of the day was bent on reducing the number of pits under its ownership, and the result was the creation of D-villages – places identified as being candidates for the axe along with their collieries. The letter 'D' assigned to such villages was intended to classify their ranking – 'A' 'B' and 'C' being a category where villagers could expect some degree of capital investment for maintenance and repair: soon however 'D' was being taken as meaning 'Death' or 'Destruction.' When you took away the pit why keep the village it had sustained for no matter how long? Many perfectly sound villages received a death notice shortly after the one served on its pit. D-notices effectively destroyed a culture that had been built up over generations. The pit-shaft was sealed along with the fate of the villagers, who unable to move on were left with little else than their memories, the slag heaps and the skeletal remains of the pithead winding gear. Perhaps Jack Redding, positioned as he was at NCB headquarters, had after all proposed the Durham coalfield to Mary Louise, knowing it held out prospects of recording in a permanent way something that would soon be gone.

Arriving at Hodren colliery on the day of the visit, Mary Louise was handed her safety helmet and yellow overalls, then checked-in at the cage which whisked her vertically downwards to the pit bottom. The miners accompanying her, forewarned of her arrival, showed little surprise at her presence amongst them and began loading her up with information about the pit. But little of it stuck as she moved from the cage to sit on a conveyor belt which was to take her deeper into the mine:

> 'The roads leading to the different coal faces were huge. Travelling on the conveyor belt was like going on the ghost train at a fairground. We went through a number of doors and gates which I was told were to secure the pit in the event of water flooding in from above. I was amazed to find they still used pit ponies down there, not many but still seen as doing a job. As we moved further into the workings the roads got narrower and narrower, the ceilings nearer and nearer to our hats. We had all to put on our lamps then. The journey seemed to take ages and we finally had to get off the conveyor belt and walk. I don't mind saying it was scary. We must have been a long way under the sea by then, but I didn't care to think about that. I must have looked worried because after walking for a while, stooping down in places they said that was as far as we go. The miners went on but I stayed behind with a couple of the officials, and after a bit more chat we headed back. But in another part of the mine they got me right up close to the machinery, the big cutters that churned away at the coal seam bringing down rocks and dust along with the coal. They called the

coal 'dusky diamonds.' At that section I was able to just about stand up and did a few quick drawings. Of course, the miners there spotted me and started doing these exaggerated poses as if they were having their photos taken.'

There was no suggestion of showing her into the pithead baths when she eventually resurfaced. Instead they took her into to the pit deputy's office and gave her tea. *'I had this complete loss of my sense of balance and direction after coming back to the surface,'* she said. *'I felt totally strange. When I left the pit I wandered the streets of Hodren for ages not knowing where I should be going. All I remember was buying sweets and chewing them one after the other for comfort.'*

Back home she followed the same pattern she'd established after Hull, working-up the images she had obtained in Durham ready for the etching plate: except in this case there was an important difference which was to shape her approach to doing art thereafter. The onset of claustrophobia at Hodern and the difficulty of doing no more than a few quick sketches there meant she had to rely on her memories of the place and what she had seen. Drawing from life, her usual modus operandi, had not been possible. It was an approach some artists in the past had insisted upon. Degas, for example, had declared that recalling from memory liberated '….one's recollections and invention from the tyranny which nature exerts.' Things metamorphosed in the imagination, and precise representations such as amateurs do when wielding a paint brush only revealed their pictures as fraud, or 'deceitful fiction' according to Degas and others.

Using her recollections of the trip underground she began producing another series of coloured prints from her studio at Chestnut Cottage. The Boadecia in London's Knightsbridge was the first gallery to exhibit the entire oeuvre – around 30 images, which included Hetton-le-Hole and scenes of other D-villages.

The miner's union as well as the press got interested, and the then President of the National Union of Mineworkers, Joe Gormley, bought a couple of her works. Not to be left out the men from NCB headquarters re-appeared and through Jack Redding invited her to give a talk at Hobart House with slide projections of her images. And yet more good news was in the offing.

Jack Redding had contacted an acquaintance of his to make a short film about Mary Louise focused mainly on her Durham art, but widening out a little to include her rationale for producing the series and her enduring memories of spending a few hours with the miners in the shadowy sinews of their workplace. The movie was partly-shot at Chestnut Cottage, and when she opened the door to the film crew there was her old fellow-student from the Slade, Dehta Hsuing, now under contract from the NCB to lead the charge.

After passing through the cutting room the film's duration was just short of nine minutes: it was then distributed to all the major cinemas in the country where it was shown before the main feature. What had started at Hull and then moved morenorthwards to East Yorkshire was now being brought to people in all parts of Britain.

CHAPTER 19

While all this was happening for Mary Louise, I was making progress with my own less-illustrious ambition to enter university. My application to do so had taken several months to pass through the Brobdingnagian-intestines of the university clearing system which had then voided the offer of a place in a civil engineering course. It was at Birmingham University. With mixed feelings I packed my suitcase, gave up my room in a shared flat in Kentish Town and said a painful goodbye to Mary Louise. Birmingham was just a hundred miles up the M1 motorway, but it might well have been in the Empty Quarter of the Saudi desert as far as I was concerned.

I arrived in Birmingham in plenty of time for the start of the term, but knew instinctively I wasn't going to like it. I got digs in Edgbaston and neither it nor the university itself suited me. I rang Mary Louise and told her so. However, being the possessor of just a single brain cell I sought to remedy the matter by moving even further away by transferring to Manchester University. Although I was later to love the people of that marvellous city, all I did there after arriving was a repeat performance of Birmingham. The off-hand attitudes of the lecturers, and finding myself in a world of mostly 18-year olds when I was 26 were certainly factors in my decision to quit, as I soon informed Mary Louise on the telephone. She tried to dissuade me by sending amusing cards she'd designed of me toiling over my studies and looking slightly bewildered at my new surroundings: but I was too pleased at the prospect of being back with her again to pay any attention.

Calling her again the next day, however, she told me she'd been in contact with someone at a new institution being set up in London which was likely to be given university status at some point in the near future. No one had decided on a name yet but it was probably going to be called the University of the South Bank.

I remained sceptical after she told me she'd fixed an interview for me in a couple of day's time when I'd returned from Manchester.

Following instructions I duly pitched up in a rather drab street in Brixton, South London at the far end of which sat an old brick building, formerly a local college but now an annexe of the new institution. I entered with serious misgivings and plenty of arguments as to why I shouldn't accept the offer of a place there. As it turned out, I took to it and the staff I met like a sailor home from the sea. The lecturers responsible for the main subjects were mostly young and energetic, and amongst the others I met was a Welshman whose preference for barrack-room language was immediately obvious, a retired solicitor who could actually make the law sound amusing, and a man of French descent who would later teach communication by reading Chaucer aloud to his students, pausing to let us roar out the naughty words in the Miller's Tale by ourselves. The ethos of the place and the vitality of the surrounding district (Brixton was a largely black community) convinced me that perhaps my objective of gaining a degree was not in tatters after all, and I happily signed-up for the three-year course.

In the couple of months I'd been away from London my old place at the shared flat in Kentish Town had been filled with someone else. They let me sleep on the floor for a few nights but it was never going to be a permanent arrangement. Mary Louise and I talked it over and we decided I should move in with her at Chalcot Square. I quickly secured a student grant from London County Council, so I was able to pay my share of the rent. But rather than it being an arrangement of convenience, I think we both knew our relationship was one with a future. In a couple of years' time we would marry, and a couple of years after that the first of our two children would be born. I was now more content than a cat in a creamery.

The flat in Chalcot Square, previously occupied by Mary Louise's brother George and his wife Christine, was in four-storey house which had once been in the ownership of just one family.

We were at the very top where the maids used to sleep. A small kitchen with a bedroom off it lay to the rear of the property: a large living room with high sloping ceilings was at the front: and due to the width of the living room, someone in the past had partitioned-off one side of it creating space behind which Mary Louise had a workroom and where she kept her acid baths and art materials. Jammed up under the roof beams overlooking this area was a platform about the size of a double bed. I used to climb up, stand on the platform and pretend to be Sir William Coldstream who had a similar arrangement, of course, overlooking the life-studio at the Slade. Although I say so myself, I think I did a pretty good job of mimicking his tight-lipped enunciation.

Mary Louise said the view from the front windows of Chalcot Square reminded her of the Parc Mont Souris in Paris. Certainly there was a large expanse of grass supporting some flowerbeds and several trees which formed the centre of the Square: but it was flat and miniscule compared to what sat adjacent to the Cité Universitaire. It was also fenced round so no one could get access to it but together with the tall, smooth-rendered houses gathered around it, it gave the neighbourhood a charm and peacefulness not always to be found in London. Perhaps this was what attracted a certain type of person to live in the area.

Diagonally across the Square from us lived Joan and Michael Bakewell, both working for the BBC at the time. A few doors down from them lived a couple who danced with the Ballet Rambert, and on the opposite corner was a flat occupied by Roger Graef and his wife. Graef was soon to be making a reputation for himself as an investigative, documentary filmmaker whose work for television began gathering awards in line with his programmes gathering audiences. In a few years time we'd all be baby-sitting for each other, or chatting at the local nursery.

Close by lived a variety of other people who made life in Chalcot Square interesting and amusing. The actor Joe Melia, for example, would appear on the pavement outside our front door wheeling his baby in a buggy and calling out 'Hot ice cream for the winter! Get your hot ice cream here!' The burly Scottish playwright, Peter MacDougall would also be seen barrelling along to the pub down the street, long hair and fierce looks scattering the neighbourhood cats. And the day was hardly complete if you didn't see the writer, Alan Bennett, wobbling by on an old upright bicycle on his way to the local library. Living as we did up under the eaves our flat was over-warm in summer and pretty damned cold in winter. But at least in warmer weather, as we sat by the window for air, there was always something to watch happening on the pavement far below.

Having a permanent base in London allowed me to get to know my future in-laws better. Mary Louise and I would make regular visits to the Vale of Health, often at the weekends when the Sunday afternoon visitors would gather at Chestnut Cottage. Her father would always offer me a whisky which I consistently declined. Scotsmen and the amber liquid are usually seen as indispensable companions: but I had a long standing aversion to booze generally stemming from experiences with drunks on the streets of Glasgow. My mind-altering substances now came in the form of politics and, increasingly, from art. And drugs, despite their increasing availability I looked on as a sheepish, almost cowardly way of dealing with life. Boring it may have been, but the invitation to 'Turn on, and drop out' just wasn't for me.

At Chestnut Cottage I had a chance to meet a range of interesting individuals drawn from the worlds of film, theatre and television: actors like Leonard Fenton (eventually to play Doctor Legge in EastEnders) and Dennis Quilley – an incredibly nice man, who after successful runs in various television dramas had now been given a contract by the Royal Shakespeare Company. Ralph Richardson too came a couple of times on his motorbike clad in his leathers as did Louis Heron, at that time deputy editor of the Times newspaper. And once the Labour stalwart and later leader of his party, Michael Foot came to tea after his addiction to walking daily on Hampstead Heath had been satisfied.

One man I was to get to know quite well over the next few

years was the actor Alan Bates, who lived with his wife in a house diagonally across the narrow alleyway separating it from Chestnut Cottage. Their garden was fairly exposed so I would often see Alan's wife doing her meditation routines on the lawn alongside Alan's father who sat muffled up in his suit and tie puffing away on his pipe. I sometimes tried talking to him but he remained largely unresponsive, due I think to the onset of age and memory loss. Alan's two sons, Benedick and Tristan, came to paddle with our children in the large reinforced-plastic swimming pool in the garden at Chestnut Cottage. Tragically the Bates were to lose one of the twins in a drowning accident some years later.

When the Sunday 'all talk but no action' sessions (depending on who was visiting that day) got a bit too much for us, Mary Louise and I would drift off to her studio to rail against the armchair-revolutionaries, then settle into a more positive frame of mind by discussing art. The Ashmolean Museum in Oxford had purchased one of her Hull prints for their collection, and there were sales too to some more big institutions like the banks and several of England's local authorities. Her part-time teaching contracts continued to be renewed, and through these she'd heard of a 'Prints for Schools' project which she was keen to contribute to and soon did. We were both optimistic about the future and I suppose it showed in the way our relationship developed. 'You're so alike, like peas in a pod,' some people would say. 'You're such opposites, no wonder you get on so well together,' others said at different times. We scratched our heads trying to reconcile these contradictory views before deciding just to get on with it in the way we had been doing.

Our optimism hadn't been dented by us both being formally deleted from membership of the YCL. We both got letters to confirm it. The root cause of our disaffection lay back at the beginning of the Sixties when cracks appeared in the international communist movement due to differences between the Chinese and the Soviets. If one man was to blame I suppose it was Nikita Khrushchev. As head of the Soviet Union he preached peaceful co-existence with the West: Mao Zedong the Chinese leader on the other hand, vehemently disagreed. It would be like inviting a wolf to play with your children, he might have said, or presenting your hard-faced boss with a thank-you card on the day he made you redundant. In short, the Soviet Union was saying oppose capitalism but live with it: China was saying overthrow it.

This fundamental difference rumbled on throughout the 1960s dividing communist parties throughout the world. The British Communist Party, like others in Europe, came up with arguably the most risible strategy of all. They reckoned that providing people voted into Parliament enough left-wing Labour and communist MPs, then socialism could be legislated for by the simple precedent of passing a motion in the House of Commons. One day we'd all be toiling under an exploitative capitalist system: a few days later we'd be out on the streets celebrating a new socialist state. There was a greater chance of the bookies going bust, or the Queen moving to a semi-detached in Stoke Newington. At any rate, the state of play politically towards the end of the Sixties was firmly set. Those supporting the Chinese line were the real Marxists: those who did not were declared 'Revisionists.' Mary Louise and I both fell into the former category. Who wanted to be a Revisionist? It didn't sound at all nice.

Unbeknown to us others in the Communist Party of Great Britain were also being expelled, or were resigning due to the dispute. One of these, a senior trade union official took with him a tiny handful of fellow engineers belonging to the Amalgamated Engineering Union and set-up the Communist Party of Britain (Marxist-Leninist). They dropped the 'Great' bit on the grounds that there was nothing very great about Britain's colonial and imperialist past. Once they got to hear about the forming of the CPB (ML) the disaffected YCL group Mary Louise and I had belonged to joined the new party. We didn't get as far as waving Mao's little red book at people: but we came pretty close at times. Shortly, Mary Louise was receiving an invitation to have lunch with the cultural attaché at the Chinese Embassy in London:

'I was surprised at that. They must have seen me as someone with the potential to exert influence on the cultural world in England. They showed films about the heroic workers in China, which was part of the Cultural Revolution underway there at the time. I realised the films were simplistic and over-emphatic: but I enjoyed the positive attitudes and the belief in what ordinary people could achieve. We had red mullet for lunch.......'

Our involvement with the new party very quickly took its toll on any time we had to spare, and to a growing extent on our self-regard. When we weren't out selling the party's newssheet and trying to get others to join we were in meetings. These could take up to four hours and wouldn't be ended, just adjourned until a later date. However, as Mary Louise put it '*...youthful energy can dim. We began to wonder if we really could manage a fifth meeting that week, or if we needed to go shopping on Saturday mornings instead. Personal and artistic life began to be important to us as well as political life.*'

In addition to this we had to contend with a growing awareness that we were of secondary importance to the industrial workers in the party. They were mostly skilled engineers whose unionised strength had been palpable in past industrial disputes and who now formed the Party's central committee. The rest of us – a motley collection of students, office and bank workers, printers, draughtsmen and the odd artist or two – felt quite cowed by it. I had been a building worker, but this didn't count for much because construction was regarded as a service industry and not at the hub of manufacturing. If this was the case I didn't exactly volunteer to pass the news on to the Irish navvies, carpenters and concreters I'd worked with, nor to the miners of Lanarkshire whom I'd known from early in life. Not that they would have bothered much anyway. A coherent political ideology had never been a strong feature of the British labour and trade union movement.

As time went on I began seeing that the party functioned on these two levels – the industrial members, and the back-up troops. It disconcerted me and I began contributing less and less to the interminable meetings I attended. If I had thought of chucking it in I was soon disabused of that idea by being told no one could resign from the party: your membership could only be terminated by being expelled. Having just recently been expelled from the YCL I wasn't quite ready yet to endure the same process over again.

Saturday nights were different though: not even the CPB(ML) felt they could call a meeting on the night of all nights for most working people. Mary Louise and I went regularly to the 'Singers Club' – a folksong venue which gave public performances in a pub near Kings Cross. It was run by Ewan MaColl (father of Kirsty who joined the Pogues) and Peggy Seeger sister of the American singer, Pete Seeger. MaColl was a genius, and a stickler for authenticating his work by deep and painstaking research in the field of traditional song. He also made several radio ballads for Charles Parker at the BBC highlighting the work of the miners, railwaymen, haulage drivers and the travelling people as the gypsies were called. The gypsies were of special interest to him because they were among the last remaining sources of traditional songs and the ways in which they were sung. These radio ballads still exist on old vinyl recordings and are well worth searching for.

When the 'Singers Club' was closed we went to classical music concerts and the opera, closing our eyes as we paid over the exorbitant ticket prices they charged. Usually though, it was money well spent. I'd seen Sickert's pictures of the insides of theatres, often music halls, particularly the views of the orchestra pit against the footlights and the curtain just about to open. Going to an opera enabled me to share what Sickert must have felt at such moments – the anticipation, the magical atmosphere as the house lights dimmed and the overture reached its climax. It blew my mind. I just willed that curtain to swish back and the place to fill with some thumping great arias. It's a reaction I never fail to have to this day.

At Chalcot Square we had a growing collection of classical records which we'd play constantly: everything from Baroque to Beethoven, from the wistful piano concertos of Schubert to the crashing conclusion of 'The Moldau' by Smetena. No few of these records came courtesy of Mary Louise's father who was a regular mid-week visitor to our flat. He rarely came without something for us, although sometimes it was in less-than perfect condition. He'd met up with a couple of old friends from California who'd returned to England during the days of Senator Joseph McCarthy, and were now establishing themselves in London. The man, Jake Schwartz and his partner Anita Sharp-Bolster, ran an antiques business nearby and were among the weekend visitors at Chestnut Cottage. But there were antiques and antiques, and below that… well, frankly just plain junk. Whatever George Coulouris brought us had usually been 'fixed up' either by Jake or himself. There was a chipped ceramic plant-pot, a couple of wobbly dining room chairs and a side-table which we could never get to sit on the level. We both agreed with George that it was the uneven floors at Chalcot Square which lay at the heart of the problem. Nevertheless, we loved him for it and if we made it disappear from view after a bit he never took it upon himself to ask why.

In the years to come he and his son, George Jnr. would help us in a variety of ways that made our lives even better. George Jnr. sourced a second-hand car for me – a dark blue Triumph 13/60 – which we managed to buy cheaply: and shortly thereafter George Snr. gave me lessons in how to drive it. Trouble was though, he insisted on keeping up a constant barrage of opinion from the passenger seat on everything from politics to acting while I was trying to perfect my three-point turn, or reverse without squashing passers-by on the pavement. The result was I failed two (it may even have been three) successive driving tests before I slinked-off to pay for private lessons with a driving school. Following that I got my licence without any problem.

CHAPTER 20

In between political meetings, anti-war demonstrations and selling the party's newssheet, Mary Louise had to get on with doing art and I had to attend to my study course. It proved difficult most of the time: at other times, impossible.

The planners of my course had designed it to help reduce the chaos in a construction industry where contractual disputes were reckoned to keep half the lawyers of the country in work. They did this by making all students heading for professional jobs in construction study together on the same course until their final year when they focused on their chosen specialism. Many of my fellow-students at Brixton, therefore, would end up with jobs in specific disciplines after appreciating the nature of the problems faced by their colleagues in other areas of construction. That was the idea and marvellous though it was it couldn't help but fail.

Two consequences soon made themselves known. First, I had to cover a vast array of subjects which kept me hard at it. Secondly, I knew a lot of what I'd be examined on in the first two years I would never use. A civil engineer, for example, would hardly ever expect to deal with issues facing a quantity surveyor: a builder would rarely venture into soils-analysis, or a structural engineer into design and architecture. True, I did get to appreciate the responsibilities my future fellow-professionals would carry: but as far as helping to avoid disputes? That left me sceptical. The origins of those lay elsewhere.

In building a structure you can't always predict what problems may arise which have to be dealt with at extra cost. And there were other things adding their weight to the industry's headaches like bonus schemes and 'The Lump' – an arrangement where gangs of building workers were hired for money paid straight into their hands, no questions or tax considerations being made. One building worker who went to jail and was blacklisted for his opposition to 'The Lump' later became a familiar figure on our TV screens. He was Ricky Tomlinson, better known as 'Jim' in the hugely-successful 'Royle Family.'

But it was one other inescapable requirement of my degree course which caused me the greatest anxiety: that was finding a job during the six-month period when the course was in recession. And not just any old job! I had to secure employment with a firm that undertook work in my chosen discipline of civil engineering. If I didn't comply I wouldn't be allowed to graduate and that would torpedo all my plans to become a construction professional. The staff at Brixton came to my aid helping me job-hunt, and soon I was to be wearing a different sort of donkey jacket from the one I'd had on the first time I met Mary Louise. This one had 'John Laing Engineering' written across the shoulders, and after confirming my contract they told me I was to be sent to a site of theirs in the Lake District where they were carving an extension to the M6 motorway through the hills there. In due course I was again packing my bags and kissing Mary Louise goodbye. This pattern of arriving and leaving was to be a feature of our life together for several years to come.

I returned to London after my spell on the motorway in a pretty battered condition. Six months of stressful employment had seen me lose weight and develop all the symptoms of having a stomach ulcer. Working long hours in the hills with food fitfully supplied from the back door of a Landrover (if it remembered to come), and the strain of being expected to design the temporary support works for a bridge, had begun taking its toll.

An engineer was also the safety officer at that time and I related to Mary Louise by mail my frequent angry exchanges with 'Blaster Bill' – the man who had the job of positioning explosives which broke up the rock standing in the way of the new carriageways. The main railway from Euston to Glasgow Central ran through part of my section and I lived in terror that 'Blaster Bill' would instruct his shotfirer to detonate the charges, which he frequently did, after I'd told him the signalman further along the line had informed me there was an express approaching. It shredded my nerves. At nights, before sleep, I could imagine the railway line shifting with the blast and a train becoming de-railed. In the nightmares which followed I saw 'Blaster Bill' pointing a finger at me with his shotfirer nodding over his shoulder. If my course at Brixton was meant to end such conflicts, no one had told the blaster about it.

I soon began recovering my health after re-installing myself in Chalcot Square, where Mary Louise brought me up to date with what she'd been doing in my absence. A further exhibition of her work at the Boedicia Gallery in Knightsbridge was more or less agreed for the following year: and this time it would show works she'd produced over a wider range of subjects. She'd been working hard and there was barely an area of the flat that wasn't covered with drawings, zinc plates awaiting the acid bath and finished prints going through their final drying-out. In between these lay a considerable number of etching tools, jars of printing inks, paint brushes and pieces of charcoal, lithography crayons, pastilles and sticks of chalk. In my time away she'd begun experimenting with other media besides printmaking.

But there was one other thing she'd got around to thinking about while I was away: that was getting married. '*Don't you think we should*?' she said, blinking the way she always did when not sure about how others might receive something. '*Gosh*!' I answered '*I had the same idea a couple of times recently, but forgot to mention it.*' We laughed. '*You fool,*' she said '*always joking, never taking anything seriously.*'

'*You should have been on the motorway with me,*' I retorted '*there weren't a lot of jokes going around there most of the time.*'

Next day we went to one of the street markets she loved to draw and bought a ring. It was a simple band of gold. My savings didn't run to much and Mary Louise volunteered to defray some of the cost. It would have to act as a wedding ring as well as an engagement ring: but that didn't matter. There is some deep psychology involved apparently in a woman deciding to get married, and following that have children by the man she's hooked up with. As far as I understand it, *she* decides when the time has come to do both, not the bloke. So, it was eminently correct for her to pop the question. Not that it mattered! I was just too pleased to have the privilege of agreeing.

One thing our engagement meant was that I now really *had* to take her to meet my family in Scotland. With all my moving around I had felt obliged to postpone it, but now I could delay no longer. Shortly before Mary Louise's teaching started up again and I was due back in Brixton, we took a train northwards – one which would pass under the bridge whose temporary support I'd been set to design. I pretended to have nodded off just before the train we were on reached that point on the route.

Once arrived in Glasgow we made the short journey to the new town of East Kilbride where my parents lived along with my younger sister and an older brother who was born with a mental handicap. As Mary Louise remembers it:

> *'Their house had three bedrooms but was small. (Gordon's) mother was an exceptional and lovely person. She always had a 'nice piece of fish' ready for us. I shared a bed with his sister and Gordon slept on a pull-down bed in the living room. They all made me feel very welcome. I suppose in a way Gordon's family was the extended family I never had. There were no close relations in my family on either side. They seemed to die young or be of little interest to my parents......'*

I took her on a tour of Glasgow, ending in a visit to Springburn in the city's N.E. corner where I'd been born and had spent the first six years of my life.

> *'Springburn (was) where Hyde Park Works had been. It built huge steam locomotives that were shipped to all*

parts of the world. We looked at the remains of it, the huge rusting hulk of the building. It was fascinating to wander round it seeing the remains of this industrial history. We also looked at the back-closes and tenements similar to the one Gordon grew up in with the washhouse at the back where boys played: it was a dare to jump off the washhouse roof. There were still children around playing there and they lined up for their photos to be taken…..'

During the all-to-short week's visit we made enquiries about getting married in the town and where we would hold the reception afterwards. We settled on having a civil ceremony in the predictably austere premises of the local authority, followed by a shindig at a grand old country house in a neighbouring village which was now a hotel. When I say 'shindig', of course, I really mean a ceilidh where the idea is to dance to a folk-band until that, or the whisky, leaves you in a state of temporary dysfunction. That doesn't apply to the bride and groom, however, who have to leave for their honeymoon in some semblance of sobriety. But on the night of the big day (April 2nd 1971) I remember both of us being greatly reluctant to leave the celebrations: only the beseeching of the cab driver waiting to carry us off finally wrenched us away. We spent our honeymoon in the Peak District of Derbyshire.

On our return to London we were free to resume our lives as normal. This meant among other things resuming our responsibilities within the CPB(ML). If there was any consideration given to art within the party, they made a marvellous job of not showing it. Perhaps they suspected, as Stalin had, that art in modern times was a subversive infiltration of the purity of the party and the ideological goals of the working class. If a draughtsman or civil engineer was seen as being a 'non-industrial' and therefore playing second-fiddle to the central cohort of the organisation, God knows where an artist stood! Mary Louise, borrowing from the 'socialist realism' art of the

Soviet Union, designed the covers of a couple of pamphlets and made a few posters containing graphics in the same vein. But her artist's integrity was at risk: the working class she'd celebrated in her Hull docks and the miner's series were very far from the stereotypes appearing in state-approved Russian art which had spanned the period of the Bolshevik Revolution to the Second World War and beyond. The Chinese displayed similar attitudes.

Yet art would have been a powerful force in what communists and socialists wanted to achieve. Good art provides the means of carrying out a scrutiny of ourselves with transformation in mind. Looking at an artwork should pose questions we wouldn't normally ask ourselves. These start with trying to understand the artist's way of seeing something, then move on to having a dialogue between ourselves and the subject of the work which amounts to a transforming self-examination. It's a very 'Marxist' process really. It takes us from the lower levels of consciousness to the higher, from the merely visual to stimulating the latent imagination. It all depends, of course, on the work and the artist who produced it. A good painter doesn't always make a good artist. In China art was instructed to 'serve the people': but in what way, it might be asked? After all a butcher's shop and a health service serves the people. Representational realism seemed to be the only answer provided, hence images of powerful figures (men mainly) wielding big hammers or yelling out slogans which you could only guess at unless fluent in both the Russian and Chinese languages.

One evening, sitting over our meal at Chalcot Square Mary Louise blinked before fixing me with a brown-eyed stare. '*Now we're married*,' she said '*don't you think we should try for a baby*?' I furiously struggled to stifle anything remotely like a facetious reply, but without success. '*I'm very agreeable to that,*' I said '*but can you wait till I've finished this delicious supper you've cooked me*?' I still have a dent in my scalp where the soup spoon hit.

The following year our daughter Saro was born to be followed two years later by our son Duncan. I attended both births at University College Hospital in Gower Street, just a stone's throw away from the Slade. Shortly, babies were to be added to the clutter of artwork and materials scattered around our flat. Barbara Hepworth would have recognised the scene immediately.

Babies have an annoying habit of completely changing your lifestyle without a word of apology afterwards. Suddenly, the five flights of stairs from the front door of Chalcot Square to our rooftop eyrie began putting a strain on us. Prams, carry-cots, packs of nappies and baby food – not to say the babies themselves – had to be hoisted-up or lowered down every time we decided to go somewhere. In addition, we shared a bathroom with two other lots of tenants – below us a widowed lady, below her a young couple like ourselves but yet to have children. If you wanted to bath the children you virtually had to follow a booking system: if you needed the loo it was best not to think about it too much.

The bathroom itself was antiquated with an old copper boiler you had to fire up hours before you could even start to think about submerging yourself in the ancient bathtub with its crowfoot-legs. Taking the children to Chestnut Cottage for the day, or staying there when Mary Louise's father was performing at a theatre somewhere outside of London, was a pleasure and a joy. But we were moving inexorably to the conclusion that our days as a family at Chalcot Square were coming to an end. The question was where were to go to next? The answer wasn't too long in coming.

CHAPTER 21

She sorts through in her mind what it is about the place that's different. Is it the scale of the town – small, but still with too few people to fill the spaces within it? Is it the quietness which descends for the rest of the day after the morning rush-hour traffic has gone? Or is just the faint scent of pine trees that has her mind instantly returning to a land much different from this one, yet in many ways similar. While her children play around her feet she stands at the big bay window facing out in the direction of the town's main street. Her eyes move over the buildings then up to the landscape beyond. It could be a wide-angled snapshot a tourist would take, or a view an artist might paint.

Above a broad expanse of water, broken into bits like fragments of a mirror by the intervening buildings on High Street, a steep hill rises to a summit clothed on one side by trees and on the other by sloping farmland where the crops sit waiting to be harvested. Today, when the sun struggles through the low cloud the fields are like long blond tresses on a girl's head, or where the harvesting has begun like solid geometrical shapes configured by the low stone walls enclosing them.

She studies them for a long time before letting her eyes return down the slope to the middle-distance where a ruined royal palace sits on raised ground beside a medieval church with a startling new spire made in laminated aluminium strips. Does she like this mixing of the new with the old: will she grow to like it, or hate it? She leaves the question aside and transfers her gaze to the north and west, looking beyond the smoking stacks of a distant oil refinery to where the high hills and mountains begin. She already knows the names of some of them: others she'll have to be coached in. In this country where she now is ancient titles persist despite attempts to drop them or alter the way they're pronounced. She doubts though if she'll ever manage to get all of them right.

After lunch she takes the children out in the double-buggy choosing no particular direction to walk in, letting her feet lead the way. She finds herself going up a steep incline and on to a bridge which spans the canal that wriggles through the town. Volunteers have already restored the towpath: and the basin nearby has several old boats under renovation. The canal brings back a memory of her husband's former obsession with inland waterways. But where is her husband now? In one of the cities which lie at a distance on either side of the town, places the men of the town go to for work. 'We're deserted wives,' she'd overhead another Mum laugh the previous day. 'They are all over us until we marry them and the kids arrive: then they're off enjoying themselves somewhere else.' To the woman work was an escape route from the dragging routines of family life.

She hasn't quite settled into any regular pattern of daily life yet: but perhaps when her eldest child is in playgroup then she'll have a chance of doing what she most wants to do. And that wasn't making a start on taming the garden, or unpacking the remainder of what the removal van brought.

Above the canal is a small public park which is a treasure. Apart from cutting the grass in summer the council let it roam free. She unbuckles the children from their straps and they whirl around while she sits on a stone and just looks. Through a belt of tall oaks and chestnut trees she can glimpse the ruined palace, the medieval church and a sloping field where cows graze below spectral pylons carrying high voltage power lines. She traces the pylons away into the rolling countryside, struck by the juxtaposition of the rural and the industrial. She'd noticed this before from the window of the train which had brought her and her children from London – a power station with its steaming cooling towers set against the background of the sea: an oil refinery belching flame and smoke while sheep grazed on the green sward around it. She had stored these glimpses in her memory. There would surely be a time when retrieving them would mean more than just casual remembrances.

Back home she lets the children climb the creaky-Slingsby ladder which pulls down from the ceiling at the far end of the hall so they can enter the dusty domain of the two attic bedrooms as yet unused. There are suitcases here still waiting to be emptied, two black hold-alls containing the tools of her trade, the contraptions and contrivances she's collected over the years and which she's determined will at some point be given renewed life. 'Even if it's just half-an-hour a day,' she recalls someone like her saying many years ago, 'then that is better than doing nothing.'

She is still in the attic room when the front door bangs open and a familiar voice bellows out a greeting. The children make an immediate dash for the landing which leads to the top of the Slingsby-ladder. 'Daddies home! Daddies home!' The man comes quickly up the ladder to steady them and guide them slowly down to the safety of the hall. The woman is the last to descend, smiling, pleased that for once her husband has taken an early day from work. They embrace and go into the living room where the floor is scattered with toys and games. She thinks he looks tired and tells him so. 'Never mind,' he says 'the job will be finished by Christmas and then I can rest here with you and the children.' What will follow in the new year of 1978 he has no way of telling.

After supper he reads the children a story, his son on his knee, his daughter squashed beside him in the armchair. 'Not that one again!' he wails in pretend-anguish. 'We've been reading that story for the past six nights!' But they insist, and as he reads his daughter mouths the words silently to herself from memory. She must know it off by heart by this time! The children are as different from each other as a teddy bear is from a model racing car. The girl talks all the time even if her language skills haven't caught up yet with her ideas and opinions. When she doesn't know the words, she sort of lah-lah's along before sticking what she can say on the end of the sentence. The boy is quite the opposite. In receiving the answer to a question he stands in the middle of the floor looking off into a high corner of the room as if testing the veracity of what he's been told. In his brown dungarees – too long for him so they have to be turned-up at the cuffs – he cuts a figure that makes his Mum laugh. It makes the man smile too: both his children have that effect on him, although strangely this is often accompanied by him getting something in his eye. At least that's what he tells his wife when she sees him wiping it away with a handkerchief...

Chapter 22

Added to the inconvenience of having to lug our children up and down several flights of stairs at Chalcot Square was the fruitless search for somewhere better to live at a price we could afford. But there were a couple of other things which encouraged the idea of us living elsewhere outside London. These were the heat-wave summer of 1976 and a period I was obliged to spend in prison.

Before any eyebrow-raising begins over this latter fact, I should explain quickly it was Holloway Women's Prison that detained me, and I was allowed home every night without supervision. No record of the time I spent at Holloway will ever appear on police files: only my fingerprints might remain somewhere on the structure of the new prison I was hired to help build alongside the old one in North London. It wasn't to be my only involvement with construction matters within the prison service, but it was certainly one which helped bring about substantial changes in my life and that of my family.

All our thoughts about moving, however, became irrelevant when we were told that Mary Louise's mother had been diagnosed with cancer. Although she must have been ill for some time she never let it be known to us and was always on hand to care for our children whenever we asked. She was taken into the Royal Free Hospital in Hampstead and within three weeks she passed away. Along with other family members we visited her almost every day in hospital, emerging into the bustle of London's streets leaden-hearted at her rapid decline and the pain she had to endure. She had been a mother-in-law to me and a grandmother to our children few could equal. A calm, ineffably-kind person who seemed as if she would always be there for us, Louise Franklin Coulouris was someone you just couldn't possibly forget: and we never have.

By this time I'd graduated and was working full-time on a

number of large construction contracts in and around the capital. For a six-month spell I'd also worked for the Building Research Station in Hertfordshire, who presumably thought highly-enough of my spell there to offer me a permanent contract. I thanked them and said no. Despite my experiences on the M6 motorway I still yearned to actually build things…see them emerging from the ground…watch them grow like I did my children. I couldn't get enough also of the talk and banter of the Irish labourers who swarmed over construction sites wherever I went. They are surely the most lyrical race in the world! Consequently, I took jobs with a string of well-known contractors skipping on when a site was 'out the ground' and only the boring finishing trades were left to do. Several large buildings and other structures in London which have serious faults, or don't work the way they should can probably be put down to me being the engineer.

But at least I was close to home and Mary Louise even if by now things were getting pretty hard to manage. Just taking our children for a walk in Regents Park amounted to a logistical exercise comparable to organising a military campaign. Bikes, buggies, bags, bottles, babies…they all had to be carted up and down, and you prayed you didn't meet a neighbour coming in the opposite direction. On top of that the Chalcot Square area was changing from having lots of people like us who rented to those who could afford to lash out several hundred thousand buying a property there.

The landlord of our flat was quickly on our case, offering to buy us out for sums that seemed to increase incrementally with his feverish plans to renovate the entire house and sell it off to a single purchaser. Mary Louise and I decided we ought to jump before we were pushed. We considered moving sideways: but what was the point in risking the same thing happening elsewhere in London's leafier districts? Why not move away altogether to a place where we could grow in larger spaces, and where 'gentrification' – that ridiculous euphemism for turning whole areas over to the wealthy – wasn't even a gleam in a property speculator's eye?

Very early one Friday morning I got into my old Triumph Herald and headed up the A1 to Edinburgh. I'd decided that if we relocated to Scotland's capital city with its history of supporting the arts that would soften the blow for Mary Louise of leaving London. In my excitable state I'd completely overlooked how adaptable she was: born New York, lived Beverly Hills followed by Port Chester and Connecticut, then London, Paris, Berlin and other places like Moscow in between. '*To me (going to live in Scotland) seemed an adventure and a challenge*,' she was later to write.

Arriving in Edinburgh I was appalled to find how expensive the houses were, and wasted little time moving on. I was due back at work the following Tuesday so I didn't have the leisure to hang about. I got back in the Herald and began driving west on the M9 motorway. '*First decent place I see I'll pull off and take a look*,' I told myself. That opportunity presented itself about twenty-miles out. Through the passenger seat window I saw a small town sitting by the side of a loch with what I took as a ruined castle by its banks and an old church with a modern metal spire towering above it. I took the next slip-road exit and doubled back on a pleasant tree-lined road running between fields of grazing cattle. Shortly, a sign told me I was entering the Royal Burgh of Linlithgow. It was news to me: even as a Scot I hadn't heard of the town before.

'Edinburgh' People and their modern appurtenances set against the spires and towers of a previous age seldom failed to evoke a response.

I parked my car on the High Street and almost fell from there into the office of a solicitor-cum-estate-agent directly opposite, explaining to the lady inside what I was about and how limited my time was. She listened, then rising to her feet grabbed some keys from a board on the wall and told me to follow her. '*I might*

'Feeding Ducks' On the snowy slopes below Linlithgow Palace a family endeavour to see that more than the swans get their fair share.

just have the place you're looking for,' she declared.

We walked just a short distance uphill to a street called Strawberry Bank where she showed me around a house there along with its owner – a man who was the local joiner and funeral undertaker. Jimmy Bennie was a short, bustling, cheery individual who couldn't have been further away from the sharp-eyed property merchants in London. I warmed to him immediately and guessed Mary Louise would do the same.

The house at number 5 Strawberry Bank had a hall like a long spine running through the middle of it off which sat two bedrooms, a dining room and a large lounge with egg-and-dart cornices and a large, moulded-plaster centre piece on the ceiling. A wide, three-sectioned bay window looked on to the street from the first storey, and although the main railway line between Glasgow and Edinburgh ran on the opposite side of the road it appeared to be anything but intrusive. Later, Mary Louise was to recall:

> *'The house was a fine solid house about a hundred years old. In fact it was a large upper flat with a small garden at the back. The view from the living room window was magnificent. Linlithgow has a medieval centre, a palace where Mary Queen of Scots was born and a loch whose surrounding park is called 'The Peel.' Viewed from the window, especially in winter when there was a scattering of snow over the hill behind, its medieval quality came to the fore and you could easily imagine people (from that time) going about their business and the (Royal) court arriving from Edinburgh bedecked with jewels and hunting in the surrounding country. I did several large watercolours on the spot with my easel in the living room.............'*

Before finishing my tour of the house, Jimmy Bennie showed me the *piece de resistance* by taking a long pole with a hook on the end and pulling down what I thought was a large section of the hall ceiling. Attached to the back of it was a wooden Slingsby loft-ladder giving access to two further rooms in the attic. They were both large with sloping ceilings and dormer windows and ran the entire width of the house. This made 5 Strawberry Bank a six-apartment dwelling and well worth the asking price of £12,500. A few weeks later Mary Louise, bringing our daughter Saro with her, came to take a look and shortly after that we were up to the ears in house surveys, deposits, mortgages, insurances and all the other paraphernalia which goes with property purchase. Soon, it was to be the removal men who became the focus of our endeavours.

Back in London I gave my boss six-weeks notice before setting my chin firmly back in the direction of building Holloway Women's Prison. I didn't manage to stick it out, however, until my official leaving date. A fairly large number of 'bad girls' saw to that.

The new section of the prison was being built alongside a large chunk of the old, and was overlooked by dozens of cell windows behind which lived the female prisoners. From these windows came an almost constant stream of voices offering us marriage or sex, irrespective of who we were in terms of age and physical condition. The two Home Office engineers I worked with at the site had told me to expect this and not to respond, not even to indicate I had heard it. When it came to requests of a different sort, however, few of us could just shrug them away or absorb them in muttered, sometimes humorous, undertones.

A day never went by without us being asked to contact the prisoners' children through telephone numbers the women called out from their windows. We assumed these were the numbers of grandparents or other relatives caring for the children while their mother was inside. '*Her name's Kimberley. She's only four. Tell her Mummy's still in hospital but will be home soon.*' I was assured by my engineering colleagues that many of the women concerned wouldn't be re-united with their families until their children had grown into their teens on account of them serving long sentences.

But try as I did to let such requests fall on deaf ears, I found it increasingly difficult to blot them out entirely. I had two small children of my own and knew only too well the wrench of being away from them for much shorter periods than prisoners had to cope with. It all started getting to me, and I would find reasons to stay in my office rather than go out on site. On top of that was the weather – the hottest summer on record. The heat and the heckling prisoners was enervating and becoming too much to handle.

What really did for me though, causing me to infract my period of notice, was when I re-routed a pipeline through the site and had an excavator dig a trench which unearthed an old cess-pit from Victorian days containing scores of rings, bracelets, necklaces, earrings and other such items. On closer inspection they proved to be worthless prison 'jewellery' fashioned from bits of wire twisted into all shapes and sizes. Over a century and more, whenever a cell-search was forewarned the women prisoners had hurriedly washed these illegal objects down the lavatory where they'd collected in the cess-pit. It was pathetic and for me too sad a sight to contemplate. A few days later I left the site and never went back.

Before I left, however, a stroke of luck befell me. I bumped into a man who was a director of a civil engineering firm. The firm was known for its 'design and build' approach to contracts, meaning their staff was as used to the construction site as they were to the drawing office. And I knew also they sometimes went in for 'quirky' contracts – ones which were a bit out of the ordinary and often very challenging.

Ian McEwan, one of two senior directors at the company, was a gem of a man – intelligent, thoughtful, someone who would never give up on a problem until he'd teased out a workable solution. At home he cared for the needs of his invalid wife: outside of that his interest lay only in bringing difficult civil engineering projects to fruition. He described a job the firm had starting soon, and asked if I'd be interested in being the engineer and contracts manager on it. I asked where the job was. '*Oh, in Scotland,*' he said. '*If you were interested I'm afraid you'd either have to resign yourself to long periods away from home, or else move there.*'

Ian was a fellow-Scot, so I suppose he recognised the little jig I did in front of him. I explained how I was moving my family soon to Linlithgow, a town he knew well him being an Edinburgh man. '*That would probably suit you fine,*' he replied '*the site is in Glasgow just 25 miles away. You could guarantee being in your own bed every night.*' I repeated the jig, though had I been given the numbers I'd have danced a full Eightsome Reel.

At Chalcot Square I told Mary Louise about what had transpired. She was as pleased as I was. We were even more delighted when Ian sent my contract a few days later. It showed that my salary was set at considerably more than I had been earning at Holloway. I guessed though I would be expected to give a pound of flesh or more for the money. But for the moment I was too happy knowing I had a job to go along with the house we'd bought. It made the London heat wave and my experiences at Holloway seem like no more than passing inconveniences. '*Next step is to ring the removal men,*' I said to Mary Louise '*and then start the whole business of packing-up our stuff.*'

As I hung out the window overlooking Chalcot Square trying to get cool, I had the feeling things were all changing for the better. It might be 1976 would turn out to be a good year after all: except, of course, it couldn't. Whatever else happened, no matter how exciting, it would still be the year we lost Louise Franklin, my very sweet mother-in-law. There was nothing anyone could do to change that.

CHAPTER 23

Leaving London behind also meant leaving some of Mary Louise's art equipment behind us as well. Not being able – at least for the time being – to bring her star-wheel printing press to Scotland was a particularly hard blow: it was like leaving a treasured heirloom behind on the train. Fortunately, the resurgence of interest in the art of the print had preceded us up the A1 and she quickly found newly-established print studios, part-funded by the Scottish Arts Council, in both Edinburgh and Glasgow. The studio in the capital was adequately resourced and located in a former-laundry at the east-end of Princes Street: so the smell of inks and acid baths hadn't yet eclipsed those of soap powder and bleach in some corners of the premises.

Mary Louise recalled the experience of going there:

'I was one of the first members of the Edinburgh Printmaker's Workshop, and loved going there to work on my prints. They were still my primary interest at the time, and the workshop was a friendly place and I felt able to do creative work there in etching. There was space to experiment and I began trying different approaches like the juxtapositions of plates I had developed of the Central Belt of Scotland as I saw it for the first time. I produced a series of 34 etchings which were all an expression of my reaction to the area. One of the ways I saw it was an area of strong contrasts – tractor factories seen next to cows in a field: a medieval palace against a petrochemical plant. I experimented with different combinations of plates resulting in titles like 'Central Belt 1', 'Forth Valley' and 'Flower of Scotland'.'

A touring exhibition of these works was hosted by several venues in Scotland with the artist receiving a fee on each occasion. Thanks to a gallery curator called Jenny Crawford who saw the significance of them, Mary Louise's work was later to be given a one-person show at the Crawford Centre in St. Andrews and following that parts of the series along with other thematic images of hers appeared in a three-person show at Glasgow's Print Studio. Alexander 'Sandy' Moffat, Head of Fine Art at Glasgow Art School wrote the exhibition's catalogue and it received good notices. Sandy has a formidable talent which ranges across several subdivisions of the arts in Scotland: but he was ever approachable and never short in giving people his broad grin. He remained in contact with Mary Louise's work for many years afterwards, and helped her in several ways to get her career moving forward in what she described as *a new culture, a new ethos.*

That 'new ethos' had issues for her which were shared by all young mums – what about the children? Going to the Edinburgh Printmaker's Studio was the equivalent of leaving home for a part-time day job in the city. We soon made contact with other couples in the Linlithgow area who faced a similar situation. They had already formed a child-minding group which worked on a point's basis – one-hour's baby-sitting earned one point, after midnight two points. When you had accumulated enough points by this method you spent them having a member of the group seeking points for themselves, look after your children. It worked out fantastically well, and meant father's had direct participation making them familiar child-minders in your home whether in daylight hours or at night.

It was also a source of making new friends and a way of enlarging our knowledge of the district and seeing how other people lived. There were around 12 couples in all. Some of them lived out in real farming country surrounding Linlithgow. Some of my baby-sitting nights were spent in large farmhouse kitchens. I rode a horse for the first time at one place. Self-sufficiency was being tried by some of the couples who'd bought old houses or farms in the area. One had pedigree sheep and spun her own wool. Many of them were in the anti-nuclear movement and we certainly felt a rapport with them.

During this period I was working on the site in Glasgow Ian McEwan had told me about. When I first saw it the jig I'd done for him in London now became something quite different: nothing like a funeral march but something that might be heading in that direction. It would prove to be my toughest job yet, but as I got into it I took on the stress that's part of every civil engineering contract and began to enjoy the challenges of working there.

The contract was to build a floating breakwater in Alexander Stephen's Graving Dock in Govan – a dry dock that had been used over many years to repair and renovate ships of all sizes and descriptions. When you think that ocean-going vessels had been put in Stevie's yard, then you'll know how big it was. I'd say it was almost the dimensions of the pitch at nearby Ibrox, home to Rangers F.C.

My job was to manage the process of constructing the breakwater in sections using concrete and steel with giant sections of polystyrene inside to give it buoyancy. When we'd completed the construction phase, the dock would be flooded and tugs would tow the entire structure, section by section, down the river Clyde to a marina at Rhu where they would be assembled providing a barrier which would protect the vessels there from the battering sea. It was one of my firm's 'quirkier' contracts – in fact, a prototype for other, even larger structures needed by the oil industry in the Middle East and elsewhere.

The trouble was I had to work to a very tight completion date so that the entire structure would be built and in position at Rhu before the seas there got into their winter mode. That meant long hours on-site and what with travelling to and from Glasgow, I was only seeing my children when they were ready for bed and my thoughts were turning in the same direction.

My new job was adding nothing to Mary Louise's struggle to find her feet in an environment that was still strange to her.

So, in the few weekends I had off I took her to visit my family. Mary Louise recorded her impressions of these first visits and the others which followed:

> '*My father's origins were humble amongst the immigrant population of Manchester, but by reason of his success as an actor we (his family) had become middle-class. Gordon's family had more of a sense of being part of the broad sweep of the working class. At family gatherings it is expected that everyone will have a song or poem prepared to entertain the group. We were all expected to contribute something, but I failed hopelessly on this score because I simply don't have the skill. Our children grew up in this tradition. It suited Duncan because he's musical and later in his teens became quite the star when he took along his guitar. Our daughter Saro wasn't so keen........'*

For all her talent as an artist with a growing reputation and her love of music and dance, when it came to singing Mary Louise was what people call 'tone deaf'. We used to joke about it, but I knew how far I could go in teasing her on the matter. Unlike her mother who had a light, melodious voice and her father who'd seen his ability at singing as worthy of gracing a theatre stage, Mary Louise just couldn't 'hold a tune' well enough to stop the cat running for cover. It didn't stop her trying though, singing along to the music that was ever-present in her studio as she worked.

The start of 1977 brought heavy snow to Scotland, and although we didn't realise it at the time it was to lie for around three months blanketing our house and garden to a depth of two-feet. The canal running at the rear of our house froze over allowing Mary Louise to strap on her skates (the very ones she'd used in Los Angeles) and take to the ice. Her Father arrived from London at one point with two sets of children's skis – one set each for both of our children. '*In London he had always supplied us with 'finds' he'd made in junk shops and was still doing it!*' Mary Louise recalled. '*The skis were second-hand but quite serviceable, so I took the children to a park with a bit of a slope and they loved it.*'

Our house at Strawberry Bank was in need of renovation which had to be carefully budgeted-for and carried out mostly when I was away building my breakwater. First to go was the old Slingsby ladder leading to the attic rooms which was dangerous for children. In its place we had a proper staircase built. Next was to put in central heating replacing the old open-fireplaces which were a feature of every room. We kept the surrounds and mantelpieces although they were nothing spectacular to look at, but had gas-fired radiators fixed to at least one wall in each room. '*It was difficult for me,*' Mary Louise said '*but somehow also fun and exciting coming to Scotland. It was often quite chilly in the house even with the radiators on and I got chilblains and there were times when I badly missed my Mum.*'

But there was always something in her art which made up for the shortfall in other ways. '*Two of the big watercolours I did of the view from our bay-window sold. The first was bought by a Procurator Fiscal (roughly the equivalent of the Director of Public Prosecutions in England) and a second one was commissioned after somebody saw the first one.*'

Our first Christmas in Linlithgow was celebrated in my absence: the breakwater construction was behind schedule (when is a civil engineering contract ever delivered on time!) and Ian McEwan collected me from home on the 'big day' to take me to the dry dock. Not that this was an unfamiliar occurrence in Scotland: even in the late-Seventies most people with jobs went to work over Christmas and took a week off at New Year. But this tradition was already beginning to crumble as the consumerist society waxed ever-stronger. Our children expected both parents to be in attendance as they opened their presents, or emptied their sock as we still did. Mercifully, despite having floodlights to work under at Stevie's graving dock, I got Ian to drive me back home a bit before supper-time on Christmas Day. Poor Mary Louise… she didn't complain or even give me a reproving look. I made a silent vow, however, never to let it happen again.

In what should have been the spring of 1977 (the snow still lay crisp and deep and even), my breakwater was ready at last to be launched. To say I felt apprehensive about it qualified for the award of 'Understatement of the Year.' I was tired and pretty washed-out, and only nervous energy seemed to be keeping me going. The reason I was verging on exhaustion was not just due to the long hours, the travelling and the bitter cold on the Clyde waterfront. It lay also in whether the breakwater would actually 'work.' By that I mean would something made in part from heavy materials like steel and concrete actually float with the 'freeboard' – the amount it showed above the water – specified, which was plus or minus one-quarter of an inch? It wasn't much to play with and if it didn't achieve the required freeboard then in the words of my colleagues on the site – I was 'scoobied.'

On the day previous to the launch we flooded Stevie's dry dock, and on the day itself I was on the site earlier than ever along with Ian McEwan, senior staff from the firm and the people who'd financed the project along with many others with an interest in floating breakwaters of the sort we'd put together. The media turned up, of course, and I'm sure I wasn't the only one there holding his breath and telling his heart to shut-up and settle down!

After several anxious periods when the sections wouldn't separate without intervention by a couple of brave souls armed with crowbars (I'd suspended health and safety regulations for the day) the first piece of breakwater suddenly broke free, plunged like a drunken swimmer into the murky water of the dock and disappeared completely from view only to re-emerge on the surface a few seconds later, where after a lot of roiling and bobbing about it finally settled down. From where I was standing high up on the dock steps I could see it floated, but although I could only guess at the freeboard I knew at worst it wasn't a cat's whisker short of the one specified.

Did a cheer go up from the men who'd worked with me to reach this result? I can't remember. I expect it did but I wouldn't have heard it anyway above the great wave of relief breaking over me. There were handshakes all round and faces which had previously looked worried now broke into wide permanent smiles. I declined the offer of going aboard one of the tugs towing the sections downstream and went home on the train to my wife and children. As it turned out it was a train journey which not only headed me towards Linlithgow and Strawberry Bank but pretty soon afterwards changed the direction of my working life for ever. I was to continue with life in the construction industry, but in an entirely different capacity. It was one where a hard-hat and protective clothing would never again be set against personal expenses on my tax-return.

CHAPTER 24

After adding up all the lost holiday entitlement I'd accrued due to building the breakwater, I told the firm I was having a month off following its launch. They weren't chuffed but neither were they hostile about my decision. They said my next contract hadn't really got going yet and could well live with me being absent for a bit. I knew it was a bridge job but neglected to ask where it was assuming it would be somewhere in Scotland. As it turned out it wasn't, but because I'd failed to ask it didn't cast the slightest shadow over my anticipation of a delightful four weeks of idleness.

Being around Strawberry Bank every day meant I was able to see at close quarters the vicissitudes of Mary Louise's life as an artist, wife and mother. Our daughter Saro was now attending playgroup which ought to have freed-up time for her mother to start applying the 'Hepworth Principle' – a view expressed by the English sculptor Barbara Hepworth which maintained that doing a bit of art everyday was better than doing none. But it didn't always work out that way. Saro was a difficult child to manage – lots of nervous energy coupled with problems over making relationships with other children. She was rarely happy in group situations and as often as not Mary Louise's plans were blown apart by the need for her to stay with Saro at the nursery. The frustration at seeing her planned and paid-for sessions at the Edinburgh Print Workshop turn to dust must have been intense even if it rarely showed. With me around the place, however, she could book a place at the workshop confident it wouldn't have to be cancelled at the last minute.

Her series of prints on Scotland's central belt went on being added to, developing out in several different directions to include urban street scenes, buskers and eventually inside a local factory which made shirts for some of the big High Street retailers. With our children in the back seat of the Triumph Herald I'd drive her to the shirt factory just as the backshift there was clocking-on, leaving her to return later on the bus. Out of this came a further set of images which later became a series of prints devoted entirely to the female employees at Sneddon's shirt factory

It's in the way of the art world, however, that an artist's work is often compared to what critics and reviewers see as influences from other artists in the past. Mary Louise wasn't to be spared what can be an irksome tendency in those writing about art for the journals. For a while at least her choice of images (if not her rendering of them) was compared to that of her old visiting tutor at the Slade, L.S. Lowry. He too produced art depicting industry and urban life, in his case of Lancashire where he was born and stayed all of his life. In choosing to be a loner and an outsider, however, meant that not a single picture of Lowry's depicts workers inside the mills and factories whose sooty architecture appears in many of his pictures. He never passed through the gates of any industrial premises, and although once seen his artwork will rarely be forgotten, the difference between his approach and Mary Louise's couldn't be greater. Reviewers who attempted to make a connection ended up confusing themselves as much as anyone else.

Around this time the entrepreneurial female proprietor of a ceramics company opened a modern showroom-cum-café on Linlithgow High Street, and later invited Mary Louise to have an exhibition of her work there. It was the first of two one-person shows she was to have at 'Portfolio 4', and it was really her first exposure locally as a professional artist. More than that, among the people who came along to the openings were those who bought her work and others who were in a position to commission artists for specific projects. In future years some of these contacts were to become collectors of her art as well as friends of the family.

As the faltering spring of 1977 arrived I found myself still on the payroll of the firm who'd employed me to build the breakwater, although my work at Alexander Stephen's graving dock was largely over. I wondered about the bridge contract they'd mentioned and began fretting a little over not hearing more from them. Then I got a call from someone at their head office saying they had got the bridge contract underway although things were proving difficult.

'How do you mean difficult?' I asked.

'Well, the foundations for the bridge are made from pre-cast concrete piles,' came the reply 'but when we drive them into the river bed they just disappear. We thought if you went there you might find out where they're disappearing to...'

I suppose I ought to have been flattered that they thought I could achieve such a thing considering other engineers must have taken a look at the problem: perhaps the troubleshooting I had done on the floating breakwater had something to do with it. Anyway, before they rang off they told me that the bridge under construction was in Yorkshire which stunned me. That meant once again I'd need to live away from home. It reminded me of a former Greek monarch whose crown was on a shaky nail, and who'd once answered the question as to what the best tool was for governing the Greeks by saying '...a packed suitcase ready to go!' I felt much the same way. No sooner was I settled in one place than another place demanded I leave. I discussed what the prospects were with Mary Louise: she looked disappointed but as usual made no fuss or tried to dissuade me. It was me who did all the agonised, head-clutching stuff. As it turned out, however, a solution was close at hand.

Returning home one day from final operations at Stevie's dry dock I boarded a subway train which connected to the mainline rail service to Linlithgow. On one of the seats of the subway carriage I found an abandoned newspaper lying open at the jobs-pages. On one of them was an advertisement seeking lecturers for Glasgow's College of Building & Printing. Since my subway stop was practically in the same street as the college, I nipped in and returned home with an application form. A few days later I handed it in and then forgot about it. Lecturing wasn't a burning ambition of mine, although my days at Brixton had certainly taught me what could be achieved when it was delivered by people who'd done time at the dirty end of the construction sector.

Within a few weeks I was invited for interview at the college which ended with me being offered a job. It hadn't been an easy decision to arrive at according to the chairman of the interviewing panel – a short, corpulent man who I imagined had never donned a hard-hat even for a fancy dress party never mind go in search of lost concrete piles. What had clinched it in my favour he said, was a very positive reference he'd obtained from Dr. Skoyles at the Building Research Station where I'd once worked. Good old Eddie Skoyles! I added him immediately to my list for Christmas cards.

Apparently my experience in handling large contracts like Guy's Dental Hospital in London, the Skyline Park Tower Hotel in Knightsbridge and a range of other construction projects including the M6 Motorway had counted for little with the interviewing panel. The chairman's personal opinion was the college needed a builder, not an engineer to teach its students who were aiming to be professional quantity surveyors, site agents and clerks-of-works. In a way he was right, of course, and when I looked at the subjects I was expected to teach I quickly realised I had a fair bit of learning to do myself before standing in front of a class. The house building process (called 'cottage walloping' by engineers) which I'd so strenuously shunned figured highly on the list of subjects I'd be expected to teach. Fortunately, I was given several months to prepare myself before facing my first class of students.

It was smiles all round when I arrived home in Linlithgow with the news: huffy silence when I phoned through my resignation to my current employer. But there was a major downside to my satisfaction at becoming a college lecturer – at a stroke my salary reduced by 25%. Had I been cool-headed enough to work this out in advance I may well have decided to decline the college's offer. It seemed paradoxical for educational institutions to insist on having qualified and experienced people on their staff, yet not pay them what they would earn in industry. At any rate, my drop in income would put pressures on our family budget for years to come and send us in search of different ways to enjoy life which didn't cost too much. Despite that, however, for the next ten years or so we lived a rather penurious existence.

To help the family finances Mary Louise took on a leisure-time class in art which was held in the evenings at our local senior school. Unlike England where she'd taught at several art schools and colleges, teaching in Scotland was an all-graduate profession and as yet her Diploma in Fine Art from the Slade awaited up-grading to degree status. Teaching leisure classes was about as much as anyone in her position was allowed to do. But alongside the sacrifice of valuable time spent away from doing her own work the drain on her creative energy soon began to show. It wasn't helped by the fact that her evening class students were amateurs, sincere in wishing to learn the fundamentals of drawing and painting but amateurs nonetheless.

The majority of people who have an urge to express themselves through art, rarely get further than dreaming about enrolling in art school. The chance of learning different techniques and having the opportunity to develop their imagination through making images eludes them because competition for places in art colleges is probably fiercer than in any other discipline. Consequently, they try to make do with self-learning, or the little bit of development offered by part-time classes in their locality.

What keeps their dream going in many cases is the knowledge that some accomplished artists – though they are few in number – rose to illustriousness without formal training, fostering the idea that nothing is impossible. And, of course, much of what was produced by way of 'Sixties Art' and what followed only served to reinforce the idea that with a little concentration and a bit of luck they could be the ones filling the art supplements of the Sunday newspapers.

In reality though, amateurs strive mightily to represent

things as they appear to look - a favourite bit of landscape…a bowl of fruit or flowers…their pet dog or cat…is what they try to produce with photographic accuracy. The results may sometimes be nice but completely unchallenging. Any idea of such things being merely the form taken by them and it's the artist's vision which translates them into something arousing the imagination is often received like a list of atomic numbers appearing on the Periodic Chart. The idea that a still-life can express the passage of time: that a sunflower is emblematic of what sustains our planet: or that wind-racked trees and a stormy sea can represent a person's state of mind, all tend to remain locked away for most amateurs. Nonetheless, as her father had done with film roles well below his capability as an actor, Mary Louise stuck to the task of teaching beginners without relinquishing her professionalism. She even went on a course which provided her with a qualification in community education which she remained proud of though she never had cause to use it again.

Some weekends we drove across country to visit my mother, now widowed and living in a house with caged-birds and furniture much of which went back to what she and my father had bought on the never-never. Our visits were often scheduled to coincide with one of the extended family get-togethers where it wasn't unusual to encounter up to three animated conversations going on in the same small room: it wouldn't have been a 'gathering' without it! In these surroundings Mary Louise had to fast-learn the meaning of words and expressions in the Scots vernacular used by her fellow guests. Perhaps her most difficult moments in that respect came in conversations with old neighbours of my parents, Geordie Wallace and his wife Mary.

Geordie was a miner and immediately interested in Mary Louise's prints of the Durham coalfield. A man who'd self-taught himself many things including an appreciation of classical art by using the public library service, he was already enduring the onset of 'black lung' or pneumoconiosis from having been a face-worker at his local pit. When Mary Louise met him he'd just been reassigned to the first-aid and rescue team at the same colliery. The mild-mannered and quietly humorous Geordie was loved and respected by everyone encountering him: and that went also for his wife, Mary, who flatly refused to anglicise her language for anyone peppering her speech with Scottish idioms no matter who she was talking to. Mary Louise had to work hard keeping up! Afterwards I'd run through some of these with her giving the English equivalents where there were any – people were 'thrawn' not stubborn, 'oose' was what gathered under beds not 'dust' and 'hirplin' was what you did if walking about with an injured leg.

In many instances the Scots word for something was more-apposite than the English. We never went 'shopping' for example but set out to do 'the messages' which in a way was very much part of the whole business of community – carrying back from the 'stores' all the latest news and gossip gathered in the queues. Supermarkets equipped with self-check outs would have been anathema to Mary Wallace and her like. Mary Louise was later to write:

> 'I suppose in a way Gordon's family was the extended family I never had. There were no close relations in my family on either side. They seemed to die young and I only remember meeting my mother's twin sister and her family in New York when I was in bed ill at the Waldorf Astoria, and she came to say goodnight. Once in London she showed my mother and I her operation scar for breast cancer and I met my Uncle Carl who drew cartoons for me. He knew I would like them because of my talent for art had already been noticed....I quite liked him, but unfortunately he became an alcoholic after being appointed the CEO of the Anglo-American Corn Company in South Africa. He totally accepted the politics of apartheid and turned a blind eye to the suffering of the black people there........'

As far as our own politics were concerned Mary Louise and I both remained members of the CPB(ML) although there being only one other member of the party in the entire population of Scotland, we weren't faced with the prospect of spending time in endless meetings such as we had done in London. Occasionally, the other member would traverse most of the central belt to be with us in Linlithgow and we'd talk about things – not just the political situation - until he had to catch the last train home. And as the 1970s ground to an end there was a lot to discuss.

A neighbouring town to the south of Linlithgow called Bathgate was having a really rough time. Once a coal mining town it had seen several of its 'replacement' industries last a few years then like the pits, close down and disappear – usually to England. Among these was British Leyland's truck-making plant along with the last remaining steel and iron foundry in the town. Shortly after we arrived in the area the big electronics company, Plessey, was heading in the same direction. As best we could we lent our support to the Plessey workers by joining their protest rallies and open-air meetings on the closure.

It was at one of these we met our local Labour MP Tam Dalyell who many will recall was a thorn in the side of every government throughout his career. An Old-Etonian (Tam openly confessed to having been a fag at Eton to Nicholas Ridley, later an arch-conservative member of the Tory cabinet), his maverick approach to politics endeared him to many voters so that his constituency seat was never seriously challenged at election time. His nose for government cover-ups and deception and his way of drawing them to the attention of the public and the press was un-rivalled.

On one occasion friends of ours, one of whom was one of Tam's aides invited us to attend the MPs rally at Linlithgow's town hall after a local canvass for his re-election to Parliament. The event took place during the Falklands war between Britain and Argentina. It was a heavy, humid day and Tam's door-to-door canvassers weren't the only ones feeling fatigued. Looking around I could see eye-lids drooping all over the place. They didn't stay that way for long though as Tam declared that he had it from the highest authority (presumably the intelligence services) that the Conservatives were prepared to carry out a nuclear missile strike on the Argentine city of Cordoba if that's what it took to win the war. The media-men present let Tam continue for only a few seconds before interrupting and bombarding him with their own 'missiles' hoping to elicit more about this astonishing piece of information. But Tam never revealed who his sources were as the journalists present knew only too well, although he never made claims that weren't backed by evidence which later usually proved to be true. On retirement he expounded a bit more on his comments about the war against Argentina, telling his biographer '*Politicians and proud naval officers facing possible humiliation and defeat could resort to mad and immoral decisions.*'

My only 'difficulty' with Tam was when he phoned in response to some issue I'd raised with him. He spoke slowly (though never boringly) choosing his words in a way that meant he never had to repeat a point once he'd made it. However, in most cases this made it hard to decide when the conversation was at an end. When you thought that was it…it wasn't! It was just an extra-long pause he'd inserted into the conversation.

Linlithgow was pleased to have him living close to the town and seeing him about the place when he was due to have a surgery or a few days away from Westminster. The man who replaced him as our MP certainly had a hard act to follow. But then, who could possibly fill the shoes of such a singularly exceptional man?

CHAPTER 25

The early 1980s saw Mary Louise with more time to do art than had been possible for several years. Our children were both in primary school, I had found my feet in a new job and we had settled into life in the small town of Linlithgow with its 17,000 other souls. I did my best to convert a downstairs room at Strawberry Bank into a work area for her: it wasn't great but at least it was somewhere she could retreat to in order to paint and develop her ideas in relative peace. Though it didn't compare with what she'd had in the garden at Chestnut Cottage we called it 'the studio' anyway.

It was around this time that I began understanding more of how an artist works – not in the technical sense, but how they went about choosing what to paint. Why they made the choices they did, however, would remain a mystery like it does for many people. On walks around Linlithgow and travels elsewhere there was plenty to look at and see. I tended to look: Mary Louise did the seeing. The difference often surfaced after we'd returned home and talked about various things we'd encountered on our outing. Frequently, Mary Louise would look as though I was recounting something I'd come across when out on my own rather than in her company. '*But you've got to remember that huge explosion of rhododendron by the old stones of the church,*' I'd say '*and that field of cows being rounded-up by the farmer's dog!*' Often she'd look particularly blank about recalling such things. '*How can an artist go around not seeing things like that?*' I'd protest.

Of course, she had been seeing other things which had gone unnoticed by me or I'd dismissed as insignificant – the grip of a passing cyclist on the handlebars of his bike: the way barrels had been stacked on the pavement outside a pub: someone's features under a cap pulled down tightly against their scalp. These and a score of other images would be drawn quickly on the pages of her sketch pad soon after arriving home, later to re-surface in one of her art works. In time I would get to be more observant of these things myself, seeing deeper into the most 'ordinary' objects and their contexts and deriving a much greater sense of awareness and reward from them than I'd done previously.

On the eve of her departure from London in 1976 Mary Louise had been told by the London Borough of Camden that a picture of hers 'Spirit of London' had won second prize in an open competition: it was a further addition to several art works done by her to enter public collections held by local authorities. Now Edinburgh City Council informed her that another work of hers, 'Spring Fling', had been bought by them after being given a prize in a painting competition. The finished work got coverage in the Scottish newspapers because radical councillors in Edinburgh had taken down the picture of a venerated naval warship on the main staircase of the council's headquarters and put Mary Louise's picture in its place.

Her second solo show at Linlithgow's Portfolio 4 took place, and the MacRobert Theatre and Gallery situated on the wonderful campus at the University of Stirling gave her a one-person exhibition. These were added to by participation in a Scottish Arts Council funded exhibition at the Royal Scottish Academy in Edinburgh, and further afield by her contribution to a show of mini-prints in Barcelona. Although her colour-etchings and lithographs figured much in these shows, increasingly her work in a variety of other media such as acrylic, pastel, and oils found their way on to the walls. In time these were to become the predominating elements of her exhibited work.

An interesting offer to provide work for the Wavendon Centre at Milton Keynes in England came along in 1983 and an exhibition of her work was hosted there the following year. Mary Louise was particularly pleased with the proposal because the Centre was both a theatre and a live music venue, the brainchild of the jazz musician Johnny Dankworth (later Sir John) and his singer wife, Cleo Laine. Both appeared regularly on television and Cleo's richly-unique voice expressed much of her heritage as a black performer on stage and in clubland. Dankworth was a pioneer of modern jazz but also wrote music for films and an endless stream of television adverts. His penchant for appearing on-stage dressed immaculately in suit and tie earned him a reputation for being 'couth, kempt and shevelled' in contrast to how most jazz musicians looked.

The Dankworth's were on hand when Mary Louise arrived to hang her exhibition and attend the opening at the Stables Theatre which was built in the grounds of their home. The work on show consisted of prints she'd done of Simon Rattle and the Birmingham Philharmonic Orchestra rehearsing their performances for the Edinburgh International Festival along with older work depicting nights at the 'Tally Ho' jazz pub in London's Kentish town – a proving ground for future stars of the British jazz scene who usually ended up playing in many of Dankworth's jazz ensembles.

Back in Scotland she prepared work for an international exhibition of prints in Germany and for a one-person show at the Glasgow Arts Centre. But her continuing desire to give her art a community dimension led to her working with a team of local women to design and paint a mural on the wall of a recently-completed leisure facility in Linlithgow. The women were each given a section of the wall to work on, being free to choose what subject they liked providing it had local references. Mary Louise had a section of her own but also responsibility for seeing that everything integrated by adding anything she saw as achieving that objective. The scheme took ages to reach completion and involved Mary Louise in many hours of unpaid labour. But it was something she loved doing because for once the local women were talking about things to do with art and not their children. But it also marked a turning-point of sorts in her career – one that led into public art. Soon she'd be commissioned to design and paint several more wall murals and other public art works at home and abroad.

Living on a lecturer's salary and the fitful earnings of an artist meant family life had to be lived within the constraints of a tight budget. When the old Triumph Herald breathed its last smoky breath of burnt engine oil I bought a Lada – a car designed by Russians and manufactured in East Germany. I knew lots of people who would have chosen the electric chair rather than being seen in the driving seat of a Lada. But although it was heavy on the steering I found it otherwise an excellent car considering its relative cheapness and lack of sophisticated gizmos other than a cigarette lighter on the dashboard. Not so our children, however. If they'd slumped down trying to look anonymous in the back of the old Herald, now they took to lying almost in the well between front and back seats until we were far enough away from the town not to be seen by any of their school-chums.

Our limited budget also got in the way of something Mary Louise and I both believed in – exposing our children to other cultures by taking them abroad. As a child in a large working-class family I had been denied such opportunities and it looked as if my own children were to follow suit. In a stroke of good fortune, however, a work colleague drew my attention to a scheme where families could swap houses in the summer months leaving just the air-fares and the daily expenses to be covered. We quickly made contact with the scheme's organisers, paid for a small advertisement to be placed in their brochure and waited. Dozens of responses came in the mail, just about all of them from teachers enduring life on the same reduced levels of income as ourselves.

We chose to swap our Linlithgow home with a family living in the Champagne area of France. It was our first foray into this sort of arrangement, but certainly not the last. Such was the care taken by swap-families to each other's homes that we repeated the experiment over and over again spending four-week vacations in several European countries throughout the Eighties. Added to the low cost was the fact our children could experience life outside the cities even if it meant on occasions not being able to have more than a day or two viewing the famous sites. In many ways though the sunflower fields of Charente-Poitou tended by peasants in traditional clothes, or the volcanic sand forming the beaches of lakes near Italy's Rocca di Papa were as intriguing and instructive as the well-known landmarks of Paris and Rome. We'd return to Linlithgow with lots of memories and find our own house even cleaner and tidier than we'd left it.

Needless to say Mary Louise returned with drawing pads crammed with her perceptions of the places we'd seen, although among them would be pencilled notes questioning her approach to her work:

> 'I should reflect more on why I'm attracted to something, why I'm doing it.
> What did I want achieve in that Italian village?
> The house up on the hill? The little square? The people lounging on the corner? Too much for one painting!
> I have to decide what goes in and what doesn't. You know when it's right. It all clicks. Automatic pilot.'

In her new-found studio at Strawberry Bank some of these drawings would be worked on until ready for the brush, the crayon or the etching plate.

In 1984 the Conservative government under Margaret Thatcher precipitated a strike in the British coalfields as part of a battle with trade-unionism she was determined to win. In the Conservative's view unions were the chief cause of economic failure and decline and had to be taught a lesson. This war with the unions went along with the policy of de-industrialising Britain and turning the country into one with a services-based economy. The resulting havoc caused by their attacks on workers in the coalfields will always be remembered as the 'The Miners Strike.'

Mary Louise wrote:

'There was a lot of strong feeling locally. We were (close to) mining communities at Kinneil and Bathgate and I cycled over to Kinneil with small quantities of food which was being collected at the Miner's Welfare. The mining families were really that close to hardship! The government had seized the union's funds. Mining communities are very warm and close-knit groups and there were lots of examples of effective organisation not least among the women, the miner's wives........'

As history records, of course, the strike failed and today there isn't a traditional coal pit left in Scotland.

Group shows, where Mary Louise shared wall space with other artists, became more-numerous as the 1980s wore on. After a brief return to Paris where her work was included in the exhibition 'L'estampes Aujourd'hui' at the Bibliotheque Nationale and at the 'Platform for Artists' at the Royal Society of Arts in London, she returned closer to home with solo exhibitions at the Smith Gallery in nearby Stirling and the Artis Gallery in Edinburgh. She also contributed to an art/poetry venture at the Scottish Poetry Library, a connection which was later to take her into producing artwork in an entirely different medium from what she'd been used to.

Meanwhile, her touring exhibition of Central Belt images was coming to an end. Before it did so, however, Grampian Television – a station operating mainly in the major oil town of Aberdeen – decided to do a short film of her work. The digital age had already arrived but most television companies still used their heavy outdoor broadcasting equipment and a sizeable crew of sound and lighting technicians. For the best part of a day the children and I had to step carefully over cables snaking through the hall and down the outside stairs to the street. The six-minute edited outcome to this showed Mary Louise in her studio at Strawberry Bank but also leaving the house to draw outdoors, and even to go food shopping at the supermarket! The item appeared the day following on Grampian's evening magazine programme and was also networked to other commercial television stations. For a few days at least she enjoyed a bit of celebrity, or as Mary Wallace might have put it…'*my, yon lassie's become the talk o' the waash hoose*!' By this time, however, Mary Louise was quite able to dispense with my services as a translator.

CHAPTER 26

Screen appearances, of course, continued to be the regular diet of Mary Louise's father, George Coulouris. He had played roles in scores of films since arriving back from the United States adding to this with a growing number of television appearances. In many of these he was cast predictably as the villain, although playing opposite Steve McQueen as a doctor in '*Papillon*' and in '*Mahler*' directed by Ken Russell, he managed to break free from this sort of typecasting and turn in impressive performances. He also made guest appearances in television series such as '*Doombolt Chase*' and a '*Doctor Who*' episode called '*The Keys of Marinus.*' When he had periods away from television doing other things the stallholders at his local street market would josh him saying 'Cor guvnor, you must be skint: haven't seen you on the telly for ages!'

More aligned to his talent as a stage actor were his roles as Shylock in '*The Merchant of Venice*', Big Daddy in Tennessee William's '*Cat on a Hot Tin Roof*' and General Sikorski in the controversial play '*Soldiers*' by Ralph Hochuth where he played opposite another actor with Greek antecedents, John Colicos. The subject of the play is Churchill's sanction of the utter destruction of German cities, including their civilian populations during World War Two. Colicos made an excellent Churchill – in voice and appearance both. Mary Louise and I were in the audience on the opening night of the play and enjoyed meeting the cast afterwards.

Despite film directors seeking to fit him into roles they'd seen him play in the past, Coulouris rarely showed anything but disdain for their efforts afterwards. Even in the theatre he disputed the interpretation of plays made by directors and frequently the performances of his fellow actors. This may have made it difficult for some people to get along with him at times, but for me I found watching television with him very enlightening. In a TV drama of the time, for example, a phone would ring and someone would answer it. Viewers would hear the voice at the other end of the line saying what awful news they had to impart. To my father-in-law this was the antithesis of drama: why not let the actor receiving the call show in their reactions how awful the news was? Bit by bit this could then percolate through the following scene making the audience work at keeping up with the plot and maintaining the tension in the drama. As I sat absorbing his views on this and other observations he made, the play on-screen would have moved forward leaving me floundering! Watching anything on television with George was usually more like a master class on acting techniques rather than something entertaining.

Despite this he continued to be strictly professional with regard to his own film roles irrespective of what he really thought of them. Arguably, there is no better example of this than in the adaptation for the big screen of Agatha Christie's '*Murder on the Orient Express*' where he plays the character, Dr. Constantine. In a 'star-studded' cast which has Albert Finney screeching his lines as Poirot (you have to put your hands over your ears at some points) and a lugubrious Sean Connery dressed as a Highland laird ready for the grouse shooting season, only Coulouris along with a couple of others like Martin Balsam put in any sort of performance. At the film's premier in London, Mary Louise and I did the unforgivable thing of giving our free tickets away to somebody else. Only later when the video was released was I able to appreciate how my father-in-law incorporated in his performance some of the views he'd expressed from the sofa at Chestnut Cottage.

Perhaps Coulouris's sometimes volcanic temperament had to do with his frustration at not being able to devote his entire career to the classical repertoire of the theatre. Had he been able to however, it is doubtful if it would have changed him to any great extent. He was what he was – a restless spirit, creative and knowledgeable, a man who could spot pretentiousness and conceit in others faster than it took him to learn their names. If there was anything missing from Coulouris's make up it was ego-tripping, something usually concealed in the unassuming demeanour adopted by his fellow actors when being interviewed. Rather than take my word for it have a look at the website dedicated to him which was put together by his son George Jnr. Here he does a half-hour interview about his experiences in Hollywood and elsewhere. It gives you a pretty good measure of my father-in-law in a way words alone couldn't convey.

Mary Louise had described her father's origins as 'humble' – the only child of a Greek father who'd left the running of the restaurant he'd established in Salford to his English wife in order to open a business which bought-up junk for resale. The junk was often stuff salvaged from ships torpedoed during the First World War. The young George had plenty of stories to tell of his life during that period, including one where he was sent to dry-out an endless number of soaked cigarette papers using the hot-water boilers at the local YMCA to achieve his ends. Years later, over dinner in Hollywood, Coulouris related some of these stories to Charlie Chaplin who responded by saying 'I think your father was heroic.' It perhaps made Coulouris revise his opinion of his father: later in life he was to describe him as a 'gutsy little Greek.'

Gutsy or heroic it didn't stop Coulouris running away from home to become an actor, and although he was forced to shed his skin in terms of his strong Lancashire accent, getting rid of other complexes proved more difficult. At a memorial meeting for him shortly after his death in 1989, I was granted the privilege of being one of two speakers to address an assembly of Coulouris's friends and colleagues in Hampstead Town Hall, most of them actors. Borrowing from a comment made once about the city of Edinburgh I described my father-in-law as a man who had not learned, or indeed wanted to learn, how to consume his own smoke. It was, as Dame Peggy Ashcroft told me afterwards, a perfect description of Mary Louise's father as she and others had encountered him.

Throughout his career Coulouris had never settled terms

with the almost Junkers-like rule actors such as John Gielgud and Laurence Olivier exercised over the English theatre. Their subscription to an updated version of the rarefied 'close reading' aesthetic of Shakespeare meant it was never a matter of sour grapes with George Coulouris: it was how he viewed their interpretation of roles and entire plays where scholarly interpretation held sway over his intense personal engagement with the bard's work.

In a talk broadcast by BBC radio some time after he'd returned from America, Coulouris declared he'd never felt part of the theatre scene in England the way he had in New York. '*I thought I must go back there (to England) because I want to do some proper acting. I started out to be an actor, I used to go around reciting Shakespeare for people and I wanted to do Shakespeare and I've been sidetracked. I've been in America doing modern plays, I went to Hollywood and did all these things, and I've still not done what I really set out to do*.'

He continued to echo these sentiments despite success in some of the roles he most wanted to play – Jacques in *As You Like It*: Brutus in *Julius Caesar*: Malvolio in *Twelfth Night*: Claudius in *Hamlet*: Shylock with Dame Flora Robson: Dr. Stockmann in *An Enemy of the People*: Squeezurn in *Lock Up Your Daughters*: the father in Sartre's *Altona*: Edgar in Strindberg's *The Dance of Death*: Flynn in O'Casey's *The Plough and the Stars*: and a string of other productions which would require a chapter by itself to list. Maybe this is the actor's lot, to never feel everything's been accomplished, that there are no more challenges to face, no further interpretations to be made. Long after retirement age George was to be found in America acting, directing and teaching at drama schools in places such as Southern California.

It is hardly surprising his daughter inherited some of her father's characteristics. From George she got her deep-rooted determination never to give up on her art and the self-belief which carried her through changes of country as well as fortune, through rejection as well as success. From her Mother she was given the priceless gifts of sweet good-humour, the calm to be a mother to her children and perhaps above all that intangible hoard of creative aptitudes which made her the artist she was becoming. As inheritances go it could have amounted to a great deal less.

CHAPTER 27

At the station she chooses to sit outside watching leaves from the nearby sycamores drift slowly downwards through a weakened autumn sun. It reminds her briefly of Magritte and that picture of his which has little bowler-hatted figures poised in the air like raindrops, challenging our preconceptions of how things are, waiting perhaps for us to reconsider. It's one of the functions of art, after all, to stir our latent imagination.

On the opposite platform, however, she spots a less-sublunary character in the form of a bulky station man pushing a trolley loaded with boxes. As he turns away from her she sees how the breeze make his trousers flap high around his ankles making his legs look impossibly thin. If she depicted him as such in a painting some people would say she hadn't got him 'quite right.' What 'right' meant to them was what they expected to see, what they were accustomed to seeing in a predictable world free as possible from unsettling glimpses of the unconventional.

When he's disappeared she shifts her look for a few moments to where a woman sits on a neighbouring bench. Her perm'd hair is beginning to grow-out, straggling above the back of her neck, flopping across her forehead. Somehow though it sharpens her profile - the incisiveness of her nose, the hollow of her cheek, the compressed lines of her lips. Then the woman turns to rummage in a bag at her side and her whole appearance alters. Now her head has become a broad, sandy-coloured plain parted in the middle by an arrow-straight road ending at her crown.

What is to be made of such things?

What is an artist to make of it?

Which 'fleeting moment' if any will find its way eventually into one of her pictures?

She boards the train which will carry her to Edinburgh, capital city of her adopted country, home of David Hume founding father of the Enlightenment. The Enlightenment became the scourge of romanticism, championed science and rational thinking, provided a gateway to explaining complex things by reductionism and quantification. After two-hundred years and more it is still the tool of enquiry for many, including environmentalists, ecologists, researchers into all sorts of matters including incurable and untreatable diseases. Responses to it, she knows, has often come through art – the Romantic school, Dadaism, Surrealism, other attempts to challenge the techno-scientific basis of present-day culture.

Can artists have a foot in each camp? This is a question she poses to herself frequently. Her husband claims the human species doesn't need science, but can't survive without art, poetry, music and dance. Yet even he isn't foolish enough to deny the material successes the Enlightenment has brought about: but what about the more 'subjective' human qualities inherent in individual experience? The role of imagination, emotion, intuition, the effects of irrationality and apparent chaos over cold logic and reason? Aren't these as valid in art as they are elsewhere in human society? Wasn't her father often a 'victim' of such feelings causing him to rail against the prevailing orthodoxies he encountered in his world?

Art she decides…her art…will only succeed when it has relevance to the lives of people…people who never go near galleries…who never open a book on the subject…who think artists are outsiders, dreamers, gifted yet tortured individuals. People who think like this are most of the people in her community. In the community you have everything, warts and all. Communities are supportive, quotidian and infuriating sometimes all at the same time. People sometimes bought pictures to hang on their walls, small, intimate, private pictures for them to enjoy. But where a picture ends up has little to do with the reasons for buying it. Art, she believes, has a public aspect no matter how much it's suppressed. People buy her art because they want something with a public feel in their private spaces. In their choices they appear to defy the prevailing ideology of 'private good: public bad.'

As the train slides to a stop alongside the platform, she squints briefly at her reflection in the window. Tilting at windmills? Too idealistic? She knows she lacks coherency of thought: but then doesn't coherency of thought just return you to the prison gates of the status quo, to acceptance of the dubious divisions made between things, where a flower is either a beautiful object or a study of a living organism in relation to its environment? Hasn't it got lots more to offer than its preciseness, its palpable existence, its recognisable form and classification? You're advised to paint or write only what you know about, and she's no botanist! Attempting to do anything based on what you think or feel will only end in the bitter tears of failure…….. They say.

Moving along Princes Street she thinks…science and art, what are the grounds for dividing them? Why does one have such precedence over the other? The buildings to her left shed grey light like flakes of skin: the moon is already visible: the wind lifts her portfolio in a sudden gust causing her to grab hold of it with both hands. We are brought up to see the investigation of nature and the natural world as being the job of science. We're not taught to see that the exploration of what's called 'reality' can be done through art as well as through poetry and literature. Nature lends form and colour to things, encloses space which science and art both seek to explore. Yet in school and in her experiences of art colleges not once were the two things ever associated: forever kept in their own boxes. Why? Not that it stopped artists seeking to unite them. Monet and the Impressionists depicted the natural world in one way, the Pre-Raphaelites in a completely opposite way. Her mind circles things like an astronaut circling the globe – moved by its sublime beauty from the scientific miracle, the technological haven that will sustain him until he returns to earth.

Shortly before reaching the workshop where she'll spend the next few hours she has to navigate a wide ring of people standing on the pavement having a conversation. She notices the positions they take up relative to each other, the way one gestures with his arm, how another slumps hands in pockets, another leaning forward as if unable to wait for his chance to contribute to the discussion. Dialogue, communication, conflict and aggression all present if only for a moment or two. How is this to be incorporated in her art if at all? Capturing the moment: but for what purpose? Asked to explain what attracts her to the scene she'd be pretty much at a loss to say. Anyway, it isn't the artist's job to impose a view on others like politicians do. An artist explores without dictating. A picture is released eventually into the public domain, there to be looked at and decided upon by others unknown to the person who produced it. The concealed critic in everyone will decide if it 'works' or not.

At the studio she is met by the familiar bouquet of ink, acid fumes, paint thinners and dampened paper. She sniffs at it like a hungry person in search of dinner. Where does a picture begin to form in her head? Sometimes it's from a single detail – fruit in a bowl: someone munching a sandwich: a man's gesture: a woman's hair, two impossibly thin ankles. A picture then grows outwards sublimating the detail which triggered it to the whole. Then there are the demands of colour and harmony, the balance between subject and space, setting out the means by which the eye is swept into the focus of the entire image. At that stage there is nothing 'dreamy' involved, only concentrated work and the expenditure of nervous energy.

She buckles on her apron and ties back her hair. This is her time to create work that'll bring together the sharpest and subtlest colours, to make aesthetically pleasing things and create something that has the potential to make life better. If asked what makes her an artist, she believes that would be the best explanation she could manage. To make life better. For the time being that'll have to do........

CHAPTER 28

No sooner had the paint dried on Mary Louise's team-led mural at the community centre than another mural beckoned. This time, however, it was a fee-paying commission that was being offered and the artist was to choose the subject for the work, make the design and carry out the painting of it entirely by herself. In no small way the resulting mural on the wall at Linlithgow railway station was to mark a turning point in her career, a step away from printmaking and her growing development in other media to doing public art.

The commission came at a time when the government was rigorously implementing its policy of privatisation beginning with the state-owned public utilities except for the rail network: that wasn't to happen until several years later largely because it was far from being an attractive proposition to private investors. The railway system was a shambles as anyone who used it at the time will recall in their nightmares. Scotland was only marginally-more disadvantaged than other parts of the United Kingdom, travellers there having to endure regular break-downs in locomotives, obsolete signalling systems and rolling stock which on occasions offered passengers bench seats composed of horse-hair stuffing dating back to pre-war times. In an attempt to improve their image as serial incompetents the British Railways Executive embarked on a campaign to improve the 'passenger experience' by carrying out, among other things, refurbishment of old stations from the Victorian era. Linlithgow Station was one of those and Mary Louise's mural was seen as an important step in that direction.

The wall given to her for the mural measured around 20 feet long and 12 feet tall at its highest point. It was a large area to fill and it faced passengers as they climbed the stairs to the eastbound platform and took their seats in a newly-appointed waiting area. The main question though was the content. People in the town had plenty of suggestions. Railway enthusiasts suggested commemorative scenes of the steam era: others proposed an amalgam of the town's history marked by its many buildings dating back to medieval times. Yet others recommended a simple landscape scene based on the rolling farmland and low hills surrounding Linlithgow. Mary Louise listened, but it is doubtful if she ever considered anything other than the idea which had sprung immediately to mind as soon as she heard she'd been given the commission. The mural would contain many of the suggestions people made: at its heart, however, would be the whole idea of people in the community.

Unlike other towns in the county of West Lothian, Linlithgow had managed to survive losing what industries it once had due in no small way to the people of the town – many of them volunteers – who were determined not to let the distinctive character of the place sink to a level where its past would only be accessible through museums and historical records. Linlithgow continued to have its own newspaper, maintained two town bands, hosted a consistently successful Junior football team and despite at least one major planning disaster, had held on to some of its old buildings including the Royal Palace of the Stewarts and St. Michael's Church.

On the first Tuesday after the second Thursday in June, in commemoration of its past Linlithgow put everything on hold to celebrate 'Marches Day' – a day dating back to the time when the boundaries of the burgh were confirmed by a march led by the burgesses, to all four corners of the parish. Today, despite Linlithgow having become a dormitory town, 'The Marches' are still celebrated with great enthusiasm helped along by the consumption of spirituous beverages supplied by just about the only commercial premises open on the day – the pubs.

Mary Louise's mural depicts the town and its residents at their peak on 'Marches Day.' Floats, vividly decorated and representing a host of local organisations move along the High Street and circle the Cross. The streets are filled with music as pipers waggle past in their kilts: the burgesses of today don traditional costume: and on the pavements crammed with people flags wave, handshakes and greetings are exchanged and people tap their feet to the town's adopted anthem – 'The Roke.' All of this is depicted in Mary Louise's mural making it a constant source of interest and comment by locals and visitors alike. It took her several months of energy and tiring effort to complete it in time for the newly-renovated station to be opened by our constituency MP, Tam Dalyell. Regrettably, a few years ago a chunk of the mural was destroyed by the decision to install a lavatory for passengers adjacent to the artwork. Perhaps the serial incompetency of those running our railways today continues, unabashed.

The proceeds from the mural commission came at a time when they were badly needed. Since starting work as a college lecturer I had remained stuck at the bottom of the salary scale making my reduction in earnings acute. I had already re-negotiated the terms of our mortgage extending the pay-back period by five years, and family holidays continued to be possible only through the house-swap scheme. The Lada I'd bought duly succumbed to the depredations of a wet climate and became a rust bucket that was as embarrassing to me as it had always been to the children. For a year or more we went without any form of personal transportation. Mary Louise discussed with me what might be done about it all:

> *'We pondered the question of me getting a part-time job in anything that might have vacancies. Earning money from selling art was a precarious existence: sometimes it happened, sometimes not. And prints, because of their nature, sold for less than say oil paintings and other forms of art. But we agreed that no one does art expecting to get rich. And as for producing stuff to suit the so-called 'market', forget it! That led to bad art and stifling an artist's creativity. The day I took that route everything would change, probably for the worst...'*

I agreed. These were views we were to repeat over the years to come whenever the issue of artists and their income surfaced.

Nonetheless, all we could rely on was my lecturer's pay and that was stretched often to the limits. With both partners earning a steady income – as was common amongst most of the families we knew – then perhaps we could have made more headway in providing what a family in consumerist society expected. But we didn't linger long on the idea of Mary Louise changing course or becoming a part-time shelve-stacker at Tesco.

Some alleviation of our pecuniary situation, however, came in the form of me teaching night classes. I took on two, sometimes three, evening classes at my college and Mary Louise had her contract renewed to teach a leisure-time art class at our local school. After deductions what was left didn't amount to a great deal: but it helped put sultanas in our muesili and get us around even if it was on buses and trains. At least on the train our children didn't have to hide themselves from any chance of being seen by their friends and school chums.

Mary Louise worked on the station mural during the time our children were in school, but there were periods when other duties called. She prepared work for a one person show at the Glasgow Arts Centre, entered work for a Scottish drawing competition, mounted her second solo-exhibition locally at Portfolio 4 and took up the offer of a residency at the Smith Gallery and Museum in Stirling where she taught and had an exhibition of her latest works. The combined income from these events made us feel as if maybe a choked pipe was starting to unblock itself allowing things to start flowing again.

I enjoyed being at the openings to her shows and exhibitions, circulating among the invited guests whose comments about Mary Louise's work were made ignorant of the fact I was her husband. Often there would be no words exchanged at all between people viewing her art: looking at art often requires silent contemplation and it gets it as often as not. Moving within the crowded spaces of a gallery taught me a lot about how people, especially women,

'Edinburgh Castle' The night sky blazes with fireworks. The image demonstrates Mary Louise's handling of colour, a feature of her work from her earliest days.

responded to the images Mary Louise produced.

Three more mural commissions then appeared in quick succession – two at the Royal Edinburgh Hospital, the other at the Commonwealth Pool in the capital. This latter one was a temporary affair which lasted only for a time after the 1986 Commonwealth Games came to a conclusion. The two at the Royal Edinburgh Hospital were different. Her commission there included the involvement of long-term patients at the hospital which had a long record of caring for people with enduring mental health problems:

'I found the whole thing fabulously interesting. Once I'd found my feet and got to know the patients who'd been chosen to work with me I really looked forward to going there two days a week. The nurses told me the patients wanted to work on their bit of the mural outside of that but were told they couldn't until the artist was there. I think as therapy it worked although it was hard keeping control of the content so it would look like a coherent whole when it was finished. The success of the first mural was what gave the hospital management the idea of doing another one.'

And there was more good news about to come her way. By the mid-Eighties the city of my birth, Glasgow – the industrial giant which had once claimed to be the second city of the empire – was on the rack and looking for ways of regenerating itself. Its main industries, shipbuilding, steel making and manufacture, had become a shadow of their former selves. It seemed every few months another closure was announced, another thousand or more skilled workers signing the dole. Few communities were unaffected by the decline, everybody knew somebody whose job had been taken away or was about to. So what did the city fathers of Glasgow decide to do? Why, create a year-long garden festival that's what! Not only that they chose to locate it on land which had once rung with the hammers of riveters and caulkers building ships. Many of the city's population were surprised when the news broke, then appalled, then downright indignant. Surely the expenditure could be used on creating new jobs, or protecting those still hanging by a thread.

To be fair, the Glasgow Garden Festival of 1988 was one of the most imaginative concepts the city council ever came up with. Amid the gloom of de-industrialisation they sought to lighten things with a touch or two of nature's blessing: and if you weren't convinced by that argument then there was always the money to be made from locals and visitors alike who travelled to the banks of the Clyde to see this wondrous creation rising from the decaying remnants of the old Glasgow.

The project exceeded all expectations. Four million people (40% more than targeted) with a fair proportion of them from overseas, paid the entry fee then proceeded to consume 100 tons of chips, three-hundred thousand pints of beer, four-hundred thousand ice creams, 130,000 doughnuts and 26 miles of hamburgers. Thus fortified they departed on the Festival tramway to see the six themed areas ranging from science to health and from recreation to sport, all built on soil dredged from the River Clyde. The only thing missing from the hundred-acre site was large, ostentatious pavilions to industry and engineering so much a feature of great public displays in the past. Considering the parlous nature of Glasgow's recent history that was hardly surprising.

Families with small children visiting the Garden Festival would invariably pitch up at one feature near the main entrance which aroused much curiosity. This was a series of giant inflatables joined together and given the name 'The Soft Island.' It covered a fair bit of ground and if you access Youtube you'll see a short clip of it shortly before the Festival opened to the public. You will also see a woman putting the final touches to the inflatables dressed suitably in clothes designed to keep out the chill coming from the river nearby. As she turns to see if the camera crew have got enough of what they want you could well recognise her if you'd already made her acquaintance. She is the designer of the 'The Soft Island' and her name happens to be Mary Louise Coulouris.

CHAPTER 29

She has to think of creating something that departs radically from the art she normally produces. And although the project is for children to play on, it has to have an appeal for adults as well. It has to be vivid, colourful, amusing, able to entertain and engage people's minds irrespective of age. As she sits by the bay window looking over the slopes with their first scattering of snow she has at least an idea of the general shape of what her proposal will contain. It also has a provisional title – 'The Soft Island.'

Artists have to keep on proving themselves, not just to others but also to themselves. The last exhibition, the most recent sales, the last reviews leave them a bit like a footballer who is said to be only as good as his last game. A new exhibition means new work not images dated in the past. Knowing eyes will look for development, for greater levels of accomplishment, for signs that an artist is maturing in handling paint, in using colour, mastering the architectonic composition of her work. Yet here she is about to surprise and shock them by turning to something quite different and properly three-dimensional. Well, at least 'The Soft Island' won't be exhibited within the circumscribed boundaries of a gallery but in public space like her murals where anyone who cares to can have a look and pass a comment.

She goes through to the room which acts as her studio and looks again at the preliminary drawings she made of what might appear on the inflatable base to the island she has decided on. Animals and birds, of course, but for once no people. But what sort of creatures should they be, what form should they take? They have to look very different from how they usually do.

'The world that surrounds me and the world that is in me.'

She thinks Emerson wrote that when talking about how artists and writers set about 'the reproduction of the world' in their work. But art, she knows, is not simply about reproducing: it must proceed from the desire for transformation. The mimetic and the symbolic have their places, but enduring art must transcend them. She smiles: all this is taking things a bit far, isn't it? What she's proposing isn't going to be 'enduring.' It will last no more than the best part of a year then be dismantled: and it will be a bit of 'conceptual' art, won't it? She smiles again at the irony contained in the thought.

The Soft Island will consist entirely of her ideas although others will put it together before getting it to the site. She picks up a handful of crayons. She's getting far too far ahead of herself. She hasn't even submitted her proposal yet and has no idea how it will be received by those who'll take the decision. To be honest she doesn't even know the names of those who will decide who gets the commission.

'Central Belt 1' The contrasting effects of industry in a rural setting provoked a series of prints which toured the country and were bought into several public and private collections.

Over the next few days she works on nothing other than the creatures for The Soft Island. They become odder and odder. They pay no heed to any sort of evolutionary development. Or perhaps they do, in a way. A bird acquires rockets to propel it rather than wings: a fish is given the head of a rhinoceros, a cow-like animal the beak of a parrot. And other bizarre things begin making an appearance - a set of backward steps, a waterfall which runs upwards, a tree whose branches are formed from fingers and thumbs and the penguins which roost on them. There is also what she's decided to call 'groaning grass' and a cave with a secret thing inside unknown to anyone. Some of these she does in full colour, others remain only in sketch-form.

Finally she fills in the forms which go with her submission and waits for the courier who will take what she's parcelled-up to those who will decide who gets the commission. From someone, somewhere, she's heard artists from all over Britain and beyond are submitting proposals. There may be in the order of 60-odd schemes for the decision makers to go through. So what? The experience of putting together 'The Soft Island' has stretched her in ways she wouldn't have imagined. It has taught her to release her imagination in directions never before travelled. It really doesn't matter much what the end-product is: travelling is often more exciting than arriving. She only hopes others will come to see it that way too.

CHAPTER 30

The competition for a play-area at the Glasgow Garden Festival was organised by the Scottish Development Agency who were responsible for deciding just about everything that went on to the site. Their letter telling Mary Louise she'd won first prize delighted her no end. Such was her excitement at the news she completely overlooked the fee offered for her design of 'The Soft Island' and her running costs during its installation. When she did get around to noticing it her pleasure took another leap forward.

In a way though the hard bit of the contract she was given was just about to start. The inflatable structure and the weird and wonderful creatures she'd decided to populate it with were to be made in England by a company whose highest achievement to date had been the production of 'bouncy castles.' Its proprietor – a rather grumpy individual who feared the costs involved in producing what the artist wanted would run away from him – proved to be the first and probably the biggest hurdle Mary Louise had to get over. He came to our house once to discuss the manufacture of the island's various components and left scratching his head and muttering words like 'impossible' and 'ridiculous.' Eventually he turned the task over to a younger member of his staff who was much more up for the challenges involved. I would arrive home at times to hear Mary Louise and he deep in discussion about the 'Sad Donkey', the 'Fast Snail', the 'Side Pinking Retro-Rocket Bird' and how many 'Boomerang Trees' should be included. '*And what exactly do you have in mind for Groaning Grass?*' I heard him say once looking down rather nervously at the detailed plan Mary Louise had provided him with. I'm not sure he got any further forward with that one before boarding his train back south.

In between a couple of visits with her to the site during the installation of 'The Soft Island' I had the thought that something might still be added to it. What that might be continued to bug me until one day sitting on the subway (the Glasgow underground railway seems to have positive effects on my synaptic activity) the idea of what that might be suddenly came to me. When I got to suggesting it to Mary Louise she went for it like a bee to the hive.

Ever since my teens I'd written stuff which I then proceeded to pester publishers with. Some of these were incautious enough to accept them which only fuelled my desire to produce more. Now, I suggested to Mary Louise I could pick up my pen and write something appropriate to her festival sculpture. But what? And for whom? She came up immediately with the idea of us producing an activity pack which could be sold at the Garden Festival inviting children to attempt solving the many puzzles it would contain within its covers. The puzzles I left her to decide on: I concentrated on writing stories about the strange and wonderful creatures whose images appeared in the pack hand-crafted by the artist before being printed on stiff card. One story went like this:

'Once the Tree Penguins lived on the shore of the Soft Island where they ate so many fish they could hardly stand upright. They waddled and wobbled and often fell flat on their faces. Then one day they found some old boots the sea had washed up. When they tried on the heavy boots the Tree Penguins looked very odd. But it cured their wobbling and never again did they fall flat on their faces no matter how many fish they ate. Now the Tree Penguins clump around the Soft Island looking for new trees to build their nests in. And they never take their boots off...not even for polishing!'

There were stories also about the Harris Tweeder, the Fast Snail, the Almost-Completely-Flat-Animal and the Yearning Bird who spent all its day just yearning, yearning, yearning.

A BBC radio interviewer asked me to read a couple of these stories aloud on his programme which was broadcast from the Festival site. He was Jimmy Mack who hosted an afternoon show called, well...'The Jimmy Mack Show' as it happens. I did so in a two minute slot sandwiched between an update on Scotland's road works and a song by Shakin' Stevens. Fame doesn't come much better than that!

Buoyed by the success of the Garden Festival, Glasgow took another bold step by applying to be European City of Culture in 1990. Amid a forest of raised eyebrows and astonished looks from the cultural cognoscenti elsewhere in Britain the city had its bid accepted – the only non-capital city to have done so up until that time. The idea was to showcase its cultural life although behind this was the increased urgency felt by the West of Scotland to revive its local economy by bringing itself to the notice of mainland Europe. So, among the first things to be organised was a concert with Frank Sinatra. Well, it was about culture after all! He performed in front of a largely middle-aged audience who'd once swooned at his screen appearances but now fainted at the fee he charged - £575,000. 'Old Blue Eyes' was soon followed by Pavarotti and the Bolshoi Opera, so it wasn't all bad.

In Mary Louise's area of fine art exhibitions of work by Van Gogh, Degas, Henry Moore and Pissarro were mounted in various venues, and an old friend reappeared to do the publicity for these and other cultural events. He was Charles Saatchi, who for around £2.5 million in fees came up with the official slogan 'There's a lot of Glasgowing on in 1990.' Don't worry if you don't get it the first time round, or the hundredth. It was almost impossible to interpret the slogan for overseas visitors who came by the planeload to the City of Culture, and it sat so uncomfortably on the lips of Scots that it failed to make any impression at all. Subsequently, Saatchi confined himself to designing newspaper ads for the year-long event from his offices in London, although some uncharitable folk reckoned he must have had more than a little to do with a much publicised exhibition featuring among other things dustbin lids, filing cabinets and fur-covered spoons. Perhaps hosting Frank Sinatra hadn't been such a bad idea after all.

It can't be said Mary Louise had much input to make to Glasgow's cultural jamboree, not least because around the late-80s her father was diagnosed with having Parkinson's disease. For an actor the loss of equilibrium and speech quality which Parkinson's brings about is almost equal to a death sentence. Grievously in April 1989 he died. In passing away he took with him a talent which had never been used to its full extent, a temperament which could soar as well as sink and who had insights to his profession which only towards the end of his life was passed on in teaching, mostly in America. Mary Louise and her brother George lost their Father, I lost a father-in-law of inestimable value and our children had lost a loving Granddad. Considering all the things George Coulouris had packed into his eighty-six years, perhaps Charlie Chaplin might also have seen him as being more than a little 'heroic.'

The name 'Coulouris' is, of course, Greek and when Glasgow's City of Culture invited artists to apply for an exchange with artists elsewhere in Europe Mary Louise was quick to respond. She suggested Athens as a place she'd like to exchange with and in many ways this made sense to those making the exchange scholarships available because it had been the Greek actress and politician, Melina Mercouri, along with the French government minister Jack Lang who had originated the concept of a European City of Culture. Athens had been the first to have the honour bestowed on it in 1985.

Around the mid-point of Glasgow's year of events Mary Louise was informed she had been granted an allowance which would support her for six-months in the Greek capital. The granting of the scholarship quoted the quality of her work, her reputation as an artist and the experimental approaches she used in printmaking which characterised much of her art. The decision to send her to Greece helped alleviate a little the grief at losing her father.

But it left me as chief-cook and bottle washer to two teenage children in Strawberry Bank at a time when my own fortunes at work were changing and had catapulted me from the lowest ranks in lecturing to become the head of a new department set up at the college where I worked. I was as bewildered by the promotion as Mary Louise was excited about leaving for Athens. But I didn't stay in that mental state for long. Apart from anything else our income increased several fold, and although it was probably miniscule compared to the wealth of Charles Saatchi and the creator of fur-lined tablespoons, we felt that perhaps we could now look more optimistically at supporting our children now heading for university. To give you an idea of how well-off I suddenly felt I went off and bought a second-hand car. It was a chocolate-coloured Austin Allegro though: but that mattered little to our children. They still refused to be seen in any outdated contraption and went about their business travelling on the bus.

CHAPTER 31

On the eve of her departure for Greece Mary Louise asked me to mail off a proposal she'd put together for the Churchill Memorial Trust. The trust offered around half-a-dozen scholarships every year to people who wanted to deepen or extend their knowledge in areas of activity pre-designated by the Trust's decision makers. They provided generous funding for any proposals which conformed to their criteria, and in 1992 they sought applications for research in art which bore relevance to the lives of ordinary people. They've always been like that at the 'Churchill' – you could be researching cell biology or canoeing on the Canadian rapids, so long as what you proposed added to current knowledge and what you learnt was passed on to others in the same field you were in with a chance.

When Mary Louise returned from Athens she found a letter inviting her for an interview at the Trust's headquarters in London. Her choice of subject was 'public art' and her focus for study was the United States. In due course her interview took place and her proposal was accepted. She began preparing for yet another trip overseas.

'*But I've no sooner given you back your kitchen apron,*' I protested '*than your handing it back to me. You're not staying around long enough to even have it laundered!*'

Soon I was getting down her suitcase again, ripping off the 'EasyJet' labels from her Greek visit leaving space for American Airlines to affix theirs. She flew out in early Autumn of 1992 with Chicago as her first stop. In the two months which followed she was to look at art in the public sphere of 8 major American cities and one in Mexico. Different cities had different approaches to commissioning public art, and in the account she wrote for the Churchill Trust after completing her scholarship she wrote:

'One of the things I noticed was how various projects grew up organically fitting the needs of the local people: public art organisations were formed as a need was felt for them. It would have been very boring if every city had a system imposed on it from government level so that everybody got standard art. The way things worked from the grass roots up and how administrators and artists were involved from the start made a big impression on me. Noting that each city voted for its own 'Percent for Art' ordinance endorsed this.'

Her investigations began in Chicago, a city I'd been in myself a few years previously as part of an educational exchange scheme between Scotland and the U.S.: so I was interested in her views of the public art I'd also seen there. Unlike me though she stayed in 'The Loop' with its decaying 1940s architecture, the 'El' bounding between modern skyscrapers and the gregarious black population greeting each other on the streets with much banter and humour. The first public art commission in the city was 'The Chicago Picasso' which Mary Louise told me had triggered 17 new public art sculptures in 25 years, including those by Joan Miro and Jean Dubuffet: she set about tracking them all down.

From Chicago she moved on to California, specifically the cities of San Francisco and Los Angeles. In San Francisco she made straight for the Art Institute and one of Diego Rivera's first wall murals. Later she went on a planned visit to the Mission Area with its mainly Hispanic population where more murals done in 'hot colours and complex, interwoven designs' grabbed her attention. She was also impressed by a giant wall painting next to the City Lights Bookshop, once the main hangout for a generation of 'beat poets.'

In L.A. however, fellow guests at her hotel virtually barricaded her in her hotel room when they heard she proposed visiting an especially dangerous part of the city unaccompanied.

A compromise was reached by one of them agreeing to drive her through the area. In one place it was possible to slow down enough to get a view of the half-mile long mural designed by Judy Baca and over a hundred artists contributed to. Because many of these were local artists the images on the wall depicted icons of the community in terms of portraits of familiar individuals, styles of dress, taste in food and posture.

Following L.A. came a grand tour of North American cities which included Phoenix, Arizona, where so many districts looked the same that only public art gave them a separate identity: Seattle, a new city who had spotted early the social function of art: Washington where she found her own work recorded in the National Museum of Women in the Arts: Boston, whose Red Line subway system boasted 20 major artworks and where the Director of the Arts Council there told her that '*public art that no one notices, talks about or writes about is art that's safe and boring.*' Eventually she reached Philadelphia, her mother's birthplace and the first American city to allocate a 'per cent' for art in their annual budget. Her tour ended in New York where the communication technologies used by Bill Fontana imported sounds from the waterfront like lapping water, seabirds and the creak of scuppered ships into the heart of Manhattan. She just happened to be there during one of the biggest storms to hit New York in 90 years.

Arguably the highlight of the entire tour however, was the detour she made to Mexico City. She was determined to meet the Linares brothers, members of a family who had been grand masters of folk art since the 18th century:

'I just couldn't be in the region without making an attempt to meet at least one of the brothers. I'd heard they had fallen out and kept different premises, but that didn't bother me. One would be enough. Against all the advice I went there on my own. Mexico City isn't the best place for a female on her own, especially a foreigner. So

'Conversation'
Family and
friends meeting
on the pavement,
banishing the
grey winter's day
with colourful
conversation.

I took a taxi to roughly the area where their workshops were and then walked looking neither left nor right but straight ahead at great speed until I got there. I was so pleased I did!'

The Linares specialise in making giant papier-mâché figures, traditionally fantastic monsters ('Alibej') with sharp teeth, incredible wings, clawed hooves, and long winding tails, all produced in strong vivid colours. They also make skeleton figures usually in celebration of the 'Day of the Dead' in November when returning souls are welcomed back home to a domestic altar loaded with marigolds, candles, figures fashioned from bread, fruits, prepared foods, soft drinks, clothing and the work tools of the deceased. Flower petals are scattered inside the house and also on the approaches to it.

Today, giant 'Judas' figures made in the image of unpopular politicians, devils and bandits are equipped with fireworks which will blow them to bits on Holy Saturday symbolising the fury of the people and the destruction of evil. With a bit of careful planning Mary Louise arrived in Mexico City for the Day of the Dead and was privileged to be at the 'altar' built to welcome back Pedro Linares, who invented the 'Alibej' and had died just a few months previously.

Returned safely to Scotland she slept for what seemed like a fortnight. It wasn't just the jet-lag and the vast amount of travelling she'd done in the U.S. which had exhausted her, but the sheer nervous energy she'd expended on viewing and recording the public art she'd encountered. I hovered on the landing outside our bedroom door with the kitchen apron all neatly pressed and ready to be handed back. I might just as well have gone off and like the Mexicans made figures out of the bread I'd left to go stale on the window-sill.

As things began returning to normal news came from Greece that a picture of hers had appeared in a newspaper called

Kathemerini, four pages of which in English were stapled to the back of the International Herald Tribune. The image of a Greek stallholder selling his fruit and veg on an Athens street corner along with an article about Mary Louise took up most of one entire page. A copy of the paper was sent from a contact she'd made during her six months Glasgow-Athens exchange scheme. She was Leonie Vidalli, who had a senior position in the graphics and printmaking division at Athens School of Art. Leonie, who was a fantastically warm and outgoing individual was to remain a close and helpful friend for many years to come.

Around the mid-point of 1993 an opportunity to extend her public art activities came in an invitation from an organisation called 'Healthcare Art' to provide work for the walls of a remodelled hospital in the town of Arbroath in north-east Scotland. The brief for the commission didn't specify any particular approach to subject matter, style or medium: but it said five artists would be invited to submit ideas and samples of their work. All were to be interviewed separately on the same day after being shown round the new hospital and its grounds. There might be worse things than being forced into direct contact with your peers who are also your competitors, but there isn't too many I can think of. All of the other candidates invited to Arbroath were established professional artists carefully selected by 'Healthcare Art': so all of them were equal favourites to win the commission. A few days after the interviews Mary Louise had a phone call telling her she had been chosen to do the work.

'*The artwork was for Arbroath Infirmary's Outpatients Department*' she recalled '*and the two things that were foremost in my mind was to produce a limited edition of prints for the people who went there, and interest them in how prints were produced. I wanted them to see what I had learned about their town in an enjoyable and imaginative way. As far as I knew this had never been done before in Arbroath.*'

The outcome was a series of 14 prints, two of which were linocuts, three monoprints, five small etchings, three lithographs and one woodcut. All of them had to fit appropriately into their chosen site and she had to provide a detailed design plan of where every image would be displayed. '*This is one of the important things about public art,*' she'd told the interview panel. '*It's what makes it different from 'other art' which is produced speculatively and may not suit the site chosen for it, or lose a lot of its effectiveness by bad siting.*'

Before anything could start, however, much in the way of domestic arrangements had to be made. Both our children were now at Edinburgh University – Saro most of the way through an honours course in Archaeology, Duncan progressing in his aim to becoming a lawyer: so I was less stressed on the home front since both had moved out of Strawberry Bank into student accommodation. I helped their Mother track down a comfortable bed-and-breakfast in the centre of Arbroath, and due to the town being within reasonable travelling distance from Linlithgow looked forward to paying her visits there at weekends. In a sense our lives had been reversed: once I'd been the one to work away from home, now it was Mary Louise's turn to live out of a suitcase. I saw her off on the train to Arbroath and returned to our house in Strawberry Bank with a sigh. Now, where exactly had I put that kitchen apron again…….?

CHAPTER 32

The last thing she does before going outside is to put the strap holding the camera around her neck. Then she zips-up her anorak, pulls a pink-coloured beret over her ears and steps out over the threshold of the guest house. This isn't Paris in winter, or stormy New York: its summer in Arbroath and no one yet has thought of telling the weather. Up here in this little town pinned to the north-east coast of Scotland anything can happen – rain followed by a cloudy sun, relaxing mildness suddenly stabbed by a biting wind. As she heads out she can hear the lash of the sea echoing in rocky gullies, waves breaking over immaculate sandy beaches not likely to see sunbathers today.

Yesterday she spent time in the local museum admiring the job that's been done in recording the town's past. But as she snaps a shot of the building's impressive tower she knows her work is not to record history but concentrate on the present, infusing it with her own interpretations, rendering it in line and colour such that people will pause and reconsider their view of familiar surroundings. It's what art is mainly about, after all.

She wanders down past the faded elegance of a ballroom which has fond memories for many of the town's older residents, and turns her camera on a row of properties beyond which will eventually produce 'Facades' – an etching pulling together disparate images of the townscape, many of them buildings important to the town, past and present. Then at the very bottom of the hill running down to the harbour she discovers the boatyard with a fishing vessel on stocks awaiting the scraping and cleaning services she remembers from Hull. This will form the basis of two lithographs. Already these are taking shape in her mind - how the artefacts of fishing will form the border to an image of one boat instead of just leaving it plain.

Nearby she passes a row of cottages with large stone-built sheds at the rear. The smoke sidles from their chimneys carrying the sudden, strong aroma of fish. Here, fresh caught from the North Sea, herring are being smoked before packaging and sent to the cities in many corners of the world where they'll appear on the menu as 'kippers.' She tries to get a peek inside one of the sheds but the reeking smoke drives her back, makes her eyes smart, catches in her throat. Maybe she'll take a closer look some other time......

Presently she finds herself back at the ruins of an abbey she'd looked at the other day, a collection of stone walls without a roof, arches which seem supported by nothing but the air, windows long deprived of their frames, gables still standing above the rubble, neat little patches of very green grass dotted defiantly across the site.

She draws quickly two views of the abbey shielding them from a low cloud dropping a little of its load, using the moisture to smudge the stronger lines with her fingers. She will composite the two views into one image that will convey her feelings for the place, the spalled-stonework revealing its vulnerability, its variation in colour, the blank windows like eyes framing her the way she is framing them, the solidity of stone against the movement of a wheeling seagull, wings flickering white above trees all bent over in the same direction by blows delivered by the prevailing wind.

On a bench by the banks of a smooth-flowing river she rests beside another ruined structure, a textile mill scheduled for demolition. Nature has already begun the job, vegetation grows vigorously from even the slightest cracks in its walls, reclaiming what was taken from it over a century ago. At one time thirty-four mills stood on this burn. Now just the faintest reminders of where they once were remain in overgrown heaps bulging the ground like swellings on the back of an old weaver's hands. She will put the figure of a man in the picture she'll make of this, 'Brothock Burn.' He'll be standing looking upstream towards a mill no longer there, but whose existence made him in large part the person he was to become.

Back in the town she eats in a fashionable café which hopes to represent part of a renaissance which will help the town on its way to a new future far from smoking fish, textile manufacture and old men who still sit occasionally on the steps of their houses smoking pipes and looking out towards the stormy reaches of the sea. Then she walks in a local park, Springfield by name, where dog walkers and children playing criss-cross her field of vision until she's into more open space with steep cliffs which plunge to the shore as if declaring to the water below '...this far but no more!' All of this will find its way in some form into her commission for the hospital.

Her camera is now redundant even if it still contains unexposed film. What she's used up of it will become simply an aide memoir, a trigger for her imagination not a replacement for it. But as she retraces her steps back towards her bed-and-breakfast it's a photograph she'd lingered over the day before in the museum that swirls through her mind. It is a small, yellowing picture from decades ago of a young local girl dressed in a smock and carrying a wicker-work basket containing fish strapped to her shoulder. Soon a large, strong and imposing linocut of the girl will make its appearance on the wall of the Outpatients Department. Copies of the image will eventually travel to different parts of mainland Europe and be bought by people who fall in love with it. Mary Louise will give it the title 'Fisher Lassie.'

CHAPTER 33

The Arbroath commission saw her produce several limited editions of her prints – 140 prints in all – which went on sale to the public. Some were to appear in solo and group shows shortly afterwards but not to such wide-ranging reviews as her previous work or that which was yet to come. 'Fisher Lassie' was probably the biggest exception to this. It was to find a place in several private collections, including those held by art lovers living in Greece, Denmark and Switzerland.

Around this time Mary Louise met and became friends with a quite remarkable woman whose vision and dogged determination was to eventually provide Edinburgh with something it lacked yet badly needed. She was Tessa Ransford and the guiding light in bringing into existence the Edinburgh Poetry Library. The library was shortly to provide Mary Louise with the opportunity of applying her talent to a much different form of artistic expression. And if people looked at it stooped over rather than standing up then that was all part of the idea.

Tessa Ransford is a respected poet who was married to the publisher Calum MacDonald who used the proceeds of his printing business to finance a poetry journal called 'Lines Review.' It provided space for Hugh MacDiarmid among others to showcase their work, 'Lines Review' being about the only journal at the time to do so. Tessa bought a van and travelled the less-well provided areas of Scotland as a mobile library. It was stacked with Scottish literature and poetry including, of course, her husband's publication. Due in no small way to Tessa's persistence over many years, Edinburgh finally got round to providing its citizens with a state-of-the-art poetry library, now located near the parliament building at the bottom of the city's Royal Mile. After producing a portrait of Calum MacDonald, the friendship and mutual respect between Mary Louise and Tessa, artist and poet, was to remain for many years and led to some unique collaborations which ranged out to include at one point involvement with extra-mural courses on human ecology at Edinburgh University.

Before that, however, Mary Louise was asked to produce 3 carpets for the children's story-telling section at the library. '*I was so pleased to be awarded the commission,*' she told the press. '*It was a big leap for me to do designs for the rugs, but the challenge was exciting and stretched me to the limits.*' For the storytelling area she drew on several different poems by Hugh MacDiarmid, including one '*Hungry Waters*' which he'd written for a little boy in Linlithgow, our adopted town. Combined with it was another of the same poet's work '*Somersault*' where he says:

I lo'e the stishie	(love, rumpus)
O' Earth in space	
Breengin' by	(bursting)
At a haliket pace	(headlong)

MacDiarmid's poetry is always vivid in images and allusions as well as intellectual depth, and the other two carpets borrowed from his work again but this time with a theme of medical science.

The designs Mary Louise produced for these drew on the poet's awareness of Dictyostelium discoideum a slime mould which was used to test anti-cancer drugs and immune cell diseases: and Belousov-Zhabotinsky which led to an exciting new field of research into problems with human biological systems. The spiralling, oscillating colour changes in the case of this latter example held a particular fascination for an artist like Mary Louise. In due course the designs were woven into the carpets by Lynn Kirkwood, an Edinburgh-based weaver using the tufted-gun technique. Like the man who had huffed and puffed over Mary Louise's 'Soft Island' design. Lynn complained much about the difficulties involved but saw the project through brilliantly to completion.

In a period of five years starting in 1989 Mary Louise had five

solo exhibitions in private galleries on both sides of the Scotland/
England border, exhibited in a group show at the Bankside
Gallery, London, home of the Royal Society of Printmakers where
she'd been made an Associate member, and seen reviews of her
work published in a variety of newspapers and art journals. Even
the stern critic, Edward Gage, had positive things to say about her
work: and reviewing her solo exhibition at the Kingfisher Gallery,
Edinburgh, Richard Jacques compared her way of lending dignity
to everyday scenes to that of the German artist Josef Herman. He
went on to describe Mary Louise's temperament as being '*pitched
somewhere between the classical and romantic*' inferring she ought
to choose one or the other so critics, who put artists in categories
and 'schools' ringed round with clear lines of demarcation, might
be satisfied. People viewing her work though didn't appear to be
over-wrought by the issue and went on buying it.

Further encouraging news came from Greece. Her contacts
there, including those in the British School at Athens where she'd
stayed during her exchange visit, told her about the opportunity
of obtaining a Greek government scholarship in art, something
she responded to with alacrity. She'd already had one show at the
Jill Yakas Gallery in the opulent Kiffisia district of Athens and
another one at the same venue was in the pipeline: so she was
beginning to envisage some sort of future in the country of her
grandfather's birth. Added to this was the news that another
image of hers had been used on the cover of the magazine 'Greek
Weekly' this being the picture of a pavement kiosk (or periptero)
with its owner sitting at his tiny window surrounded by stacks
of newspapers, sunhats, soft drinks and chocolate bars. Leonie
Vidalli had also been in touch picking up the threads of an idea
Mary Louise had inspired where a group of Greek artists including
those working with Leonie at Athens School of Art would come
to England in exchange for a similar group of British artists going
to Greece. This duly took place a few years later, the Bankside
Gallery playing a major role as host for the venture.

In 1997 after completing the second of two, month-long

residencies at the Fundacion Valparaiso in Southern Spain she entered designs for a competition run by the Sainsbury's retail chain for labels which would adorn their proposed new-millennium line of bottled wines. She won it and in due course displayed the designs at a launch held in London. Along with the fee came two cases of the new product (12 red, 12 white) delivered by courier to Strawberry Bank. Well, at least one resident there was overjoyed by his wife's success and insisted on toasting it at indecently-close intervals thereafter.

1997 soon turned into one of the busiest years in her career. *'Do you know I'll be sixty in a couple of years'* time?' she asked me one night over a tasty meal she'd cooked for our supper. Her flair for cooking, like her love for music and dance, was something which engrossed her at times almost as much as her art. *'No, I didn't,'* I replied *'you must have lied to me about your age when we met. Still, I suppose there's advantages in marrying an older woman, it's just I haven't discovered them yet.'* She threatened to lace the next meal she prepared for me with arsenic.

Throughout our married life she'd been the victim of a number of fairly familiar but nonetheless irritating illnesses such as hay fever, sinusitis, allergies to cigarette smoke and certain foodstuffs. She also got sore legs from standing so long on hard floors at her etching press. As a consequence she became an exercise fiend, joining aerobics classes at our local gym and adhering to a diet which had the phrase *'trust me, I'm healthy'* written on every molecule of food.

She also went cycling to stay fit and during an artist-in-residence at Scottish Natural Heritage in Perth, and similarly at the Haworth Museum and Gallery in the north of England, put in several miles daily on a bike to and from these venues. Thankfully, the noxious chemicals used in traditional forms of printmaking had now been entirely supplanted by a range of less-poisonous substances: so she no longer needed to wear a mask when stooped over the acid bath.

In addition to the Sainsbury commission and her residencies

in Spain, she participated with an old artist friend Polly Ionnides in the 'Brockley Open Studio' event in London, was represented at the London Print Fair, had two solo shows – the Albemarle Gallery, London and Thompson's Gallery in Suffolk – and contributed to a photo-mural 'A Mad God's Dream' at that year's Edinburgh Festival. Arguably though the highlights of the period came in rapid succession - her rugs for the Poetry Library, and the application for a Greek government scholarship which was accepted for two years rather than for one as she'd expected.

The award of the Greek scholarship and the longer-term prospects of what that might result in really excited her. In the years ahead I was to see her buzz with enthusiasm at being back in Greece after attending to commitments elsewhere in the world. She couldn't sit still on occasions and her eyes would look as if they were turned inwards scanning any number of plans and possibilities yet to be structured into meaningful options.

Everything artists of the past had said about the quality of the light in Mediterranean countries was just a part of what she was responding to. She loved the relaxed social interaction Greeks had with each other, the latitude they gave to everybody to do what they wanted and, of course, their mannerisms and turn of phrase which used much of the body – hands, shoulders, features, voice. I had to agree with much of this. '*I hear more laughter in Greece,*' I told her once '*than anywhere else in the world I've been to.*' And this time I wasn't kidding.

By this point I was in need of a few laughs myself. I had built my college department (now called a 'unit') from just me and a half-time secretary, to one that employed four full-time staff and up to 25 part-time lecturers (now called 'tutors' or 'advisors') most of whom were from business and the professions. Sadly, apart from a small and heroic group of college-employed staff (still called 'lecturers') I was forced to give contracts to people from outside post-school education. The simple reason was my colleagues at the college were often hopelessly out of date and far behind what my adult students needed in the way of updating training in areas ranging from using new technology and quality assurance to health & safety, gas engineering and management skills. Recognition of this out-datedness was the rationale for me being appointed Head (now 'Director') of my unit. It was hoped I would drag the 'dinosaurs' into the new millennium by example. It was hard work: dinosaurs as you know have tough hides and are not averse to snapping at you with their jagged teeth.

When I did have a break from work I usually made it a long one, say around a month, whereupon I'd go off to find Mary Louise wherever she happened to be at that moment - in Scotland, or overseas. I joined her at the Valparaiso residency in Spain, for example, where I was able to experience first-hand the rivalries, petty-jealousies and ego-tripping that sometimes goes on in such places. It is never a great idea to put several artists in close proximity to each other in a baking hot environment with shared studio space. In similar places I'd been to the mix had been leavened by including a couple of writers or poets, although that didn't guarantee anything in the way of ego-free zones. Throughout these events however, Mary Louise carried on doing what she'd set out to do. Her irritation at what her fellow-residents got up to at times often surfaced, but her excitement at doing art remained undiminished.

One interesting trip took us to an artist's colony, Atelier Four Winds, near the tiny hamlet of Aureille in Provence. It was run by two women one of whom was a Native-American who'd retrieved her former name and was now known as Donni Buffalo Dog. She and her partner Ursula were both sculptors and had created the colony in 1993 by clearing 5 acres of land and converting a large chicken shed into four studios. And a brilliant job they'd made of it! Alongside the studios was living accommodation for six artists.

For the first few days while Mary Louise was busy organising her studio and work-schedule I talked a lot to Buffalo Dog and learned quite a bit about her background and why she'd decided to leave the United States to live permanently in France. It was a story only a heart of stone would not have been moved by, and as she recounted it I could understand her anger at how she and her fellow Native-Americans had been treated. In a sudden fiery U-turn however, she began attacking me one afternoon calling me racist, homophobic and the equivalent of a male chauvinist pig though I was too shocked to remember her exact wording on that last accusation.

I was profoundly shocked by these allegations, then became indignant, then extremely worried that anyone should think such things of me. I spoke to Buffalo Dog's long-time partner who tended to brush it away by suggesting Buffalo Dog had 'moods' that were unpredictable. But I began worrying that my presence would affect Mary Louise's creative time at the colony and took myself off every day to Aureille and its surrounding settlements, tramping a number of truly wonderful country roads which curved and twisted and had little traffic except for the occasional cyclist or rider on horseback. Other times I went with Mary Louise into the foothills of the nearby Petit Alps where she set up her easel and painted while I found a comfortable pitch beside one of the irrigation channels and read a book. If I don't remember how many books I got through in this period, I do recall vividly the insect bites I received by sitting too close to the ground. Their attacks on me were only slightly less-annoying than those of Buffalo Dog's.

Ironically, the area around Atelier Four Winds was a stronghold of Jean Marie Le Pen the extreme right-wing French politician. Poster-portraits of him were often displayed in shops and fixed to walls. What Buffalo Dog made of that I never got the chance to find out. Among other things Le Pen was known for his advocacy of racist policies: and he wasn't all that approving of gays either. Seemed that maybe Donni had jumped free of her homeland without being entirely clear about where she was about to land. But at least there were positive results from our stay at the colony – Mary Louise produced a number of beautiful oils which eventually found their way on to the walls of two galleries in the U.K.

CHAPTER 34

The 'stipend' paid at intervals to Mary Louise by the Greek Ministry of Culture wouldn't have kept a caged bird in breadcrumbs. But added to the income she made from selling her artwork and using her savings, meant she could meet her accommodation costs and travel which usually meant taking a bus or going by ferry. We had a joint bank account which met all our daily needs with a bit left over, but she refused to use it for any expenses related to art. She held her own account separately for that: it felt at times as if she saw doing art almost as an indulgence no one else should be expected to pay for.

She also got paid for teaching art to groups recruited by small, entrepreneurial businesses who offered 'alternative holidays' abroad in sunnier climes. She took her place among a variety of subjects ranging from meditation and environmentalism, to sculpture and watercolours. One of these took place on the Greek island of Skyros which saw Mary Louise take on the challenge of making art from small pieces of marble which on completion is known as a 'mosaic.' The bench and ground slab which she turned into a mosaic on Skyros featured a figure half-female, half-fish and was subsequently referred to as the 'Mermaid Mosaic.' She was pleased at how it looked on completion, especially since it represented her first full-scale experiment in producing a mosaic. She also accepted an invitation to teach on another Greek island called Hydra where I joined her for a fleeting visit. Our time there convinced us Hydra was a place we'd like to have as a second home.

Apart from mosaics other innovations, which might legitimately be traced back to Hayter and his approach to image-making, began appearing as her scholarship residency in Greece moved on. In the garden of the British School of Archaeology at Knossos in Crete, she put oil with water in a shallow tray and after adding a pinch of certain colours immersed sheets of fine quality art paper below the surface. What she drew out of the tray eventually was paper bearing a delicate marbling effect whose patterns suggested the shape or outline of objects which she then worked up into images for a number of pictures, usually with a Greek theme.

At other times she would soak the paper in warmish-water then scatter the sharpening's of coloured crayons over the surface letting them melt and dissolve into fantastic shapes she could attribute in her art to mythical creatures. Many of these would go on exhibition in Greece and appear in a book she produced chronicling parts of Homer's Odyssey in amazing coloured plates. 'The Cyclops Series' was launched at a special event in the Technohoros Gallery in Athens.

The flexibility of her Greek scholarship meant she could attend to things elsewhere. A solo show at 'Artistic Licence' in London took a lot of preparation, and because she was now a Fellow of Royal Society of Painters-Printmakers she had to be involved in helping organise the National Print Exhibition at the Mall Galleries where she exhibited one of her works 'Tube People 3' based on travellers using the London Underground. Soon, she was to be given the commission to design a large tapestry which would hang in the foyer of Vale College in Wrexham. Back in Greece she fulfilled her promise to organise the visit of 7 Greek printmakers to exhibit their work at the Bankside Gallery, which duly took place in 2003 as part of the Painters-Printmakers Annual Exhibition. But even before this took place other opportunities were arriving some of which were too good to ignore.

If Mary Louise was busy, a similar degree of energy was being expended in my role at the college where I worked. I was earning money for the college from the courses I designed and marketed, at the same time making a rod for my own back. The more I earned this year the more I was expected to earn the next. This was a period when Principals of colleges and universities had become politicians and the day-to-day management of their institutions was handed over to accountants. And since 'costs' headed their list of priorities the accountants were in their element. While the Principal was away schmoozing the government's education minister and chiefs of the funding council, the accountant was busy 'reforming' pay scales, extending class-contact hours and not replacing the jobs of people who left. Everyone from the teaching staff to the admin workers felt the cold draught as soon as they entered the corridor where the accountant's office sat, usually next to the Principal's.

In 2003 I decided it was time to go. I might have soldiered-on to official retirement age which was due in around five years' time: but I didn't see the point. My resignation was accepted with no more than the usual platitudes and I was given forty-pounds worth of Marks & Spencer vouchers as a farewell gift. Fearing this might represent my true value to the college (equivalent to a few pairs of underpants), or I had somehow been incurring the displeasure of my College Council (now renamed 'Board of Management'), I searched back over 14 years of honest endeavour as a senior staff member seeking to identify the causes for their parsimony. It wasn't until a colleague pointed out the glint in the accountant's eye that I guessed what the real cause of their meanness was. *'He'll be figuring out how much he can reduce the salary of your replacement by,'* he said. I organised my own leaving party, left my gift vouchers on top of my empty desk and went home quite excited at starting a new stage in my life, one in which Mary Louise would hold centre-stage.

Throughout my college career I'd continued to write for newspapers and journals. Then I wrote a book in which young entrepreneurs (the flavour of the times) spoke of what it was like to set out on a voyage which led to them to owning and running their own businesses. Scottish Enterprise sponsored the book and paid me to write it. Then, from a handful of grimy letters written by a soldier to his Mother from the trenches of the First World War I wrote a radio script *'Just A Few Lines'* which was broadcast on the BBC and ended up winning a Sony Award. This was followed by a couple of short stories I wrote which were also read on BBC radio, and I started sending out poetry I'd written to various small publications.

On retirement however, I set-to writing a fuller account of the soldier's story which was eventually published as a book. And not to be outdone by a mere woman I too was granted a Churchill scholarship shortly before I retired which took me to America, principally Philadelphia whose industrial and social history was staggeringly similar to Glasgow's. My research project was to compare efforts in both cities to regenerate their economies. I have to say Glasgow easily out-did Philadelphia in innovative ideas and support for new business start-up. I was inducted as a Fellow of the Churchill Foundation in 2001 and received my medal in the magnificent surroundings of London's Guildhall, an occasion I frequently teased Mary Louise about: she'd been awarded her Fellowship somewhere much lower in the rank of classy venues. I only gave up teasing her when she began making lists of who would get what when we divorced.

In 2003 Mary Louise had two solo exhibitions at galleries in Edinburgh –one at The Bakehouse, the other at the recently opened Circle Gallery. This latter event proved to be a disaster when the owners encountered financial problems and shut the place down leaving her pictures inside. I was given the 'commission' of retrieving them which I finally managed after much tedious argument and no little threat. It wasn't the first time or the last I was to get heavy with some people in the art world whose ethical behaviour left much to be desired. In our days at Chalcot Square I'd had to force my way through the door of a studio and grab a couple of Mary Louise's canvases which had not been returned to her after a show and which I reckoned the studio owner was intent on keeping. Summoning-up my near-perfect Glasgow accent I threatened him and those present on the night with all sorts of things. The two women in attendance looked on with a mixture of fear and awe as I barrelled out with my wife's paintings securely under my armpits.

2003 also saw us depart for Hydra where we rented a house and stayed for most of the year. That set the pattern for the next eight years – spending most of our time on Hydra, with a couple of months back in Linlithgow when the heat in Greece threatened to turn our brains to porridge. It was during one of those spells in Scotland that Mary Louise submitted work for consideration by the British parliament who have a large collection of artwork most of it of high quality produced by well-known and accomplished artists. She submitted three watercolours based on scenes from Scotland which were displayed in the House of Lords for peers to decide which ones to buy into their collection.

They finally decided on 'Union Canal –Linlithgow' which featured a passenger boat against the background of the canal basin near to our house in Strawberry Bank. However, the other two images were not destined to be returned with a 'Thank you but no thank you' note attached to them. They were bought privately by Baroness Crawley – a champion of legislation on women's rights – who assured me in recent correspondence that 'Hogmanay-Edinburgh' and 'Inverewe Gardens' maintained their places on the walls of her home.

On Hydra, when the jaw-dropping beauty of the island didn't succeed in luring me out into its narrow stepped streets and slanting mountains, I began writing the book based on my BBC radio script about the First War soldier. The idea of doing such a thing came from the senior official at the BBC who had presented the programme with its Sony Award. 'He should expand it into a book,' he'd told the producer of the broadcast. At the time I couldn't contemplate such a thing due to work pressures and family obligations. After retirement though the tide turned in my favour and gathering all my research notes sat down in our house on Hydra and began to write. The result was publication of 'Sonny: The Truth Behind the Lines' in 2013.

Mary Louise's first solo exhibition on Hydra took place in 2004. It was hung appropriately in the island's council-owned venue named after Melina Mercouri the Greek actress who'd inspired the European City of Culture project which had taken Mary Louise to Greece in the first place. But the Mercouri centre was a less-than ideal place for showing art. It had a long sloping floor due to its previous function as a water-storage facility, and it had many large windows along one wall which restricted available hanging space. There was no gallery lighting as such and even hammering a nail into the thick stone walls was looked on with extreme disapprobation by council officials. But it did have a large grand piano though, which dragged to the middle of the floor made up somewhat for the lack of horizontal areas that would take unframed samples from an artist's portfolio. Perhaps the worst aspect of the whole set-up, however, was the lack of discrimination on the council's part about who exhibited there. A show by an accomplished artist would be followed by absolute trash. I can honestly say some of the worst art I've ever encountered was at the Melina Mercouri Centre on Hydra.

Nevertheless, most professional artists exhibiting there sold work usually to tourists and visitors to the island who'd tired of swimming and sunbathing and wanted to view something a bit more stimulating without the necessity for wearing sunglasses. Mary Louise was never to experience a loss on any of the five exhibitions she had the Mercouri community centre, and it brought her into personal contact with people who year-on-year came back to view her latest work. Many also came to the studio she'd created on the ground floor of the house we rented. Like going backstage after watching a play, it may surprise some people just how much the public like seeing where an artist works.

When the attraction of exhibiting at the Mercouri began to fade she found a perfectly reasonable alternative tucked away behind the main port area of Hydra. The small 'Galarie Zourntos' was owned by a Greek who spent most of his time in Paris, so when it came to deciding whose work should hang on his walls he knew his onions. Bad art and artists chancing their arm got short shrift. Shows at the 'Zourntos' weren't all that frequent, but when one did open you could bet there was something inside that was worth viewing.

In Athens the William James Gallery provided her with a solo show which came shortly before the exhibition of her Cyclops series at the Technohoros Gallery in the same city. On a visit back to Britain, however, the BBC approached her to contribute to a programme called 'The Artist and Radio 4.' The rationale for the programme was 'What does the creative artist need as a background to their studio activities?' The answer the programme makers wished for, of course, was the radio! The writer and illustrator Raymond Briggs, the fashion designer Zandra Rhodes, Mary Louise and several others all said what they listened to when doing their work and why. In her case it was classical music along with the occasional switch to talk radio on BBC 4. These sound bites were broadcast throughout the month of November 2005 and published thereafter along with a picture of the artist. Mary Louise declined to supply a photo of herself and instead provided an image she'd recently finished of the closing ceremony at the Edinburgh Festival called 'Edinburgh Fireworks.'

In 2008 one of London's largest hospitals the Royal Free in Hampstead, accepted six watercolours of hers for a mixed show which combined poetry with the images arising from selected lines, which were then written across the artwork sometimes incorporated as part of the creative design. Mary Louise chose her subject matter from verses written by Dylan Thomas, Thomas Hardy and others. We travelled to the opening of the exhibition on the top of the No.24 bus in high spirits, and departed taking even more of the mood with us due no doubt to some of the excellent wine served at the reception. After a bit of pushiness we were allowed to see some of the hospital's collection of artwork, many of the works having been done by artists with connections to Hampstead.

Back in Hydra shortly afterwards Mary Louise began preparing for what was to be her last show on the island. It was called 'Kefi kai Louloudia' meaning 'Good Feelings and Flowers' and it contained all of her most recent work. Along with a good friend, Apostolos, we carried her artwork in stages from our house high up on the slopes down to the venue for the exhibition. After helping to hang it I sat on a chair in the middle of the floor and just gazed around me. I was a little overwhelmed by what shone out from the walls. *'This is the best yet,'* I told her as she went about putting the final touches to the exhibition. *'I saw it all emerging in your studio, but to see it now grouped together like this is incredible. I'm gob-smacked!'* After thirty-eight years of marriage she knew I was giving voice to what I genuinely felt. That same year one of the images from the show found its way to the Optima gallery in Athens which caters to an exclusive set of clients who mostly buy work produced only by Greek artists. Mary Louise's image 'Fig' – an imaginative rendering of a single leaf from a fig tree - was the only one in the group show to be accepted from a non-Greek.

CHAPTER 35

She rests for a moment on a low stone wall overlooking the harbour on Hydra. The crescent of small fishing boats below lift suddenly, rolling in the wash of an outgoing ferry before settling back, gunwale to gunwale, to peaceful slumber.

For while the tired waves, vainly breaking,
Seem here no painful inch to gain,
Far back, through creeks and inlets making,
Comes silent, flooding in, the main.

'Say Nought the Struggle.' It could be a description of her life which has now entered its seventy-third year.

Across the harbour sit two flat-roofed structures whose darkish-stones do as much as they can to kill the sunlight. Between them though runs a steep ribbon of stairs painted brilliant white. A figure appears on the stairs, that of a child, a short heavy child dressed in a colourful top who bounces like a ball from step to step, slipping, recovering its balance, slipping again until it reaches the bottom and disappears from view. There had been a time when she would have carried the image of that back to her studio and thought about working it into a picture. It had many of the ingredients of a picture -movement and stasis, light and shadow, colour emerging from darkness. But was art really just about recording a moment that continued to live?

She still does such pictures, but lately her mind has turned to other things. This is not the 1960s and softer campaigns are in vogue. Once it was hard -edged politics, marches, demonstrations, strikes, civil disobedience. And now? Ecology, environmentalism, sustainability, animal rights, save the whale, save the seals, save the Green Belt....

She engages with these things, tries to find ways of including

'Anoyia' Villagers at table in the Cretan village of Anoyia where the men are 'lean and easy in their movement.' The village was razed to rubble by German military during the Second War.

them in her art. But how? They set up so many paradoxes, so many dissonances. Objective observation versus creativity: a message communicated in a beautiful image: a message sent in colour and the sensuality of colour. Where did the necessary compromises lie? Should there be compromises at all? After more than 50 years, she's still having to figure it out, having to move with shifting uncertainty, excited by it as well as exasperated by it. Ah well, say nought the struggle.

Lately she's been working on a series of plant-prints. During her walks she gathers plants growing in the wild, takes them back to her studio, dips them, leaf and stem, in trays of colour then presses them on sheets of fine art paper. The results fascinate her. She quickly begins to extemporise. In one print the smudgy image of a bee or a butterfly, then in others stippled lines criss-crossing the image like trelliswork, then further on still, words written on leaves, some in French, a man's name, taken from wall graffiti near her studio, trying to humanise the cold logic behind the case for protecting the environment, trying to take it from science into the realm of aesthetics. The plant-prints series now runs to 30 images. Every one, she believes, is life affirming. Every one, she says, contains her 'poetry.'

She leaves her seat on the wall and walks on past the pines and the narrow beach where people swim, where older Greek ladies wearing sunhats make a circle in the water, sea up to their necks, talking animatedly, cooling their flesh in the low, obliging waves. Beyond that she climbs up and around until she reaches the shell of the burned-out house. Here once was the home of Nikos Ghikas, a Greek artist who painted in his suit and tie, brought luminaries from across the world to stay with him, whose pictures in his

A much different interior. Mary Louise uses colour to express her responses to what is seen inside a room on a Greek island.

country's national collection are treated like jewels and seldom lent to touring exhibitions so few can see them in real time. Is this the ultimate destination of art? Her art? To be locked away, seen only by appointment? Even public art has become part of the drive to making everything private. Some universities, she knows have already sold-off part of their collections to make-good a deficit in their funding. There is no classlessness in art any more than elsewhere in society. When they say 'let the market decide' they mean let the wealthy investors decide. Well, at least she keeps in contact with some of the people who've bought her work, people who know the value of art, not just the price

Thinking of Ghikas reminds her of other artists she admires. The German expressionists with their bright colour and emotional angst. The Russian Goncharova and her husband Larianov. Klee and Kadinsky who 'painted from the inside': Leger's 'happy paintings': Matisse with his rich still life's: Picasso, the analytical thinker in his Cubist days. Then, of course, El Greco, the way he uses paint, the way he handles his brush, laying on paint in fast moving strokes. 'I am much closer to the European tradition in painting,' she says in her publicity material, 'than anything in Britain and the United States. That's why I am happier in Greece and Paris.'

She walks on between mountains which seem to tilt towards a sea which sparkles as if invaded by millions of tiny silver fish. There are times when it all seems to gel: people respond to feeling in artworks. It was all about finding the exact equivalent in art to the feeling you want to express. She recalls a work she'd done that had failed. It was the figure of a woman cleaning windows, but she'd failed to reveal her own feelings of the woman, being alone, bored perhaps, envious of the activity going on outside the window? As an artist she has to be able to express this in paint. It's what figurative art is mostly about, despite a lot of it being not much good.

Across the broad strip of water separating Hydra from the mainland the day directs its beams like a powerful searchlight on the hills, so that every tree can be identified, every rounded slope stippled in the muted hues and shades of peaceful earth. She can even see areas that were burned during last years' bush fires. Maybe she spends too much time thinking about artwork of the past and not enough of the societies which produced them. What she believes is you get the cultural development that expresses the values of the times. Romanticism battling with the Enlightenment, rational thought and logic vying with instinct and emotion, Ruskin and the Pre-Raphaelites versus the science of Seurat and pointillism. They often crossed-over, of course, when it was convenient! The carnage of war and imperialism given a romantic gloss to salve a nation's guilt. All those 'isms' art historians attached to things, the mania for classifying things in the quest to control them, the 'arts lab' like the science lab, the need to make utter sense of something by robbing it of its magic, its mysteries. What sort of business was this she'd devoted her life to!

She passes a man looking closely at a small hand-held computer device as he walks along, his pointy shoes catching on the stones protruding from the path like the stumps of broken teeth. But he is oblivious to everything save what appears on the screen.

> Greece is like a grand collage,
> Of history layered on ancient stones,
> While deep from tranquil valleys comes,
> The fiendish squawk of mobile phones.

Thatcherism lives on, monetarism and 'free' market values live on. Serota, Saatchi, Tracy Emin, Damian Hirst, Britart, the Turner Prize, they were all given extensions to their leases in Tony Blair's Britain. How could good art be produced in such circumstances? Well, at least there were signs that some young artists were beginning to express what they felt about contemporary issues.

She recalls R.L. Stevenson's phrase 'death to the optic nerve.' The work of art was frequently submerged in a flow of words, sounds, images drawn from the technical reproducibility of this century and last. This was the epoch of mathematicians, sub-atomic *physics, a break with sense-experience, even common sense. Science predominated. As it moved forward art seemed to have been shuffled off into a corner populated by sniffy gallery owners, connoisseurs of mashed potatoes and dealers with eyes of bank-paper blue. She'd sold a lot of her work though, through some of them!*

Back in the main part of the town she sits at one of the many empty tables set out in rows across the front of several tavernas and orders herbal tea. She has a penchant for fringe theories about health such as vitamin supplements, gluten-free foodstuffs, meditation, T'ai chi, acupuncture. She thinks it's related to being an artist, responding to the immediate without having thought it all out beforehand. That can be a good thing for an artist, having the facility to respond quickly to stimulus and act on it. She has drawing pads filled with stuff to prove it.

The grace and movement of the human body is found in much of Mary Louise's art. The Greek love of dancing to Zembikika (left) and runners completing a race (right) are just two examples.

Across the way a woman with long hair sits rather self-consciously alone beneath awnings whose supports frame her against the background of a water-taxi then beyond that some tall, ochre-tinted buildings made even taller by their position on the hillside. From further along comes a man leading a mule, the tough curves of its saddle only visible in places beneath the heavy burden it carries. On the very top, in a cerulean-blue pot, perches an orange tree destined for somebody's garden, tiny fruits swinging from its branches in time to the animal's steady tread. The dreary philosophers are wrong. The beard stroking jeremiahs are wrong. Her husband is wrong. Humanity isn't losing its need for spirituality by placing it in the hands of the consumerists. We are still human beings! She believes humans will always have feelings which obtrude into rational thought and this will always be a large part of their intellectual activity. We are many-sided, complex creatures. It will probably never be possible to define us, categorise us entirely. The artist still has a value in her ability to reflect on things from an individual viewpoint. The value of subjectivity remains. Death of the optic nerve? Never!

But there are times when she wonders if anyone would really care if she chucked the whole business of visual art. It's become peripheralised and now there's a feeling of 'why all this putting of brush to canvas? So unnecessary!' The function of art had always been confused, now it was just irrelevant. People went through their entire lives without giving it more than a sidelong glance. The line between fine art and advertising was made to be blurred, yet advertising was designed to leave you feeling envious, missing out on something. Art was stimulus, made you reflect, ask questions, scrutinise yourself inwardly. 'Art-advertising' was the biggest oxymoron of the 20th century, a legacy of the brash and confusing 1960s.

Walking home, climbing the steep incline of a stepped alleyway she remembers a reviewer writing about one exhibition she'd had. 'Coulouris is a painter from the heart.' Where is her heart now, apart from this pounding object in her chest as she climbs the steps? A big part of it resides in Greece with its transparent beauty, its attempts at harmonising things with feeling, the naïve pleasure taken from everyday things. 'The world that surrounds me and the world that is in me.' Emerson again. Here in Greece it appears to crystallise. The ancient Greeks are said to have believed the souls of deceased humans inhabited animals: but the thinkers who gave a basis to western civilisation wouldn't have settled for that. More likely they were drawing attention to the interdependencies of humans and other things in the natural world. Back to environmentalism again!

She lets herself in through the studio door and stands for several minutes running her eyes across the many unfinished works which hang on the walls. How many of them will eventually reach completion? How many will be scrapped and painted over? As she views them frequently over the next few days she will decide. From the ladder that drops down from the first floor to her studio a pair of trainers attached to an equal number of legs makes their appearance. When she'd first met her husband her reaction to him had begun with his head and face. Now, forty-odd years later it's the opposite end of him that approaches. 'I thought you'd got lost and was starting to worry,' he grins, knowing that getting lost on Hydra is virtually impossible. She giggles as she follows him back up the ladder to the kitchen where they'll prepare their meal. Perhaps she had got a little lost, she thinks, but only in her thoughts. That's never a bad thing in her case. After all there is no such thing as art, there is only artists……………..

POSTSCRIPT

In Christmas week, 2011, Mary Louise died in an Edinburgh hospital. I was at her bedside when she passed away. I had helped nurse her through her final months after she'd been diagnosed with Motor Neuron Disease, an incapacitating neurological condition which results in victims losing control of muscle activity and general movement of the body. Speaking, walking, swallowing and just about every other movement we take for granted is affected. There is no cure for the condition or much in the way of treatment. MND is expected to end in only one way.

I began writing her life-story before she got ill, and despite being interrupted by the need to write another book had drafted around a third of it before she died. I was intrigued by her early life as the daughter of a Hollywood actor but this was gradually eclipsed by her experiences in becoming a successful, professional artist. I was fortunate to be in at the beginning of this and over the following forty-four years watch it grow in several different, often eloquent, directions. As a female in a world dominated by male artists, deciding to gain her livelihood as an artist wasn't just a choice for her but a necessity. I had seen her burn with excitement at the prospect of transferring her creative energy to canvas or paper, and in her public art to walls and walkways. The memory of this, being infectious, was one factor responsible for me completing her story.

Although reviews of her artwork in newspapers and journals over many years rarely fail to mention her use of vibrant colour and her commitment to figurative art, I have tried to meld these with her awareness of issues in the wider world including her approach to peace, politics and latterly concerns over the destruction of our environment. Although we will never understand entirely why artists produce the images they make or why they choose to render them in the manner they do, at least we can respond to them drawing on our own resources of aesthetic appreciation, wonder and emotional response. In some cases the reaction to certain pieces of work may simply be visceral, unaccountable to words for an explanation.

My book comes with just the briefest incursion in to the vast amount of artwork Mary Louise produced over the years. It was difficult to choose which of her images to include, and I laid aside many with great reluctance. Fortunately, more can be viewed on the Internet and on the walls of the many public and private institutions who took her work into their collections. It is to these and the individuals who also bought her work I am especially grateful to.

Acknowledgements

Most of this book is based on conversations with the artist, although I have debts to pay to several others who helped confirm matters of fact. I thank my brother-in-law, George, who provided his own perspectives on family life in New York and Beverly Hills. I am also conscious of the times I was privileged to enjoy the company of my late father-in-law, the actor George Coulouris and Louise Franklin his wife. My appreciation extends to photographer Nikolaos-Panagiotis Kiafas, and those private collectors who allowed me access to the artist's work.

OBITUARIES

MARY LOUISE COULOURIS
PRINTMAKER WHO DREW MUCH INSPIRATION FROM SCOTLAND AND GREECE

Born: 17 July, 1939, in New York City. Died: 20 December, 2011, in Edinburgh, aged 72

MARY Louise Coulouris was an acclaimed painter, printmaker, muralist and public artist whose works appear in galleries and museums, railway stations, hospitals and private collections in the UK and beyond.

Although born in New York City and raised in Hollywood as the daughter of English film star George Coulouris, she would fall in love with a Glaswegian, Gordon Wallace, and spend the latter half of her life in Scotland, reflecting its beauty in her work.

From her home studio at Strawberry Bank in Linlithgow, West Lothian, since 1976, Coulouris created works for numerous one-woman or group shows, including at the Glasgow Art Centre, the Scottish Gallery, the Scottish Arts Club on Edinburgh's Rutland Square and the city's Kingfisher gallery. She also had studio space at the Wasps studios in Dalry, Edinburgh, and at the Edinburgh Printmakers' studio on Union Street.

She had about 20 solo exhibitions in Britain, France, Greece and the US and contributed to the Edinburgh-based Art in Healthcare charity, which helps hospitals, care homes, surgeries and other medical centres obtain art work to brighten patients' lives.

Among her best-known public murals is the one – painted in 1985 and refurbished in 1993 – that adorns the waiting room at Linlithgow railway station. She also delighted parents, children and artists alike with her design for the children's play area at the 1988 Glasgow Garden Festival at Prince's Dock on Clydeside, opened by Prince Charles and Princess Diana.

The Scottish Poetry Library in Glasgow houses three commissioned carpets designed by Coulouris, while a series of her watercolours adorn a wall at the House of Lords in Westminster.

Her grandfather was a Greek immigrant to Manchester and she was delighted to visit his homeland through Greek government art scholarships, drawing and painting throughout the country and seeing her work exhibited in Athens.

When her husband Gordon retired ten years ago, they spent much of the year on the Greek island of Hydra, which became a second home to them and provided fresh, vibrant colours and inspiration for her work.

Mary Louise Coulouris and her older brother George were born in the suburb of Spuyten Duyvil in the Bronx, close to Manhattan. Their father was the actor George

Coulouris, who had been born in Manchester to a Greek father and English mother but moved to the US in the 1930s with his American wife Louise (née Franklin).

Since her father had to get to Hollywood to play the character Walter Parks Thatcher in what would turn out to be the classic Citizen Kane with Orson Welles, baby Mary Louise found herself on a train from New York to Los Angeles, where she was brought up in some luxury on North Roxbury Drive, Beverly Hills.

She found herself fussed over by friends of her father, including stars such as Bette Davis and José Ferrer. Visits to the Hollywood film studios fired her imagination and she painted her first canvas at the age of 11.

In the late 1940s, having also appeared in the film version of Hemingway's For Whom the Bell Tolls, her father became disillusioned with the witch-hunt campaigns led by fanatically anti-communist Senator Joe McCarthy and decided to take his family back to his native England.

They set sail for Southampton from Manhattan in November 1949 and began a new life in London, living first in Putney, later in Chestnut Cottage in Hampstead, where Mary Louise and her mother both painted.

(One of her father's most acclaimed roles back on the British stage was the lead in King Lear at Glasgow's Citizen's Theatre in 1952 and he would go on to appear on stage, in films such as Papillon and Murder on the Orient Express, and in countless television dramas, including Dr Who. Theatre critic Ken Tynan once wrote that "acting with George Coulouris must sometimes feel like performing in front of a blast furnace" and Mary Louise increasingly showed that fire, passion and colour in her art work).

She attended St Paul's Girls' School in Hammersmith and Parliament Hill School in Camden before doing a two-year course at Chelsea School of Art. She then won a place at the highly- respected Slade School of Fine Art on Gower Street near Euston station, a branch of University College London, where she studied under the painter Sir William Coldstream and printmaker Anthony Gross.

Her work there attracted the attention of the artist LS Lowry, the writer John Steinbeck, art- collecting actors such as Vincent Price and Stewart Granger, and an up-and-coming politician called John Smith, future leader of the Labour Party.

During her time at Slade, she was also granted a one-year French government scholarship to the renowned Atelier 17 at L'Ecole des Beaux-Arts in Paris, where she developed her own colour etching technique under renowned painter/printmaker Stanley Hayter and won praise for her drawing skills and unique use of colour.

She met Gordon Wallace, a poetically-inclined civil engineer who had moved south to London during the Swinging Sixties, while she was drawing by the Regent's Canal in Camden Town, London, in the late 60s. They lived in the city's Primrose Hill area, had two children, and moved to Linlithgow in 1976.

"Art should be the place where people can slow down, indulge their senses with a static image that can take being looked at for more than 12 seconds," she once said.

Commenting on her work, art historian Athina Skina wrote in 2009: "Mary Louise Coulouris focuses through her painting on the genesis of nature, or at least on what constitutes its beginnings. Her fluid brushstroke, through the diffusion of colour, energises space and conveys its rhythmic tensions from the depth of the optical field towards the surface. A primal lyricism meets with abstraction, casting away any sense of intellectuality."

Coulouris, who died in hospital in Edinburgh after battling motor neurone disease, was a Fellow of the Royal Society of Painter-Printmakers. She is survived by her husband Gordon and children Saro and Duncan. Her funeral will be held at 1:30pm on Wednesday at Falkirk Crematorium.

Phil Davison, The Scotsman, 2nd January 2012

MARY LOUISE COULOURIS OBITUARY
PROLIFIC PRINTMAKER, PAINTER AND MURALIST WITH AN ATTACHMENT TO GREECE

Mary Louise Coulouris, who has died aged 72 after suffering from motor neurone disease, was a prolific printmaker, painter and muralist whose vibrant images were exhibited widely. The richness of her palette derived from her love of Greece, where her family's roots lay.

Her father was the actor George Coulouris, who was born in Manchester to a Greek father and an English mother. Mary Louise was born, like her older brother, in New York. With his American wife, Louise, George had made his way to Broadway and into minor American movies before appearing in Orson Welles's Citizen Kane in 1941.

Hollywood brought the good life, away from wartime austerity. Mary Louise was introduced to George's starry friends, enjoyed visits to film studios and began painting. However, in the era of Senator Joseph McCarthy's blacklisting of suspected communists, in 1950 he chose to return to the UK.

Following St Paul's girls' school and Parliament Hill school in London, Coulouris attended Chelsea School of Art for two years. She then completed a three-year diploma at the Slade School of Fine Art (1958-61) under William Coldstream, learning etching from Anthony Gross, followed by a year's postgraduate course. After winning a French government scholarship,